Appreciating Poetry

Appreciating Poetry

Richard P. Sugg
University of Kentucky

Houghton Mifflin Company   Boston
Atlanta   Dallas   Geneva, Illinois
Hopewell, New Jersey   Palo Alto   London

Library of Congress Number: 74-12895   ISBN: 0-395-19375-3

The computer produced drawings used on the cover and chapter openers are done by Colette Bangert and Charles J. Bangert. The handmade drawings are done by Colette Bangert. The computer is Honeywell 635 at the University of Kansas.

"Stopping by the Woods on a Snowy Evening" from *The Poetry of Robert Frost*, edited by Edward Connery Lathem. Copyright 1923, © 1969 by Holt, Rinehart and Winston, Inc. Copyright 1951 by Robert Frost. Reprinted by permission of Holt, Rinehart and Winston, Inc.

"The Unknown Citizen" Copyright 1940 and renewed 1968 by W. H. Auden. Reprinted from *Collected Shorter Poems 1927-1957*, by W. H. Auden. By permission of Random House, Inc. and Faber and Faber Ltd.

"next to god of course america i" Copyright, 1926, by Horace Liveright; renewed, 1954, by E. E. Cummings. Reprinted from his volume *Complete Poems 1913-1962* by permission of Harcourt Brace Jovanovich, Inc.

"Much madness is divinest sense" Reprinted by permission of the publishers and the Trustees of Amherst College from Thomas H. Johnson, Editor, *The Poems of Emily Dickinson*, Cambridge, Mass.: The Belknap Press of Harvard University Press, Copyright, 1951, 1955, by The President and Fellows of Harvard College.

Contents

Preface

Appreciating Poetry is a text and anthology designed for use in introductory literature courses in colleges and universities. The book offers a representative selection of British and American poetry, and each poem has been chosen for its demonstrated appeal to the contemporary student. The pedagogical apparatus is intended to give both the instructor and the student maximum flexibility in dealing with the poetry.

The first half of *Appreciating Poetry* consists of eight chapters, each examining one or more of the elements of poetry. Each chapter begins with an introduction, and each presents at least fifteen poems accompanied by questions that focus attention on the ways in which the elements of poetry contribute to the complete poem. Each chapter concludes with four "Topics For Writing," imaginative suggestions for short essays on subjects relevent to the lessons of the chapter. Chapter 2 presents two student essays and some instructions on how to write an essay on a poem. There are some 130 poems in the first eight chapters of the book, 80 of which were written in the twentieth century. These 130 poems are accompanied by over 500 questions, the answers to which may be found in the *Instructor's Manual*. Finally, each chapter contains a short bibliography on some poem or subject in the chapter, so that it becomes a relatively easy matter for the student to use the library for longer papers.

The second half of *Appreciating Poetry* consists of some 100 poems grouped under seven topics: Love, Death, Nature, Society, God, Change, and Art.

The poems are arranged under each topic in a generally chronological order, so that it is possible not only to compare and contrast different poems on the same topic, but also to consider the historical development of attitudes toward that topic. This second half of the book offers numerous opportunities for talking and writing about poetry from either the thematic or the historical point of view.

Appreciating Poetry is designed to fulfill a number of requirements that are common to introductory literature courses. First and foremost, the book presents a selection of poetry which will appeal to the beginning student; and its "Introduction: To The Student" offers some reasons why poetry should be appreciated, why poetry (and literature in general) is relevant and useful to today's student. With its explanatory introductions to each chapter, and its questions for each poem in the eight chapters, the book encourages the student to come on his own to an appreciation and understanding of the poems, and thus it enables him to participate in lively and meaningful class discussions. And with the "Topics For Writing" at the end of each chapter, the student essays and instructions on writing essays, and the arrangement of poems by theme and chronology in the second half of the book, *Appreciating Poetry* offers ample opportunity for the student to perfect his writing skills in compositions on subjects related to poetry. This book, then, should be flexible enough to satisfy both the student and the teacher in any introductory literature course involving the appreciation of poetry.

Introduction: To The Student

   This book has been written in order to help you appreciate poetry. A common question among beginning students is, why appreciate poetry at all? Why study it? What good is poetry going to do me in the life I am leading now or in the profession which I am preparing to enter? These are real questions, ones which it is right for you to ask about anything you do. In regard to poetry, these questions have real answers.

  The assumption that people should appreciate poetry is based on the larger assumption that people should appreciate people. Although some students think that their present and future happiness will be based on an appreciation of a machine or a sales technique or a law book, the fact remains that your most significant relationships, the ones whose success or failure will make you truly happy or sad, will be with other people, not with machines. Of course you can learn to appreciate people in many ways, the most obvious being just living day to day. And there are various disciplines of study which tell you what people have done (history), why they have done it (psychology, sociology, and economics), and what they ought to be doing instead (philosophy and religion). But literature, and especially the literature of poetry, is able to show you what people have thought and felt rather than simply to tell you about it: a good poem is a revelation of an individual's most intense thoughts and feelings written so artfully that you, the reader, can imaginatively participate in those thoughts and feelings, can make them come alive again for yourself. And since each poet is an individual person distinct from other poets, and each of his poems is an act of consciousness distinct from all his other poems, an appreciation of poetry will give you access to a wide variety of human thoughts and feelings. To appreciate poetry, then, is to appreciate a more intense and more varied range of human emotions and ideas than you would encounter by simply standing on a street corner or studying the seventeen kings of England.

A good poem is not just about life, it is itself a form of life, a form and a force which can enliven you. Poetry, as an art, appeals to your creative imagination as well as to your intellect. It strives to make you see and feel as well as to understand. Various intellectual disciplines can list for you the causes, the features, and the futures of such aspects of the human condition as love, fear, and pride; but only art, and especially the art of poetry, can enable you to recreate these conditions imaginatively in yourself. The poet uses language to embody his thoughts and feelings, to share with you (if you know how to receive them) these same thoughts and feelings. By appealing to your imagination, the poem will enliven it, stimulating it to live out its own life. Your relationships with other people depend a great deal on your ability to appreciate them imaginatively, as well as intellectually. You don't have to feel like a machine to understand one, but you do have to make some sort of imaginative identification with other people if you want to understand them and thus become a more complete person yourself. It follows, then, that increasing your ability to act imaginatively will increase your chances for sharing your human being with others.

Not only will poetry teach you to understand and share an intense and varied range of human thoughts and feelings, it will also teach you to appreciate the possibilities of language itself. Poetry is a language art, and one which, perhaps more than any other, utilizes the fullest scope of language's possibilities. Although many people take language for granted, it is clear that the invention and use of language is inseparable from the most fundamental identity of man himself. We live in a world of words, and we have to know how to use them. Words are not only necessary to give form to, and thereby communicate, our inner lives; they also establish bonds between all the elements of the social structure. Indeed, words are the foundation of society. Just as you find language indispensable in your personal relationships, so too will you find an ability to use language an absolute requirement for any profession into which you may enter. If you can't speak, read, and write, you can't get any job; and the more capable you are at these language skills, the more chance you have of getting ahead in whatever profession you choose. To appreciate poetry is to appreciate language, which is the first step in learning to use it well. This is what poetry can help you to do: to use language imaginatively, to convey accurately to someone the precise thought or feeling that the situation calls for, to choose the one key that unlocks the door that separates your listener from yourself. Thus, the education of your imagination is the most important part of your education, for you will learn to act imaginatively in all areas of your personal and public life.

The purpose of this book is to present a representative selection of the best poetry in the English language, and to provide you, the beginning student, with aids that will help you to become more conscious of the structure and meaning of poetry. Each chapter begins with an introduction explaining some aspect of poetry and presents a number of poems which use this aspect to achieve their individual ends. At least fifteen poems in each chapter are accompanied by questions designed to focus your attention on important features of the poems. Each chapter contains a bibliography of critical essays and books on a particular poet or poetic subject; in some cases important essays are reprinted for the students' perusal. And each chapter concludes with four "Topics for Writing," suggestions for writing essays on the poems in the chapter. Chapter 2 offers specific recommendations on how to write an essay about a poem and presents as examples two model essays on the same poem. The Glossary at the end of the book defines a number of terms that might be useful in describing what you find in the poems. And the Discography at the end of the book offers a list of records and tapes on which you can hear many of the poems in this book.

All of these aids, useful though they will be, should be considered subordinate to the poems themselves. The purpose of studying poetry is to learn not to define it, but to appreciate it. A poem should not appeal to you because it uses symbolism or paradox; it should use these elements of structure and meaning in order to appeal to you. The poems in this book have, by and large, demonstrated an ability to appeal to many people. I hope they appeal to you, too.

Appreciating Poetry

1 Poetry and the World of Words

We live in a world of words. The world sends us letters, sings us songs, pushes texts in front of our noses, whispers in our ears, listens to what we say, and reads what we write. As we must learn to live in our natural environment, so we must learn to participate in this world of words. We mark a child's growth by how soon and how well he uses words, and we measure a man by his verbal accuracy and eloquence. We must learn to listen, we must learn to speak, and we must learn to measure the speech of others against our own experiences. The reward for learning these things is a more complete participation in the life system of language.

One of the first steps in learning how to live in any world is to become aware of the varieties of life it supports. The world of words is protean, generating many forms. There are alphabets, almanacs, biographies, contracts, diaries, flytings, grammars, histories, idioms, jokes, koans, laments, encyclopedias, novels, odes, poems, quizzes, questions and quotes, rhymes and readers, songs, tomes, ukases, variorums, WORDS, xylographica, yearbooks, and many others, some of which have yet to be created. These language forms make possible a verbal community which joins us politically (a constitution), legally (a contract), spiritually (a prayer), and romantically (a promise).

Among the forms of language is poetry, which Webster's dictionary defines as "writing that formulates a concentrated imaginative awareness of experience in language chosen and arranged to create a specific emotional response through meaning, sound, and rhythm." This definition identifies two important features which have made the study and appreciation of poetry a requirement for anyone who hopes to claim citizenship in the world of words.

The first feature lies in the phrase "concentrated imaginative awareness of experience." Poetry offers another person's awareness of experience, one whose appreciation and understanding will require the reader's own awareness. There are two elements in this phrase: awareness and experience. Their relationship can be understood if we consider a famous poem by Robert Frost, "Stopping By Woods on a Snowy Evening."

Stopping By Woods On A Snowy Evening

Whose woods these are I think I know.
His house is in the village, though;
He will not see me stopping here
To watch his woods fill up with snow.

My little horse must think it queer
To stop without a farmhouse near
Between the woods and frozen lake
The darkest evening of the year.

He gives his harness bells a shake
To ask if there is some mistake.
The only other sound's the sweep
Of easy wind and downy flake.

The woods are lovely, dark, and deep,
But I have promises to keep,
And miles to go before I sleep,
And miles to go before I sleep.

The experience recorded in this poem is unexciting and commonplace: a man stops by a woods in winter and watches it fill up with snow. But the awareness of the experience is unusual. The importance of awareness is suggested not only by the poem's appeal, but also within the poem. The horse, a dumb and unaware animal, is contrasted with the man, who can see in the woods something "lovely, dark, and deep," and who imaginatively can recreate his awareness of that perception and share it with others. This poem shows us that though poetry can and does deal with a wide variety of human experience, it is not the unusual experience but the unusually intense awareness of that experience that makes the great poem. Going to Katmandu or the moon will not necessarily enable someone to write a great poem.

However, a poet is not simply someone who has an intense *awareness* of experience; he must also be someone who can recreate that awareness *in language*. As the dictionary definition reminds us, poetry is "language chosen and arranged to create a specific emotional response." To appreciate poetry, we must know and appreciate the many ways in which language can be chosen and arranged. We must develop a sense of the possibilities of language, the ways that rhythm, sound, and meaning can be used. The devices of language are not limited to poetry; a person who has never read a poem before can still read Frost's poem and appreciate it to some degree. The beginning student often thinks he knows nothing of poetry, but everything he knows about language is applicable to poetry, because poetry is only one form of life in the world of words in which we all live. By studying poetry we increase our understanding of the verbal world into which we were born.

How do we study a poem? The same way we study any form of language. We respond to it and then examine our response, discovering the reasons for it and correcting and refining it as we better understand those reasons. In analyzing a poem, we are really analyzing the reasons for our response to the poem, so that the next time we respond we will be more perceptive. It is important to know what we like, but it's equally important to know *why* we like it.

Frost's poem offers a good example of the relationship between response and examination. The poem seems simple: there are no difficult words, no allusions to unfamiliar myths or cultures, no unusual verse patterns. In fact, it seems *so* simple that many people read it inattentively and thus fall into a common error. They assume that this poem, or any other, can mean anything they want it to. For instance, an inattentive reader might say that Frost's poem is about God, or death, or eternity. This response, which is really an *over-response*, can be corrected by examining the poem, which says nothing about God, death, or eternity. The poem does evoke feelings which people have associated with these subjects, but in this poem the feelings are intentionally open-ended and suggestive, not limited to any specific subject.

If it is a mistake to provide our own subject for a poet's poem, it is also a mistake to add more information about the poet's subject than he put in the poem. A poem is language chosen and arranged to create a specific response, and what a poet leaves out is often as important as what he puts in. In Frost's poem there is no mention of where the man is going, why he stops to look at the woods, how old he is, or what promises he has to keep. If this were a newspaper article, we might feel cheated by the lack of information. But if we examine our responses to this poem, we will realize that those responses are based on the very suggestibility which such specific information would dispel. If we *over-analyze* and *read into* the poem things which are not there, we will destroy the response which the language was chosen and arranged to create.

These two fundamental errors, and others as well, can be avoided by paying close attention to the poem. The simple fact is that we learn to read and appreciate poetry by doing it often, not by memorizing rules and regulations about poetry. We must begin by making an act of faith in the importance and value of studying poetry, just as we make an act of faith when we begin to speak and write, when we first enter into the world of words. Poetry has been praised and cherished from the beginning of human history, and a knowledge of poetry always has been considered essential for anyone claiming to be an educated person.

The following selections suggest some important aspects of how poetry fits into the world of words. The first three poems deal with the verbal relationship between the individual and society, with the way in which people are connected by language. The next six discuss the special importance of poetry in the world of words. And the final six selections consider the role of the poet and his relationship to life. Each selection is accompanied by questions designed to focus the reader's attention on particularly important aspects of the poems.

THE UNKNOWN CITIZEN

(To JS/07/M/378 This Marble Monument Is Erected by the State)

He was found by the Bureau of Statistics to be
One against whom there was no official complaint,
And all the reports on his conduct agree
That, in the modern sense of an old-fashioned word, he was a saint,
For in everything he did he served the Greater Community,
Except for the War till the day he retired
He worked in a factory and never got fired,
But satisfied his employers, Fudge Motors Inc.
Yet he wasn't a scab or odd in his views,
For his Union reports that he paid his dues,
(Our report on his Union shows it was sound)
And our Social Psychology workers found
That he was popular with his mates and liked a drink.
The Press are convinced that he bought a paper every day
And that his reactions to advertisements were normal in every way.

Policies taken out in his name prove that he was fully insured.
And his Health-card shows he was once in hospital but left it cured.
Both Producers Research and High-Grade Living declare
He was fully sensible to the advantages of the Installment Plan
And had everything necessary to the Modern Man,
A phonograph, a radio, a car and a frigidaire.
Our researchers into Public Opinion are content
That he held the proper opinions for the time of year;
When there was peace, he was for peace; when there was war, he went.
He was married and added five children to the population,
Which our Eugenist says was the right number for a parent of his genera-
tion,
And our teachers report that he never interfered with their education.
Was he free? Was he happy? The question is absurd:
Had anything been wrong, we should certainly have heard.

W. H. AUDEN

Questions

1. *What is the relationship between "The Unknown Citizen" and the "Greater Community"?*
2. *In what ways do the capitalized words, just by being capitalized, suggest this relationship?*
3. *Is the citizen like the Unknown Soldier, to whom the State has also erected a monument? If so, who is his enemy? Why?*
4. *What is the poet's attitude toward the citizen and society? Is he praising or attacking them?*
5. *Why, when there are so many reports on "JS/07/M/378," does the poet call him an "Unknown"? What would it take to make him known as a person instead of a number? What is the significance of the last word of the poem?*

NEXT TO OF COURSE GOD AMERICA I

"next to of course god america i
love you land of the pilgrims' and so forth oh
say can you see by the dawn's early my
country 'tis of centuries come and go
and are no more what of it we should worry
in every language even deafanddumb
thy sons acclaim your glorious name by gorry

by jingo by gee by gosh by gum
why talk of beauty what could be more beaut-
iful than these heroic happy dead
who rushed like lions to the roaring slaughter
they did not stop to think they died instead
then shall the voice of liberty be mute?"

He spoke.   And drank rapidly a glass of water

E. E. CUMMINGS

Questions

1. *What does the last line indicate about the rest of the poem, which is in quotation marks?*
2. *How does the lack of punctuation reflect the relationship of thought and language in this speech? Is the absence of punctuation a device which "arranges" the language?*
3. *Do the speaker's references to God, America, the pilgrims, and "The Star-Spangled Banner" indicate his seriousness? What is suggested by the fact that the last word of the title is "i"?*
4. *Which of America's sons acclaim her glory in the language of "deafanddumb"? Is this an effective language?*
5. *Does the poet consider the speaker to be a "voice of liberty"? How can you tell? Is the poet himself a "voice of liberty"?*

MUCH MADNESS IS DIVINEST SENSE

Much madness is divinest sense
To a discerning eye—
Much sense the starkest madness.
'Tis the majority
In this, as all, prevail.
Assent and you are sane;
Demur, you're straightway dangerous
And handled with a chain.

EMILY DICKINSON

Questions

1. *What is the attitude of the poet toward the "majority"? Does she trust their judgment?*

2. Why does the poet use "Much" instead of "All"? Does this qualify her position in an important way?
3. What two possible meanings of "divinest" could apply in this poem?
4. By rhyming the words "sane" and "chain," the poet suggests a connection between them. What kind of people used to be "handled with a chain"?
5. Does this poem suggest any reason for the silence of Auden's Unknown Citizen?

YOUR POEM, MAN . . .

unless there's one thing seen
suddenly against another—a parsnip
sprouting for a President, or
hailstones melting in an ashtray—
nothing really happens. It takes
surprise and wild connections,
doesn't it? A walrus chewing
on a ballpoint pen. Two blue tail-
lights on Tyrannosaurus Rex. Green
cheese teeth. Maybe what we wanted
least. Or most. Some unexpected
pleats. Words that never knew
each other till right now. Plug us
into the wrong socket and see
what blows—or what lights up.
Try
     untried
          circuitry,
new
     fuses.
Tell it like it never really was,
man,
and maybe we can see it
like it is.

EDWARD LUEDERS

Questions

1. How are the "surprise and wild connections" of poetry like the "madness" that is "divinest sense" in Emily Dickinson's poem?

2. *This poem suggests that the method of presentation known as* **juxtaposition** *("one thing seen/suddenly against another") is the source of poetry's life and truth. What line of the poem mentions the risks and rewards of this method? How does this method of presentation differentiate poetry from such things in the world of words as encyclopedias and dictionaries?*

SONNET 65

Since brass, nor stone, nor earth, nor boundless sea,
But sad mortality o'ersways their power,
How with this rage shall beauty hold a plea,
Whose action is no stronger than a flower?
O how shall summer's honey breath hold out,
Against the wrackful siege of batt'ring days,
When rocks impregnable are not so stout,
Nor gates of steel so strong but time decays?
O fearful meditation, where alack,
Shall Time's best jewel from Time's chest lie hid?
Or what strong hand can hold his swift foot back,
Or who his spoil of beauty can forbid?
   O none, unless this miracle have might,
   That in black ink my love may still shine bright.

WILLIAM SHAKESPEARE

Questions

1. *Why is Time the enemy of beauty, which the poet calls "Time's best jewel"?*
2. *Does "summer's honey breath" refer just to the fragrance of flowers, or to something else as well? Whose is the "strong hand" that can hold back the swift foot of Time?*
3. *What activity might the terms "plea," "breath," "hand," and "ink" be associated with?*
4. *Is there a contradiction in the poet's statement in the last line that love may "shine bright" in "black ink"? How does the fact that you are reading this poem resolve that contradiction?*
5. *How is poetry more powerful than brass, stone, earth, and boundless sea?*

THROUGHOUT THE WORLD

Throughout the world, if it were sought,
Fair words enough a man shall find:
They be good cheap, they cost right nought,
Their substance is but only wind:
　　But well to say and so to mean,
　　That sweet accord is seldom seen.

SIR THOMAS WYATT

Questions

1. *What are the two relationships between language and truth which this poem contrasts?*
2. *What is the "sweet accord" mentioned in the last line?*

PERMANENTLY

One day the Nouns were clustered in the street.
An Adjective walked by, with her dark beauty.
The Nouns were struck, moved, changed.
The next day a Verb drove up and created the Sentence.

Each Sentence says one thing—for example, "Although it was a
　　dark rainy day when the Adjective walked by, I shall remember
　　the pure and sweet expression on her face until the day I
　　perish from the green, effective earth."
Or, "Will you please close the window, Andrew?"
Or, for example, "Thank you, the pink pot of flowers on the
　　window sill has changed color recently to a light yellow,
　　due to the heat from the boiler factory which exists nearby."

In the springtime the Sentences and the Nouns lay silently on
　　the grass.
A lonely Conjunction here and there would call, "And! But!"
But the Adjective did not emerge.

As the adjective is lost in the sentence,
So I am lost in your eyes, ears, nose, and throat—
You have enchanted me with a single kiss
Which can never be undone
Until the destruction of language.

KENNETH KOCH

Questions

1. *In stanza one how are the parts of the sentence related to men and women? What is a "copulative verb"?*
2. *In stanza two is there any relationship among the three sentences in quotation marks? How does this prove or disprove the truth of the first line, "Each Sentence says one thing"?*
3. *How is nature ("springtime") contrasted with the completed sentences quoted in stanza three? Why do the Sentences and Nouns "lay silently on the grass"? What aspect of a "Conjunction" makes it different from the parts of a Sentence which "says one thing"?*
4. *What is the identity of "I" and "you" in the last stanza? What kind of relationship between poet and reader is suggested by the word "kiss"? How is the poet lost in the reader's "eyes, ears, nose, and throat"?*
5. *What is the relationship between the last two lines of the poem and the poem's title? Does Koch suggest that poetry will be permanent in the same way that Shakespeare does?*

TEN DEFINITIONS OF POETRY

1. Poetry is a projection across silence of cadences arranged
   to break the silence with definite intentions of echoes,
   syllables, wave lengths.
2. Poetry is the journal of a sea animal living on land, wanting
   to fly in the air.
3. Poetry is a series of explanations of life, fading off
   into horizons too swift for explanations.
4. Poetry is a search for syllables to shoot at the barriers
   of the unknown and the unknowable.
5. Poetry is a theorem of a yellow-silk handkerchief knotted
   with riddles, sealed in a balloon tied to the tail of
   a kite flying in a white wind against a blue sky in spring.

6. Poetry is the silence and speech between a wet struggling root of a flower and a sunlit blossom of that flower.
7. Poetry is the harnessing of the paradox of earth cradling life and then entombing it.
8. Poetry is a phantom script telling how rainbows are made and why they go away.
9. Poetry is the synthesis of hyacinths and biscuits.
10. Poetry is the opening and closing of a door, leaving those who look through to guess about what is seen during a moment.

CARL SANDBURG

Questions

1. *What does definition 3 suggest about the relationship of poetry, knowledge, and awareness?*
2. *In what way, according to definition 6, is the development of a poem (for both poet and reader) like the growth of a flower?*
3. *How would you relate definition 7 to Shakespeare's Sonnet 65?*
4. *What does definition 2 say about the nature of man, as well as about his relationship to poetry?*
5. *How does the sound of the words in definition 9 convey the meaning of the definition it gives?*

GONE FOREVER

Halfway through shaving, it came—
the word for a poem.
I should have scribbled it
on the mirror with a soapy finger,
or shouted it to my wife in the kitchen,
or muttered it to myself till it ran
in my head like a tune.

But now it's gone with the whiskers
down the drain. Gone forever,
like the girls I never kissed,
and the places I never visited—
the lost lives I never lived.

BARRISS MILLS

CONSTANTLY RISKING ABSURDITY

Constantly risking absurdity
     and death
  whenever he performs
     above the heads
        of his audience
 the poet like an acrobat
     climbs on rime
      to a high wire of his own making
and balancing on eyebeams
     above a sea of faces
   paces his way
     to the other side of day
  performing entrechats
     and sleight-of-foot tricks
and other high theatrics
     and all without mistaking
   any thing
     for what it may not be
  For he's the super realist
     who must perforce perceive
   taut truth
     before the taking of each stance or step
in his supposed advance
     toward that still higher perch
where Beauty stands and waits
     with gravity
       to start her death-defying leap
  And he
    a little charleychaplin man
      who may or may not catch
   her fair eternal form
      spreadeagled in the empty air
   of existence

LAWRENCE FERLINGHETTI

Questions

1. *What kind of circus performer is the poet compared to in this poem? What is the ladder by which he climbs to the heights?*
2. *What is the poet's tightrope? What is the pun on "sea" in line 10? What might a poet's "sleight-of-foot tricks" refer to?*
3. *How is the poet, like the tightrope walker, a "super realist"? What are the two possible meanings of "super" here? Is super real the same as unreal?*
4. *Who is the poet's partner in his high wire act? Why is Beauty's leap in a poem "death-defying"?*
5. *What does the last stanza suggest about the relationship between Beauty, the poet, eternity, and time?*

POEM TO BE READ AT 3 A.M.

Excepting the diner
On the outskirts
The town of Ladora
At 3 A.M.
Was dark but
For my headlights
And up in
One second-story room
A single light
Where someone
Was sick or
Perhaps reading
As I drove past
At seventy
Not thinking
This poem
Is for whoever
Had the light on

DONALD JUSTICE

Questions

1. *What two kinds of people, according to the poem, might have the light on at 3 A.M. in Ladora?*
2. *How is the person who had the light on different from the rest of the people in Ladora? Are there any connections between being "sick" and "reading"?*

3. *Why would the poet rather write a poem for "whoever/Had the light on" than for all mankind?*

IN MY CRAFT OR SULLEN ART

In my craft or sullen art
Exercised in the still night
When only the moon rages
And the lovers lie abed
With all their griefs in their arms,
I labor by singing light
Not for ambition or bread
Or the strut and trade of charms
On the ivory stages
But for the common wages
Of their most secret heart.

Not for the proud man apart
From the raging moon I write
On these spindrift pages
Nor for the towering dead
With their nightingales and psalms
But for the lovers, their arms
Round the griefs of the ages,
Who pay no praise or wages
Nor heed my craft or art.

DYLAN THOMAS

Questions

1. *This poem suggests some possible reasons for writing poetry, as well as giving the reason that this poet writes. What rewards are offered by "ambition," "bread," and the "ivory stages"? What kind of "proud man" sets himself apart from the movement of time and the "raging moon"? What great poets of "nightingales and psalms" might be included among "the towering dead"?*
2. *The poet associates himself with the "moon," which has no light of its own but merely reflects the sun's light. How is the poet's relationship with the unheeding*

lovers like the moon's relationship with the sun? Why is the moon "raging"? Why is the poet's art "sullen"? Is Thomas' poet as insignificant as Ferlinghetti's "little charleychaplin man"?

3. Is the poet's work of "singing light" similar to the moon's act of reflecting the sun's light? Why does he call his writing "spindrift pages"?

4. What is the source of "the griefs of the ages"? Is it similar to that of Shakespeare's "sad mortality"? Why should lovers, who are supposedly happy, hold "all their griefs in their arms"?

5. The poet declares that he works for the "common wages" of each person's "most secret heart," the knowledge shared with lovers and the moon that all things beautiful must die. How does this attitude compare with Sandburg's seventh definition of poetry? Does the poet learn this from the moon or the lovers, or from himself?

POETRY

I, too, dislike it: there are things that are important beyond all this fiddle.
    Reading it, however, with a perfect contempt for it, one discovers in
    it after all, a place for the genuine.
        Hands that can grasp, eyes
        that can dilate, hair that can rise
            if it must, these things are important not because a

high-sounding interpretation can be put upon them but because they are
    useful. When they become so derivative as to become unintelligible,
    the same thing may be said for all of us, that we
        do not admire what
        we cannot understand: the bat
            holding on upside down or in quest of something to

eat, elephants pushing, a wild horse taking a roll, a tireless wolf under
    a tree, the immovable critic twitching his skin like a horse that feels a
    flea, the
            base-
    ball fan, the statistician—
        nor is it valid
            to discriminate against 'business documents and

school-books'; all these phenomena are important. One must make a dis-
tinction
    however: when dragged into prominence by half poets, the result is
        not poetry,
  nor till the poets among us can be
    'literalists of
      the imagination'—above
        insolence and triviality and can present

for inspection, 'imaginary gardens with real toads in them,' shall we have
  it. In the meantime, if you demand on the one hand,
  the raw material of poetry in
    all its rawness and
    that which is on the other hand
      genuine, you are interested in poetry.

MARIANNE MOORE

Questions

1. *What does the speaker mean by "the genuine" which has a place in good poetry? How is the genuine "useful"?*
2. *What is the connection between life and art suggested in the last four lines of the poem?*

LINES FOR A YOUNG POET WHO FLED

Your cries make us afraid, but we love
your delicious music!

        Kierkegaard

So you said you'd go home to work on your father's farm.
We've talked of how it is the poet alone can touch
with words, but I would touch you with my hand, my lost son,
to say good-bye again. You left some work, and have gone.
You don't know what you mean. Oh, not to me as a son,
for I have others. Perhaps too many. I cannot
answer all the letters. If I seem to brag, I add
I know how to shatter an image of the father
(twice have tried to end the yearning of an orphan son,

but opened up in him, and in me, another wound).
No—I say this: you don't know the reason of your gift.
It's not the suffering. Others have that. The gift of tears
is the hope of saints, Monica again and Austin.
I mean the gift of the structure of a poet's jaw,
which makes the mask that's cut out of the flesh of his face
a megaphone—as with the goat clad Greeks—to ampli-
fy the light gestures of his soul toward the high stone seats.
The magic of the mouth that can melt to tears the rock
of hearts. I mean the wand of tongues that charms the exile
of listeners into a bond of brothers, breaking
down the lines of lead that separate a man from a
man, and the husbands from their wives, in these old, burned glass
panels of our lives. The poet's jaw has its tongue ripped
as Philomel, its lips split (and kissed beside the grave),
the jawbone patched and cracked with fists and then with the salve
of his fellows. If they make him bellow, like a slave
cooked inside the ancient, brass bull, still that small machine
inside its throat makes music for an emperor's guest
out of his cries. Thus his curse: the poet cannot weep
but with a public and musical grief, and he laughs
with the joys of others. Yet, when the lean blessings come,
they are sweet, and great. My son, I could not make your choice.
Let me take your hand, I am too old or young to say,
"I'd rather be a swineherd in the hut, understood
by swine, than be a poet misunderstood by men."

JOHN LOGAN

Questions

1. *How does the epigraph suggest the difference between the poet as a person and the poet as an artist? How do the last three lines of the poem suggest this difference?*
2. *What is the difference between possessing "the gift of tears" and possessing the "magic of the mouth that can melt to tears the rock/of hearts"?*
3. *How can poetry make an "exile of listeners" into a "bond of brothers"? How can the poet "touch/with words"?*
4. *The poem alludes to an ancient torture of cooking people inside a large brass bull; their screams, reverberating against the brass, sounded pleasing to the torturer's guests. How is this translation of intense personal awareness into pleasing and public language typical of poetry? Why is it a "curse"?*
5. *How does the relationship of poet and society in this poem compare to the one suggested in the Thomas poem?*

from I: SIX NONLECTURES

Fine and dandy: but, so far as I am concerned, poetry and
every other art was and is and forever will be strictly and
distinctly a question of individuality. If poetry were anything—
like dropping an atom bomb—which anyone did, anyone could
become a poet merely by doing the necessary anything; what-
ever that anything might or might not entail. But (as it happens)
poetry is being, not doing. If you wish to follow, even at a
distance, the poet's calling (and here, as always, I speak from
my own totally biased and entirely personal point of view)
you've got to come out of the measurable doing universe into
the immeasurable house of being. I am quite aware that, wher-
ever our socalled civilization has slithered, there's every re-
ward and no punishment for unbeing. But if poetry is your goal,
you've got to forget all about punishments and all about
rewards and all about selfstyled obligations and duties and
responsibilities etcetera ad infinitum and remember one thing
only: that it's you—nobody else—who determine your destiny
and decide your fate. Nobody else can be alive for you; nor can
you be alive for anybody else. Toms can be Dicks and Dicks
can be Harrys, but none of them can ever be you. There's the
artist's responsibility; and the most awful responsibility on
earth. If you can take it, take it—and be. If you can't,
cheer up and go about other people's business; and do (or undo)
till you drop.

E. E. CUMMINGS

Questions

1. *What does cummings suggest is the difference between the artist and the rest of
   society? Do you think he would define "poet" as a writer of poems, or as the
   follower of a way of life as well?*
2. *Why is doing measurable, and being immeasurable?*
3. *How does Auden's poem reflect the difference between being and doing?*
4. *How can you judge whether a poem, yourself, or another person is "being" or
   merely "doing" an imitation of some Tom, Dick, or Harry?*
5. *How does this passage suggest the importance of poetry in the world of words?*

Bibliography: e e cummings

Baum, S. V. ed. *E. E. Cummings and the Critics.* East Lansing, Mich.: Michigan State University Press, 1966.

Cummings, E. E. *i: six nonlectures.* Cambridge, Mass.: Harvard University Press, 1953.

Davis, William V. "Cummings' 'next to of course god america i'." *Concerning Poetry* 3 (1970)i: 14–15.

Dias, Earl J. "e. e. cummings and Buffalo Bill," *CEA Critic* 29 (1966):iii, 6–7.

Friedman, Norman, ed. *E. E. Cummings: A Collection of Critical Essays.* Englewood Cliffs, N.J.: Prentice-Hall, 1972.

Gidley, Mick. "Picture and Poem: E. E. Cummings in Perspective." *Poetry Review* 59 (1968):179–98.

Marks, Barry A. *E. E. Cummings.* New york: Twayne Publishers, 1963.

Wegner, Robert E. *The Poetry and Prose of E. E. Cummings.* New York: Harcourt, Brace & World, 1965.

Topics for Writing

1. In order to appreciate poetry, you must first appreciate the different forms of language. Write a 500-word essay in which you present two language forms on the same subject. You might choose:
   a. A yearbook description of a person and a conversational description of the same person to someone you would like that person to meet.
   b. An encyclopedia article on the color blue and a poem entitled "Ten Definitions of Blue" (modeled after Sandburg's "Ten Definitions of Poetry").
   c. A statistical report on yourself (as if you were Auden's "Unknown Citizen") and a description of yourself to be included in an application for a job.
2. Shakespeare and Koch suggest that language sometimes provides a kind of permanence, even immortality. Write a 500-word essay comparing the effects of time on the following: a newspaper story, a folk saying ("You can lead a horse to water but you can't make him drink"), a popular song (why an "Oldie Goldie" can't be a "Top Pop" any more), an ethnic joke, and a poem such as Shakespeare's Sonnet 65. Do you really think poetry should survive longer than the other forms of language art? Why has Shakespeare's poetry survived?
3. Write an essay on the relationship of awareness and experience (as discussed in the introduction) in any poem in this chapter. Cite examples showing how the poet's awareness is revealed through the language he uses.
4. Write an essay on the relationship of awareness and experience as expressed in the Cummings selection.

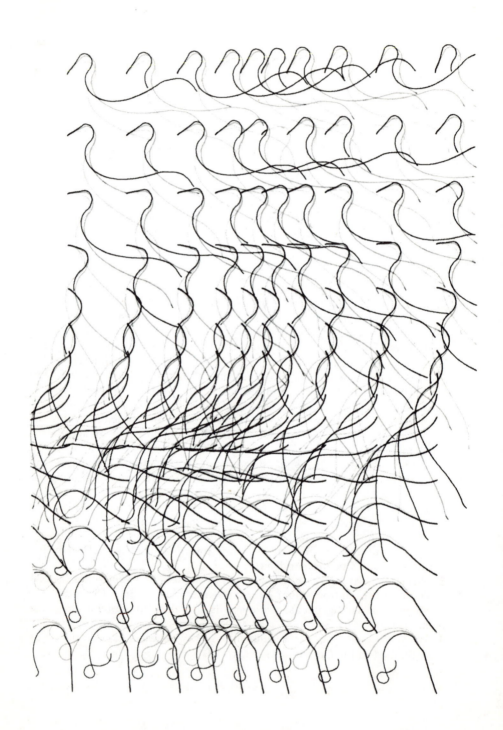

2 Poetry and the Reader

The most important aspect of language is its liveliness, and poetry is one of language's liveliest forms. The relationship between a reader and a poem has all the complexity of any relationship between living beings, and it offers similar pleasures and rewards.

Understanding and appreciating a poem is not unlike understanding and appreciating another person. We must begin by being actively open to a new poem, accepting the uncertainty which accompanies any exposure to the unknown. Then we must work toward a basic comprehension of the poem's statement. Finally, we must be able to make some sort of interpretation of the poem and our reaction to it, always admitting that interpretation can change and grow as we ourselves learn more. There are several practical steps we can take to achieve these goals.

Use a dictionary. If a word is new to you, or if its meaning is unclear in the context of the poem, look in the dictionary. Words you have never seen before, or have forgotten, are easy to recognize. But some of the most familiar words can have strange meanings and usages. Here is a line from the Wallace Stevens poem "The Emperor of Ice Cream": "Let be be finale of seem." The word "be" is used twice, first as an infinitive, then as a verb in the imperative mood (as befits an emperor). Here is another line from the same poem: "Take from the dresser of deal." The word "deal" is a noun, meaning a kind of wood; it is not the verb form, "to deal," nor does it carry other meanings of the noun, like "such a deal" or "big deal." Appreciating the uses of words in a poem will enable you to appreciate not only the poem, but each word as well. Dictionaries also give the pronunciation of words, which is as important as the meaning. In the first line quoted, the word "finale" has three syllables, with the stress on the middle one; and the final "e" is long, as in "me." An appreciation of this line demands a recognition of the correct pronunciation, as well as the meaning, of "finale."

Use your knowledge of grammar. Poetry is always responsive to the fundamental rules of grammar and punctuation. If you have difficulty understanding a sentence in a poem, look for the subject and verb, the modifiers, and so forth. You do this subconsciously every time you read or listen, and when you become confused it is wise to go through the same process consciously. Here is the beginning sentence (seven lines) of "Auto Wreck" by Karl Shapiro:

> Its quick soft silver bell beating, beating
> And down the dark one ruby flare
> Pulsing out red light like an artery,
> The ambulance at top speed floating down
> Past beacons and illuminated clocks
> Wings in a heavy curve, dips down,
> And brakes speed, entering the crowd.

The arrangement of the language gives the effect of the arrival of an ambulance at the scene of an auto wreck. A sense of time's being suspended, slowed down, while the crowd waits for the ambulance is suggested by the phrase "top speed floating down." It is also suggested by the word order of the sentence, in which the subject (the ambulance) does not appear until the fourth line, and the main verbs (Wings, dips, and brakes) until even later. The delay in presenting the subject suggests the delay in the actual appearance of the ambulance, which is first signalled by its sound (the bell) and its light (the ruby flare) as it speeds to the scene. The word order is altered for a purpose, then, but is still faithful to the basic laws of language. The sentence could be diagrammed. Poetry is not ungrammatical, it is super-grammatical. It obeys the unconscious laws of language which govern our own everyday speech, but it uses them imaginatively; sometimes it may be necessary for you to consciously trace out the imaginative application of these laws.

Use your voice and your ear as well as your eye. Read poems aloud, to yourself and to others. Listen to yourself reading, and to others reading to you. If possible, listen to a recording of the poem by the poet or by a professional reader. Many of the poems in this book are available on records, which you may borrow from your school or local library. If you like a particular poem, you might follow the advice of the poet Rilke and copy it out in your own hand. Memorize it. Speak it slowly and distinctly enough to allow its words and rhythms to echo in your head. Obey the pauses indicated by punctuation marks, and pause slightly at the end of a line, even if there is no punctuation there. Do not exaggerate the meter of the line; read it naturally, and the meter should assert itself. Read a line several different ways to see which way sounds most suitable. Your voice and your ear have standards of pleasure and common sense which can help you appreciate and understand poetry.

Use your intellect to determine your reaction to a poem, and to analyze the reasons for and the significance of that reaction. After you have grasped the plain sense of the poem, and have read and spoken it with this basic understanding in mind, it is time to determine your reaction to the poem *as a whole*. There is a mistaken notion that explaining your feelings about poetry can destroy them; this is true only when analysis becomes a substitute for feeling. A good poem is structurally sound, and the reaction it evokes is not going to be destroyed by an understanding of some of the reasons for the reaction. On the contrary, understanding increases appreciation. Further, the writing of this understanding sharpens your own sense of your reaction, which in turn reveals an important part of yourself. Just as explaining your feelings about someone else helps to explain yourself to you, so describing your reaction to a poem can and should be an act of self-discovery as well as an act of criticism.

Let us apply the procedure we have outlined to the entire poem "Auto Wreck," by Karl Shapiro.

Auto Wreck

Its quick soft silver bell beating, beating,
And down the dark one ruby flare
Pulsing out red light like an artery,
The ambulance at top speed floating down
Past beacons and illuminated clocks
Wings in a heavy curve, dips down,
And brakes speed, entering the crowd.
The doors leap open, emptying light;
Stretchers are laid out, the mangled lifted
And stowed into the little hospital.
Then the bell, breaking the hush, tolls once,
And the ambulance with its terrible cargo
Rocking, slightly rocking, moves away,
As the doors, an afterthought, are closed.

We are deranged, walking among the cops
Who sweep glass and are large and composed.
One is still making notes under the light.
One with a bucket douches ponds of blood
Into the street and gutter.
One hangs lanterns on the wrecks that cling,
Empty husks of locusts, to iron poles.

Our throats were tight as tourniquets,
Our feet were bound with splints, but now,
Like convalescents intimate and gauche,
We speak through sickly smiles and warn
With the stubborn saw of common sense,
The grim joke and the banal resolution.
The traffic moves around with care,
But we remain, touching a wound
That opens to our richest horror.
Already old, the question Who shall die?
Becomes unspoken Who is innocent?

For death in war is done by hands;
Suicide has cause and stillbirth, logic;
And cancer, simple as a flower, blooms.
But this invites the occult mind,
Cancels our physics with a sneer,
And spatters all we knew of denouement
Across the expedient and wicked stones.

After you have read the title and the poem several times, the general subject, an auto wreck and its effect on various people, should be clear. But you still may be uncertain about the meanings of several words. In the first stanza "beacons" and "mangled" may require looking up. "Deranged" is a very important word in the second stanza, and the meaning and pronunciation of "douches" may be unfamiliar. In the third stanza "tourniquets," "convalescents," "gauche," "saw" (which is not a verb), and "banal" may offer difficulties in meaning, pronunciation, or both. The last stanza has "stillbirth," "occult," "physics," "denouement," and "expedient."

You may already know some or all of these words, but you may not be quite certain how they fit into the context of the poem. Notice, for instance, how the "deranged" state of the speaker in stanza two, mentioned in the first line, prepares for the deranged vision he presents: cops "large and composed," the twisted wreckage that reminds him of "Empty husks of locusts." Notice the sound of "douches" as it fits with the vowel sounds in "ponds of blood." The context provides some help with "physics" in the last stanza, which the dictionary defines as a "science." You may wonder how an auto wreck can negate a science; but the words "cause," "logic," "mind," and "cancel" provide a context for "physics" that makes the word mean "any rational explanation of events"; and of course an irrational accident can "cancel" such "physics." In addition, "physics" sounds like and thereby reminds us of "physiques," meaning physical bodies: this pun suggests that the auto wreck not only cancels our rational explanation of natural events, but it also kills (the ultimate cancellation) our bodies as well.

The grammar of the poem presents no insurmountable difficulties. The initial "Its" refers to the ambulance, which takes the wreck victims away to the hospital. The "We" of stanzas two, three, and four refers to the observers, the crowd. The change of verb tense in stanza three (from "were" to "speak") suggests the transition from the crowd's initial reaction to the accident to its later reflection on it. This transition is also reflected in the shift from the first question of stanza four ("Who shall die?") to the second ("Who is innocent?"). These questions have no quotation marks in the poem because they are asked by all men rather than by any particular person, and because they are thought rather than uttered (they are termed "unspoken"). And the pronoun "this" in the fourth line of the last stanza refers to the auto wreck itself.

Just as words are used in a poem for their sounds as well as their meanings, so too punctuation and word order are used to create effects of sound and rhythm as well as meaning. In the first line, for instance, the absence of punctuation (commas) in the series of adjectives ("quick soft silver") suggests that the words modify "bell" simultaneously, rather than in any temporal or logical order (the bell is not quick *before* it is soft, nor is it soft *because* it is quick). The effect of the word order in the first sentence has already been discussed; but contrast this sentence's length and involvement with the relative simplicity of the three sentences in stanza two which begin with "One." Notice the rhythmic regularity of the subject-verb-object pattern, as well as the repetition of "One" at the beginning of each sentence. Does such regularity suggest a different state of mind from that of the first stanza? Perhaps it suggests the "deranged" crowd's state of shock. At any rate, the pattern of punctuation and word order is different in the second stanza from that in the first, and this difference creates effects of sound and rhythm which you will feel as you read the poem aloud. Mr. Shapiro has recorded this poem (see the list of recordings); after you have read it aloud several times, obtain a copy of the recording and listen to the poet read his poem. Notice the emphasis which he puts on certain words and phrases; compare his reading with your own.

The analysis of a poem is never by itself a satisfactory response; analysis must be followed by synthesis, by a unified expression of your reaction in terms of the information the analysis has provided. A mere listing of details is not enough: such a list would make the poem as depersonalized as the Unknown Citizen that Auden wrote about. Nor would an overemotional response serve to bring to life anything more than your own feelings, as uninformed by the poem as they were before you read it. You can't make a poem into something it is not, any more than you can make a person into something he is not. You must commit yourself to a living relationship with the poem, and this can be done by writing an essay on your informed reaction to it.

Following are two student essays on "Auto Wreck." Both satisfy the basic requirements of an essay—that it be unified and coherent in its own terms. But the essays differ in the methods of presentation. The first proves its thesis through a close examination of the details of the poem, using these details as examples to support the essay's generalizations. The organization of the essay is closely tied to the organization of the poem. The second essay selects as its thesis the conclusion of the poem, restating it so that it becomes the opinion of the author of the essay; then that opinion is explained in terms of the poem and the student's reaction to the poem. The first essay is an explanation of the poem; the second is an explanation of the student's reaction to the poem. Both are acceptable responses to a work of art, and both are models which the beginning student of poetry is capable of imitating. Read them carefully, now that you know the poem.

Auto Wreck

"Auto Wreck" presents the reaction of bystanders to an automobile accident. The first stanza describes the arrival and departure of an ambulance, and through its imagery and rhythm suggests the initial confused, shocked reaction of the people. The second stanza describes the actions of the authorities, the "cops," in writing the accident report and cleaning up the wreckage. The third stanza shows the gradual "emotional recovery" of the bystanders from their initial shock. And the last stanza describes their intellectual reaction to the accident, the questions they ask about the "cause" of any accidental death.

The shocked haze of the onlookers is reflected in the description of the arrival of the ambulance. First is heard the "quick soft silver bell beating, beating." This line suggests the distance and unreality of the sound, and seems to confuse it with the beating of a victim's heart. The "ruby flare" of the ambulance is compared to "an artery," which is "Pulsing out red light" like a human heart. The phrase "top speed floating down" suggests the difference between the actual speed of the ambulance and the dazed perception of the bystanders that the ambulance is moving very slowly. After the "mangled" bodies are put into the "little hospital," the shocked "hush" of the crowd is broken by the bell. As the ambulance pulls away, the tension of the crowd is eased: the incessant "beating, beating" rhythm of the first line is replaced by the gentler motion of "Rocking, slightly rocking," as though the onlookers' emotions were collapsing into an infantile state.

The second stanza contrasts the "deranged" onlookers with the "cops," who are efficiently and impersonally dealing with a situation they have seen before. The tasks that seem ordinary to the policemen, writing a report and cleaning up the debris, are described by the speaker in language that makes them seem grotesque. The phrases "douches ponds of blood" and "Empty husks of locusts" reflect the speaker's "deranged" vision of the scene, his extreme emotional reaction to it.

The third stanza describes the bystanders as emotional "victims" who are gradually recovering. When the accident first occurred, they couldn't speak ("Our throats were tight as tourniquets"), and they couldn't move ("Our feet were bound with splints"). Now they are like "convalescents" whom the traffic must move around "with care" while they recover. They can utter a "grim joke" through their "sickly smiles," and they can appeal to "common sense" ("Why didn't they watch where they were going?") and make some "banal resolution" ("I'll buckle up next time."), but such empty phrases are just ways of "touching a wound" that both intrigues and horrifies them.

The wound is their own vulnerability. In the last stanza the speaker applies the lesson of the accident to all mankind. The shift from the question "Who shall die" to "Who is innocent" suggests that neither has a satisfactory answer. Though there is a "cause" for "death in war," "Suicide" and "stillbirth," an accident is a "denouement" that has no cause. A "denouement" suggests the ending of a play. Even though the ending of a play may be bloody and murderous, it is the result of a cause. But an auto wreck "spatters" our sense of denouement on the "stones", and though some may, out of desperation, call such stones a "wicked" and "expedient" cause, the irony of attributing intention and purpose to stones only reveals the bitter impossibility of finding *any* cause for an auto wreck.

Auto Wreck

An automobile crashes and a life is snuffed out. Death is not a question of fairness. It strikes rich, poor, innocent, and evil. It may strike a young promise—it may strike a promise fulfilled. Death is the inevitable, mysterious something that stalks everyone and always seems to pounce at inopportune times. Death is irrational and it defeats all, even those who smugly attempt to rationalize and control its tragic grip. No pragmatist can justify death—no scientist can control it. It "Cancels our physics with a sneer/and spatters all we know of denouement/across the expedient and wicked stones." Death is the eternal mystery.

The full import of the mystery of death, its irrationality, its inevitability, and its finality, is emphasized by the word choices in Karl Shapiro's poem "Auto Wreck." To grasp the impact of the poem's message, it is necessary to read the first stanza rapidly, as the ambulance speeds to the accident scene. This rapidity creates a sense of the insistent urgency in the first stanza. The light on top of the ambulance "pulsing out red like an artery" suggests the gushing out of the victim's life blood. The second stanza slows down—the victim is dead. Normality is restored externally as one policeman records the accident and another clears the streets, "with a bucket douches ponds of blood into the street and gutter." But for some witnesses, normality is not quite so easily restored. Their throats are constricted and they cannot breathe. It is as though tourniquets have been tightly bound around their necks. They have seen shocking, irrational death and they cannot move. Their feet seem to be "bound with splints." The question of who would die has been answered, but why that person died is still a mystery. That mystery will never be solved, not even by the logic of scientists.

"Auto Wreck" engulfed me with memories as I read it, of a somewhat similar accident I witnessed several years ago when two young girls on a mini-bike collided with a pick-up truck in front of my home. One child was killed instantly. For the first time in my life, I was confronted with the injustice and the inevitability of death. I witnessed my neighbors' grief as they struggled to regain normality, following the principle that life had to go on, even though their lives had been shattered. I will never understand the mystery of death, and I am frightened. Knowing that even a scientist cannot explain death is no consolation. My horror at watching unexpected death striking down a young promise will always remain with me.

Here are five questions which you might apply to the rest of the poems in this chapter, as well as to any other poem in the book.

1. What is the subject of the poem?
2. What is the relationship of the speaker to the subject?
3. What aspects of the language (meaning, sound, and rhythm) reveal the particular awareness of experience evident in this poem?
4. What is the thesis statement of an essay you might write explaining your reaction to the poem?
5. What examples from the poem would you choose to support your thesis statement?

THERE IS NO FRIGATE LIKE A BOOK

There is no frigate like a book
   To take us lands away,
Nor any coursers like a page
   Of prancing poetry.
This traverse may the poorest take
   Without oppress of toll;
How frugal is the chariot
   That bears the human soul!

EMILY DICKINSON

Questions

1. *How is a "frigate" like a "book," or a page of "poetry" like a "courser"?*
2. *Explain the ways in which literature can transport the reader to other worlds.*
3. *What is the difference between transporting the "human soul" and the human mind or human body?*

MY PAPA'S WALTZ

The whiskey on your breath
Could make a small boy dizzy;
But I hung on like death:
Such waltzing was not easy.

We romped until the pans
Slid from the kitchen shelf;
My mother's countenance
Could not unfrown itself.

The hand that held my wrist
Was battered on one knuckle;
At every step you missed
My right ear scraped a buckle.

You beat time on my head
With a palm caked hard by dirt,
Then waltzed me off to bed
Still clinging to your shirt.

THEODORE ROETHKE

Questions

1. *What kind of motion is suggested by a "waltz"? Does the rhythm of the poem have this kind of motion?*
2. *How does the way the boy and his father dance suggest their relationship? Do they have the same physical and emotional perspectives on the dance?*
3. *What does the description of the father's hands in stanzas three and four reveal about his work?*
4. *What is the mother's reaction to the dance? What does the detail of the upsetting of the kitchen pans suggest about the mother's relationship to the dance?*
5. *Is the son terrified or delighted by his papa's waltz?*

ONE HOME

Mine was a Midwest home—you can keep your world.
Plain black hats rode the thoughts that made our code.
We sang hymns in the house; the roof was near God.

The light bulb that hung in the pantry made a wan light,
but we could read by it the names of preserves—
outside, the buffalo grass, and the wind in the night.

A wildcat sprang at Grandpa on the Fourth of July
when he was cutting plum bushes for fuel,
before Indians pulled the West over the edge of the sky.

To anyone who looked at us we said, "My friend";
liking the cut of a thought, we could say, "Hello."
(But plain black hats rode the thoughts that made our code.)

The sun was over our town; it was like a blade.
Kicking cottonwood leaves we ran toward storms.
Wherever we looked the land would hold us up.

WILLIAM STAFFORD

1. *How would you characterize the home that produced the speaker of this poem? In what ways does it contrast with the home of the speaker of "My Papa's Waltz"?*
2. *What kind of life style is suggested by the second line of the poem (repeated again as the twelfth line)? What is the effect of describing the code makers as "thoughts" instead of people in stanza one? What is the meaning of "the cut of a thought" in stanza four?*
3. *What is the difference between life inside the house and life in the country surrounding it? What are the associations of "wildcat," "Fourth of July," "Indians," and the "West"? Do they suggest elements of life which oppose the code of the "plain black hats" of Midwest settlers?*
4. *How is the lack of openness to experience which the speaker learned in his home reflected in his first sentence?*

THE MICROSCOPE

Anton Leeuwenhoek was Dutch.
He sold pincushions, cloth, and such.
The waiting townsfolk fumed and fussed
As Anton's dry goods gathered dust.

He worked, instead of tending store,
At grinding special lenses for
A microscope. Some of the things
He looked at were:
                              mosquitoes' wings,
the hairs of sheep, the legs of lice,
the skin of people, dogs, and mice;
ox eyes, spiders' spinning gear,
fishes' scales, a little smear
of his own blood,
                              and best of all,
the unknown, busy, very small
bugs that swim and bump and hop
inside a simple water drop.

Impossible! Most Dutchmen said.
This Anton's crazy in the head.
We ought to ship him off to Spain.
He says he's seen a housefly's brain.
He says the water that we drink
Is full of bugs. He's mad, we think!

They called him *dumkopf*, which means dope.
That's how we got the microscope.

MAXINE KUMIN

Questions

1. *What is the subject of this poem?*
2. *What is the speaker's attitude toward her subject? How do the last two lines of the poem reveal this attitude?*
3. *What are the "bugs that swim and bump and hop/inside a simple water drop"?*

RICHARD CORY

Whenever Richard Cory went down town,
   We people on the pavement looked at him:
He was a gentleman from sole to crown,
   Clean favored, and imperially slim.

And he was always quietly arrayed,
   And he was always human when he talked;
But still he fluttered pulses when he said,
   "Good-morning," and he glittered when he walked.

And he was rich—yes, richer than a king,
   And admirably schooled in every grace:
In fine, we thought that he was everything
   To make us wish that we were in his place.

So on we worked, and waited for the light,
   And went without the meat, and cursed the bread;
And Richard Cory, one calm summer night,
   Went home and put a bullet through his head.

EDWIN ARLINGTON ROBINSON

Questions

1. *Who is the speaker of this poem, and what economic class does he belong to?*
2. *What do the words "crown," "imperially," "king," and "grace," used by the speaker to describe Richard Cory, suggest about the speaker's relationship to his subject?*
3. *How does the regularity of meter and rhyme contribute to the shock of the sudden end in the last line?*
4. *Does the poem give any hint of why Richard Cory would kill himself?*
5. *Which of these statements seems most accurate to you:*
   a. *"Richard Cory" shows that being rich isn't always better than being poor.*
   b. *"Richard Cory" shows that being envious of others as well as miserable with your own life makes living a worse fate than death.*
   c. *"Richard Cory" shows the futility of pretending or wanting to be something you are not.*

THE PICNIC

It is the picnic with Ruth in the spring.
Ruth was third on my list of seven girls
But the first two were gone (Betty) or else
Had someone (Ellen has accepted Doug).
Indian Gully the last day of school;
Girls make the lunches for the boys too.
I wrote a note to Ruth in algebra class
Day before the test. She smiled, and nodded.
We left the cars and walked through the young corn
The shoots green as paint and the leaves like tongues
Trembling. Beyond the fence where we stood
Some wild strawberry flowered by an elm tree
And Jack-in-the-pulpit was olive ripe.
A blackbird fled as I crossed, and showed
A spot of gold or red under its quick wing.
I held the wire for Ruth and watched the whip
Of her long, striped skirt as she followed.
Three freckles blossomed on her thin, white back
Underneath the loop where the blouse buttoned.
We went for our lunch away from the rest,
Stretched in the new grass, our heads close
Over unknown things wrapped up in wax papers.
Ruth tried for the same, I forget what it was,

And our hands were together. She laughed,
And a breeze caught the edge of her little
Collar and the edge of her brown, loose hair
That touched my cheek. I turned my face in-
to the gentle fall. I saw how sweet it smelled.
She didn't move her head or take her hand.
I felt a soft caving in my stomach
As at the top of the highest slide
When I had been a child, but was not afraid,
And did not know why my eyes moved with wet
As I brushed her cheek with my lips and brushed
Her lips with my own lips. She said to me
Jack, Jack, different than I had ever heard,
Because she wasn't calling me, I think,
Or telling me. She used my name to
Talk in another way I wanted to know.
She laughed again and then she took her hand;
I gave her what we both had touched—can't
Remember what it was, and we ate the lunch.
Afterward we walked in the small, cool creek
Our shoes off, her skirt hitched, and she smiling,
My pants rolled, and then we climbed up the high
Side of Indian Gully and looked
Where we had been, our hands together again.
It was then some bright thing came in my eyes,
Starting at the back of them and flowing
Suddenly through my head and down my arms
And stomach and my bare legs that seemed not
To stop in feet, not to feel the red earth
Of the Gully, as though we hung in a
Touch of birds. There was a word in my throat
With the feeling and I knew the first time
What it meant and I said, it's beautiful.
Yes, she said, and I felt the sound and word
In my hand join the sound and word in hers
As in one name said, or in one cupped hand.
We put back on our shoes and socks and we
Sat in the grass awhile, crosslegged, under
A blowing tree, not saying anything.
And Ruth played with shells she found in the creek,
As I watched. Her small wrist which was so sweet
To me turned by her breast and the shells dropped
Green, white, blue, easily into her lap,

Passing light through themselves. She gave the pale
Shells to me, and got up and touched her hips
With her light hands, and we walked down slowly
To play the school games with the others.

JOHN LOGAN

Questions

1. *What is the subject of this poem? What is the speaker's attitude toward the subject?*
2. *How would you characterize the experience which the boy and girl of the poem undergo? How is it different from the "school games" of the others on the picnic?*
3. *Explain the following quotes from the poem:*
   a. *"She used my name to/Talk in another way I wanted to know."*
   b. *"There was a word in my throat/With the feeling and I knew the first time/What it meant and I said, it's beautiful."*

IDENTITY

(for don l. lee)

i saw a man once
tall wearing a crown
of natural   *Being accepted by white world.*
a prophet/creator of   *Being himself*
change showing identity
to negroes (the whiteminded
ones)
a black gospel he had
the message to save them
his name was   Poet

he said   -what are you-
i felt fear for what
could i say or how
should i answer what
he asked ("a negro".no.
something is wrong)

i gathered nerve and
ventured
hoping he would ask no
further as birth is a
painful process

-i am a person-

he said
sharp pain cut like ground
glass (should i lie/say
yes . . . no i need time)
(but i didn't want to
hear)

-are you B l a c k-

facing new a pet

-what do you mean-

-do you THINK BLACK-

i knew i knew what he
meant i knew but i could
not say yes in my
imitationwhite hair
i knew but my curlfree do
said .no. without my
answering

-why Poet must you
cause such pain-

he said

-Malcolm DuBois Black
African Black Baldwin
LeRoi Black Third World
Patrice Stokely Black
El-Hajj Malik
                El-Shabazz-

*new identity
wasn't easy it
came from
pain?* the pain stopped i
breathed life
birth was completed
growth was begun i
was sister i had Black
                Proud

IDENTITY

JOHARI AMINI

Questions

1. *What is the difference to the speaker between being a "negro," a "person," and a "Black"?*

2. *Is being Black more fundamental to the speaker's identity than being a person? Why?*

3. *How is the dialogue of the speaker with the poet suggested by the form of the poem? Could you read the right-hand column as a poem by itself? What is the difference in tone between it and the left-hand column?*
4. *How is "a crown/of natural" contrasted with a "curlfree do"? Which is more appropriate for the "painful process" of birth which the speaker goes through?*
5. *How is the growth from a personal to a political identity suggested in the progression of names from "Malcolm" to "El-Hajj Malik/El-Shabazz-," which is the Muslim name of Malcolm X?*

NEGRO HERO

to suggest Dorie Miller

I had to kick their law into their teeth in order to save them.
However I have heard that sometimes you have to deal
Devilishly with drowning men in order to swim them to shore.
Or they will haul themselves and you to the trash and the fish beneath.
(When I think of this, I do not worry about a few
Chipped teeth.)

It is good I gave glory, it is good I put gold on their name.
Or there would have been spikes in the afterward hands.
But let us speak only of my success and the pictures in the Caucasian
    dailies
As well as the Negro weeklies. For I am a gem.
(They are not concerned that it was hardly The Enemy my fight was
    against
But them.)

It was a tall time. And of course my blood was
Boiling about in my head and straining and howling and singing me on.
Of course I was rolled on wheels of my boy itch to get at the gun.
Of course all the delicate rehearsal shots of my childhold massed in
    mirage before me.
Of course I was child
And my first swallow of the liquor of battle bleeding black air dying
    and demon noise
Made me wild.

It was kinder than that, though, and I showed like a banner my kindness.
I loved. And a man will guard when he loves.
Their white-gowned democracy was my fair lady.
With her knife lying cold, straight, in the softness of her sweet-flowing
    sleeve.
But for the sake of the dear smiling mouth and the stuttered promise I
    toyed with my life.
I threw back!—I would not remember
Entirely the knife.

Still—am I good enough to die for them, is my blood bright enough to
    be spilled,
Was my constant back-question—are they clear
On this? Or do I intrude even now?
Am I clean enough to kill for them, do they wish me to kill
For them or is my place while death licks his lips and strides to them
In the galley still?

(In a southern city a white man said
Indeed, I'd rather be dead;
Indeed, I'd rather be shot in the head
Or ridden to waste on the back of a flood
Than saved by the drop of a black man's blood.)

Naturally, the important thing is, I helped to save them, them and a part
    of their democracy.
Even if I had to kick their law into their teeth in order to do that for
    them.
And I am feeling well and settled in myself because I believe it was a
    good job,
Despite this possible horror: that they might prefer the
Preservation of their law in all its sick dignity and their knives
To the continuation of their creed
And their lives.

GWENDOLYN BROOKS

Questions

1. *Cite specific details in the poem which characterize the speaker. What kind of
   person is he?*
2. *What is the meaning of the first stanza? Who is the "they" the speaker talks about?*
3. *What are the two aspects of the "white-gowned democracy" which the Negro Hero
   guards? If America offers, as the Pledge of Allegiance says, "liberty and justice for*

all," which virtue is imaged as the lady's "stuttered promise," and which as "her knife lying cold"?
4. Explain the contrast between "their law in all its sick dignity" and "their creed"? What is the implied threat in the last line of the poem?
5. What is the relationship between the speaker's personal and political commitments in stanzas three and four? Compare and contrast this relationship with the relationship of the personal and the political in Amini's "Identity."

TRANSCONTINENT

Where the cities end, the
dumps grow the oil-can shacks
from Portland, Maine,

to Seattle. Broken
cars rust in Troy, New York,
and Cleveland Heights.

On the train, the people
eat candy bars, and watch,
or fall asleep.

When they look outside and
see cars and shacks, they know
they're nearly there.

DONALD HALL

Question

Where is the "there" of the last line?

"ONE STREET LITE A BLOCK AWAY"

one street lite a block away
dead end street houses all dark
wintercold outside/steam dripping down windshield
men's cologne on hairless cheeks

hard cheek bones, greasy hair
face pressed hard on my chest
please/no/please/no don't/I need you/no
big hands on my tiny tits *please*
please
I would look at the monkey bites
later in my mirror & feel my cotton pants
all wet & feel cool clean sheets &
wonder who if ever & think
probably soon, probably somebody

ALTA

Questions

1. *What details suggest the age of the couple in the car?*
2. *How does the physical setting reflect the personal relationship between the two people?*
3. *What does the conversation reveal about their relationship? When you read the poem aloud, how do the two "please's" sound?*
4. *What is the relationship between the first nine lines and the last five? Does one part explain or answer the other?*
5. *What do the last two lines suggest about the speaker's attitude toward love? Is she depressed? realistic?*

MERRITT PARKWAY

As if it were
forever that they move, that we
keep moving—

Under a wan sky where
as the lights went on a star
pierced the haze and now
follows steadily
a constant
above our six lanes
the dreamlike continuum . . .

And the people—ourselves!
the humans from inside the
cars, apparent
only at gasoline stops
                    unsure,

        eyeing each other

            drink coffee hastily at the
            slot machines and hurry
        back to the cars
            vanish
            into them forever, to
            keep moving—

        Houses now and then beyond the
        sealed road, the trees / trees, bushes
        passing by, passing
            the cars that
                keep moving ahead of

        us, past us, pressing behind us
                                and
                over left, those that come
            toward us shining too brightly
        moving relentlessly

            in six lanes, gliding
        north and south, speeding with
        a slurred sound—

        DENISE LEVERTOV

[handwritten margin note, top right:] like a ghost suddenly appearing each one is locked into his own world in the car (huddled within yourself).

[handwritten margin note, left:] trapped

Questions

1. What is the relationship of nature (the "sky," the "star," the "trees, bushes") to the "dreamlike continuum" of traffic on the "sealed road"?
2. How is the dream-like state suggested by the phrases "that they move, that we/keep moving" and "the people—ourselves!"?
3. What is the effect of describing the people as "apparent/only at gasoline stops?" What are the possible meanings of "apparent"? How does the phrase "the humans from inside the/cars" (which sounds like "The Creature from the Black Lagoon" and other titles of horror and science fiction movies of the 1950s) suggest that "apparent" in this context means "ghost-like" as well as "visible"?
5. Read the poem aloud. How is the dream-like running together of things reflected in the sound and rhythm of the poem? Does the reading have the effect of "a slurred sound" by the time you reach the end?

SOUTHBOUND ON THE FREEWAY

A tourist came in from Orbitville,
parked in the air, and said:

The creatures of this star
are made of metal and glass.

Through the transparent parts
you can see their guts.

Their feet are round and roll
on diagrams or long

measuring tapes, dark
with white lines.

They have four eyes.
The two in back are red.

Sometimes you can see a five-eyed
one, with a red eye turning

on the top of his head.
He must be special—

the others respect him
and go slow

when he passes, winding
among them from behind.

They all hiss as they glide,
like inches, down the marked

tapes. Those soft shapes,
shadowy inside

the hard bodies—are they
their guts or their brains?

MAY SWENSON

Questions

1. Who or what are the "guts" of the "creatures of this star"?
2. What is the "five-eyed" creature?
3. How does the last sentence of the poem suggest the speaker's attitude toward her subject?

COMPOSED UPON WESTMINSTER BRIDGE, SEPTEMBER 3, 1802

Earth has not anything to show more fair:
Dull would he be of soul who could pass by
A sight so touching in its majesty;
This City now doth, like a garment, wear
The beauty of the morning; silent, bare,
Ships, towers, domes, theatres, and temples lie
Open unto the fields, and to the sky;
All bright and glittering in the smokeless air.
Never did sun more beautifully steep
In his first splendour, valley, rock, or hill;
Ne'er saw I, never felt, a calm so deep!
The river glideth at his own sweet will:
Dear God! the very houses seem asleep;
And all that mighty heart is lying still!

WILLIAM WORDSWORTH

Questions

1. What is the subject of this poem: the City of London, or the effect of Nature (through the "beauty of the morning") on the City?
2. What human activities are associated with "Ships"? With "towers, domes, theatres, and temples"? How can they be "silent" and "bare" and still have "majesty"?
3. In the last six lines what is the speaker's reaction to the scene he describes in the first eight lines? In what line does he move from seeing to feeling?
4. Whose "mighty heart" is he talking about in the last line? the City's? God's? his own?
5. Compare the relationship of the City to the individual in this poem with the same relationships in "Merritt Parkway" and in "one street lite a block away."

THE EMPEROR OF ICE CREAM

Call the roller of big cigars,
The muscular one, and bid him whip
In kitchen cups concupiscent curds.
Let the wenches dawdle in such dress
As they are used to wear, and let the boys
Bring flowers in last month's newspapers
Let be be finale of seem.
The only emperor is the emperor of ice cream.

Take from the dresser of deal,
Lacking the three glass knobs, that sheet
On which she embroidered fantails once
And spread it so as to cover her face.
If her horny feet protrude, they come
To show how cold she is, and dumb.
Let the lamp affix its beam.
The only emperor is the emperor of ice cream.

WALLACE STEVENS

Questions

1. *What is the meaning of "concupiscent curds," of "finale," "fantails," "protrude," and "affix"?*
2. *The tone of the poem is imperative, as the speaker gives orders on things to be done for a woman's funeral. The tone of the orders suggests finality, as does the occasion (a death), but the last line belies this. How?*
3. *What characteristics do the following phrases of the poem share with ice cream: "such dress/As they are used to wear," "flowers in last month's newspapers," "lacking the three glass knobs," and "on which she embroidered fantails once"?*
4. *Why is the woman's face covered, rather than her feet?*
5. *How does "beam" contrast with "seem"? How does the contrast suggest the relationship of life and death?*

TRACT

I will teach you my townspeople
how to perform a funeral—
for you have it over a troop
of artists—
unless one should scour the world—
you have the ground sense necessary.

See! the hearse leads.
I begin with a design for a hearse.
For Christ's sake not black—
nor white either—and not polished!
Let it be weathered—like a farm wagon—
with gilt wheels (this could be
applied fresh at small expense)
or no wheels at all:
a rough dray to drag over the ground.

Knock the glass out!
My God—glass, my townspeople!
For what purpose? Is it for the dead
to look out or for us to see
how well he is housed or to see
the flowers or the lack of them—
or what?
To keep the rain and snow from him?
He will have a heavier rain soon:
pebbles and dirt and what not.
Let there be no glass—
and no upholstery phew!
and no little brass rollers
and small easy wheels on the bottom—
my townspeople what are you thinking of?
A rough plain hearse then
with gilt wheels and no top at all.
On this the coffin lies
by its own weight.
                  No wreaths please—
especially no hot house flowers.

Some common memento is better,
something he prized and is known by:
his old clothes—a few books perhaps—
God knows what! You realize
how we are about these things
my townspeople—
something will be found—anything
even flowers if he had come to that.
So much for the hearse.

For heaven's sake though see to the driver!
Take off the silk hat! In fact
that's no place at all for him—
up there unceremoniously
dragging our friend out to his own dignity!
Bring him down—bring him down!
Low and inconspicuous! I'd not have him ride
on the wagon at all—damn him—
the undertaker's understrapper!
Let him hold the reins
and walk at the side
and inconspicuously too!

Then briefly as to yourselves:
Walk behind—as they do in France,
seventh class, or if you ride
Hell take curtains! Go with some show
of inconvenience; sit openly—
to the weather as to grief.
Or do you think you can shut grief in?
What—from us? We who have perhaps
nothing to lose? Share with us
share with us—it will be money
in your pockets.
                    Go now
I think you are ready.

WILLIAM CARLOS WILLIAMS

Questions

1. *What are the meanings of "tract"? Which apply to this poem? How does the word suggest the angry tone of the speaker?*
2. *Who is the speaker of the poem? In what lines does he seem to be one of the*

"townspeople," and in what lines does he seem to be different from them? Who is the *"us"* of the last six lines?
3. What changes does the speaker propose to make to personalize the funeral?
4. What line reveals his attitude toward the possibility of a life after death?
5. How would you compare the speaker's attitude toward death with that of the speaker in Stevens' *"The Emperor of Ice Cream"*?

Bibliography: William Carlos Williams

Breslin, James. *William Carlos Williams: An American Artist.* New York: Oxford University Press, 1970.

Miller, J. Hillis, ed. *William Carlos Williams: A Collection of Critical Essays.* Englewood Cliffs, N.J.: Prentice-Hall, 1966.

Ostrom, Alan B. *The Poetic World of William Carlos Williams.* Carbondale, Ill.: Southern Illinois University Press, 1966.

Paul, Sherman. *The Music of Survival: A Biography of a Poem by William Carlos Williams.* Urbana, Ill.: University of Illinois Press, 1968.

Ramsey, Paul. "Williams Carlos Williams as Metrist: Theory and Practice." *Journal of Modern Literature* 1 (1971):578–92.

Wagner, Linda W. *The Poems of William Carlos Williams: A Critical Study.* Middletown, Conn.: Wesleyan University Press, 1964.

Weatherhead, A. Kingsley. "William Carlos Williams: Prose, Form, and Measure." *Journal of English Literary History* 33 (1966):118–31.

Williams, William Carlos. *Autobiography of William Carlos Williams.* New York: New Directions, 1951.

———. *I Wanted to Write a Poem.* Boston: Beacon Press, 1958.

Topics for Writing

1. Write a 500-word essay comparing and contrasting the different attitudes toward "home" in Roethke's "My Papa's Waltz" and Stafford's "One Home." Discuss the various ways in which language and rhythm are used to express these attitudes.
2. Write an essay on the relationship of the individual and society. Use Robinson's "Richard Cory," Amini's "Identity," and Brooks' "Negro Hero" for guidance and inspiration.
3. Write an essay on the ways in which the technological and fast-moving city is both an oppressor and a liberator of the individual person, as suggested in Alta's "one street lite a block away," Levertov's "Merritt Parkway" and Wordsworth's "Composed Upon Westminister Bridge."
4. Compare and contrast the attitudes toward death in Stevens' "The Emperor of Ice Cream" and Williams' "Tract." Discuss the relationship between the tone of each poem and its subject. How (if at all) does either poem offer consolation to the survivors?

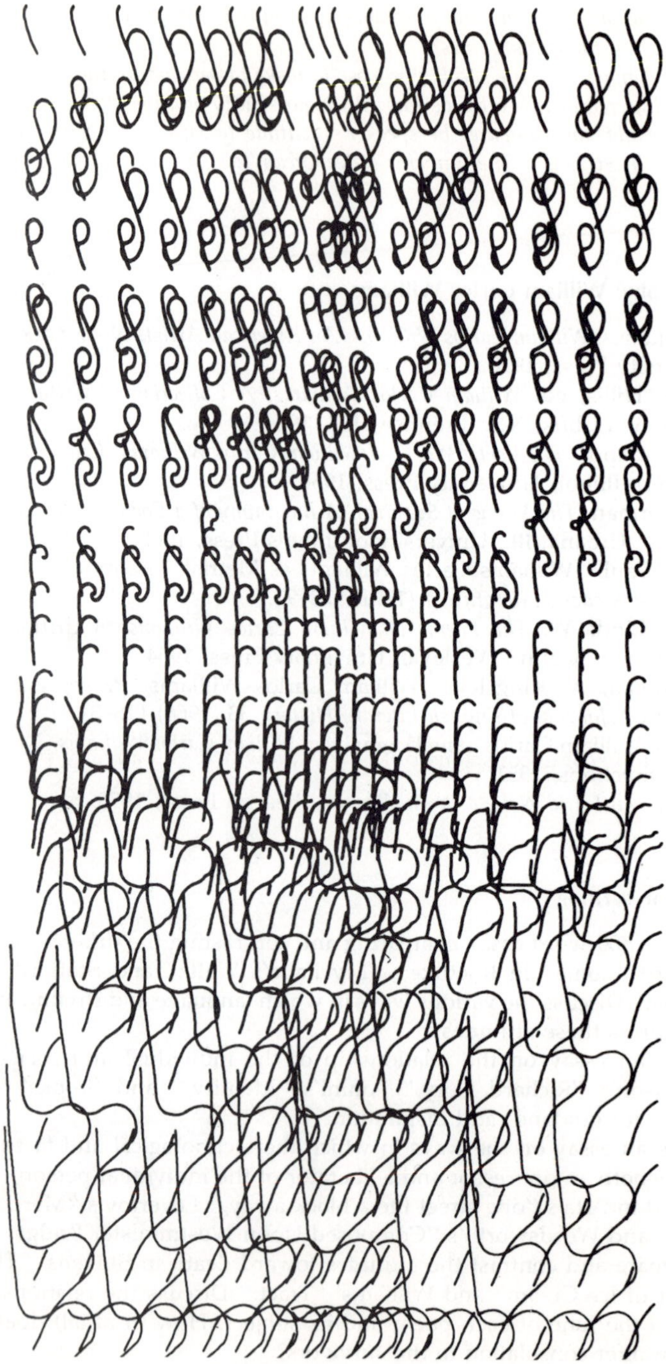

3 Image and Metaphor

This chapter and the ones that follow deal with techniques which display the liveliness of language. Though poetry uses these techniques, they are not limited to poems; they can be found everywhere. You use them every day, both in writing and in speaking. Thus you will be learning to become conscious of knowledge which you already possess and use. The poetry will reveal yourself to you.

An *image* is the revelation in language of sensory experience. How do you tell a friend how something looks, sounds, feels, smells, or tastes? By making an image of the thing, by particularizing it through vivid, concrete language. The hamburger is: a) huge, b) sizzling, c) tender, d) savory, e) juicy. "This huge, sizzling hamburger seems tender, savory, and juicy." These adjectives, now so familiar, once may have been vivid and concrete. Applied to a hamburger, they once may have aroused juices and rumblings in the stomachs of millions. Now, because they have been constantly repeated, they have become worn out, trite, boring. If you use them, they will probably sound boring too (unless you are very hungry). So invent new ones. Make an image that really works, that makes the hamburger come alive again. The world will beat a path to your door, because that's how important images are. People get tired of eating plain hamburgers.

Here are some images that we have already encountered in poems in this book. Test them. What sense (or senses) do they appeal to?

1. "flying in a white wind against a blue sky in spring"
2. "Its quick soft silver bell beating, beating"

3. "wintercold outside/steam dripping down windshield
   men's cologne on hairless cheeks
   hard cheek bones, greasy hair"

The first two quotations present images which are essentially descriptions of a definable object (a spring day, a ringing bell). The last images a scene (lovers parked on a winter night), as well as depicting certain specific objects in the scene (cheeks, hair). By now you probably have noticed that images not only evoke a vivid sensory experience, but they also can associate it with an emotion. This is because we quite often make emotional connections with sense experiences. What is a "soft" bell? Is a temperature range, described as 0–150 degrees, equivalent to the range between "bone-cold," "numb," "freezing," "warm," "feverish," and "burning"? Is a "plain" hamburger simply one with no ketchup?

In the previous examples the images make particular objects come alive. "Blue sky" images the sky, "quick soft silver bell" images the bell. Now imagine the detail without the object, the "blue" without the "sky," or at least without the "sky" *right next to it,* controlling all its blueness. Imagine:

blue

sky

Is that the same as "blue sky"? Yes and no. The arrangement of the words on the page focuses your attention on the "blue" of the "sky." It reinforces the concrete aspect of the image, which you may have neglected as your eyes raced along to find out what was blue. Stop. Open your eyes to the concrete. It is the basis of the image.

An image brings an object to life in our imagination by making concrete its sensory aspects. A metaphor brings something to life by making us imagine that thing in a way that is different from what we are used to, by comparing it to something else with which it seems to have nothing in common. A *metaphor* is a comparison between things that are basically different. A *simile* is a comparison, like a metaphor, which uses some word or phrase (*like, as, similar to, than*) to connect the two things being compared. The liveliness of metaphors and similes comes from the revelation that two things actually *do* have something in common, a similarity that we may not have suspected before.

Here are some metaphors from the previous selections of this book. What are the unlike things that are being compared? On what basis can they be compared?

1. "Poetry is the synthesis of hyacinths and biscuits."
2. "tall wearing a crown/of natural"
3. "The magic of the mouth that can melt to tears the rock of hearts."

How can "poetry" be compared to a "synthesis" of things that are so different as "hyacinths and biscuits"? Before analyzing the metaphor, test it with your mouth and your imagination, to see if it sounds correct. To receptive and perceptive readers of Sandburg's metaphor, the comparison has revealed some truth. Obviously it is not an inclusive definition of "poetry," such as the dictionary definition in the first chapter of this book. No logical explanation of the metaphor can account fully for its pleasing effectiveness. But the perceptive reader might note that the sound of the words "hyacinths and biscuits" resembles the sound of "synthesis," and that this resemblance in sound is itself a kind of synthesis, hence an example of "poetry." Also, the sense of the words "hyacinths and biscuits," and their associations with flowers and food, might suggest that "poetry" is a combination of pleasure (the beauty of a flower) and usefulness (the necessity of food). And a reader who is familiar with the poetry and ideas about poetry of earlier centuries might see a similarity between Sandburg's metaphor and an older belief that poetry should be *"dulce et utile,"* pleasing and useful. You don't have to recognize all these similarities to enjoy the metaphor; but the more you recognize, the more you will enjoy.

The ability to make and to recognize metaphors has always been a measure of human intelligence. Every day we compare new experiences with old ones, the unknown with the known. A metaphor is not only a source of knowledge, it is a source of pleasure as well. People delight in metaphors and are constantly inventing new ones. Common slang terms like "cool," "hot," "down," "up," "high," "trip," and "far out" are metaphors, and they are popular because they have effective and pleasing results in the popular imagination. When these metaphors are worn out, people will create new ones, because the human world can't survive without metaphors.

Here is a poem which is also an exercise in metaphor making. Test your imagination on it. It's a gift from the Eskimos. It invites you to "use the language of the shamans," who are people endowed with the ability to see the unknown in the known, the invisible in the visible. Shamans, like poets, are constantly inventing metaphors to tell others what they see.

LANGUAGE EVENT 1

Use the language of shamans.

Say the leash		*& mean* the father
" a road		" the wind
" someone with a something sticking out		" a man
" where things get soft		" the guts
" soup		" a seal
" Big Louse		" a caribou

" what makes me dive in headfirst	" a dream
" what cracks your ears	" a gun
" what looks like piss	" your beads
" a piece of frozen meat	" a child
" a piece of almost frozen meat	" a grandchild
" a jumping thing	" a trout
" what keeps me standing straight	" your clothes
" the person with a belly	" the weather
" the person with a belly getting up	" it's morning
" the person with a belly goes to bed	" it's nightfall
" little walker	" a fox
" walker with his head down	" a dog
" the bag it lies in	" a mother
" the bag it almost lies in	" a stepmother
" a person smoke surrounds	" a live one
" a floating one	" an island
" a neighbor	" a wife
" a flat one	" a wolf
" a shadow	" a white man
" another kind of shadow	" a person
" the dark one	" the liver
" making shadows	" a seance
" the shadow-maker	" the shaman
" he turned my mind around	" he told me something

ESKIMO (arranged by Jerome Rothenberg)

The following poems in this chapter use both images and metaphors. Read each selection as a whole poem, and note how the use of image and metaphor fits into the context of the whole. Notice the effects of using language that appeals to sensory experience, that makes us look at things in a different way.

IN A STATION OF THE METRO

The apparition of these faces in the crowd;
Petals on a wet, black bough.

EZRA POUND

1. *Pound once defined an image as "an emotional complex in an instant of time." Does this short poem present an image that satisfies this definition by the poet himself?*
2. *What senses are appealed to in this poem?*

GETTING UP EARLY

I am up early. The box-elder leaves have fallen.
The eastern sky is the color of March.
The sky has spread out over the world like water.
The bootlegger and his wife are still asleep.

I saw the light first from the barn well.
The cold water fell into the night-chilled buckets,
Deepening to the somber blue of the southern sky.
Over the new trees, there was a strange light in the east.

The light was dawn. Like a man who has come home
After seeing many dark rivers, and will soon go again,
The dawn stood there with a quiet gaze;
Our eyes met through the top leaves of the young ash.

Dawn has come. The clouds floating in the east have turned
    white.
The fence posts have stopped being a part of the darkness.
The depth has disappeared from the puddles on the ground.
I look up angrily at the light.

ROBERT BLY

Questions

1. *Does the poem simply describe what the speaker sees, or what he feels about what he sees, or both? Cite specific examples.*
2. *How does the last line in the first stanza suggest that the mind of the speaker is an active part of the scene he is revealing to us?*
3. *To what senses do the images in stanza two appeal?*
4. *Explain the simile in the third stanza. Is it merely descriptive of the "dawn," or does it reveal something about the speaker's emotional response to the "strange light"?*

5. Explain the cause of the visual changes mentioned in lines 3 and 4 of the last stanza. Do these changes suggest a reason for the speaker's emotional response to the "light"? Does the speaker's state of mind, revealed in his use of image and simile, change during the poem? How?

LOST

> Desolate and lone
> All night long on the lake
> Where fog trails and mist creeps,
> The whistle of a boat
> Calls and cries unendingly,
> Like some lost child
> In tears and trouble
> Hunting the harbor's breast
> And the harbor's eyes.
>
> CARL SANDBURG

Questions

1. *What senses are appealed to in this poem?*
2. *Explain the simile between the whistle of the boat and the cries of a child. Explain the implicit metaphor in "the harbor's breast" and "the harbor's eyes."*

WORKING ON WALL STREET

> What's left of the sunset's watered blood
> settles between the slabs of Wall Street.
> Winter rubs the sky bruise-blue as flesh.
> We head down into the subway, glad
> the cars are padded with bodies so we
> keep warm. Emptied from tall closets
> where we work, on the days' shelves
> reached by elevators, the heap of us,
> pressed by iron sides, dives forward under
> the city—parcels shipped out in a trunk.

The train climbs its cut to the trestle.
Sunset's gone. Those slabs across the murky
river have shrunk to figurines, reflecting
the blush of neon—a dainty tableau, all
pink, on the dresser-top of Manhattan—
eclipsed as we sink into the tunnel.
The train drops and flattens for the long
bore under Brooklyn.

Night, a hiatus hardly real, tomorrow
this double rut of steel will racket us back
to the city. We, packages in the trade
made day after day, will tumble out of
hatches on The Street, to be met by swags
of wind that scupper off those roofs
(their upper windows blood-filled by the sun.)
Delivered into lobbies, clapped into upgoing
cages, sorted to our compartments, we'll be
stamped once more for our wages.

MAY SWENSON

Questions

1. *What aspect of the "sunset" in the city is compared to "watered blood"? What things on Wall Street are compared to "slabs"? In the third line, if "sky" is compared to "flesh," to what is "Winter" compared? How do these metaphors work together to suggest not only the visual but also the emotional coloration of quitting time on Wall Street?*
2. *Find and explain the metaphors in the last five lines of the first stanza which work together to suggest the comparison between the employees of large office buildings and "parcels," perhaps even corpses, "shipped out in a trunk." How is the comparison between the workers and packages expanded upon in the last stanza?*
3. *Point out the verbs in the poem. Which subjects have active verbs, and which subjects are passive? How does this contribute to the overall effect of the poem?*
4. *What is the attitude of the speaker to the subject? Does this attitude, revealed in the use of image and metaphor, change during the poem?*

SPRING AND ALL

By the road to the contagious hospital
under the surge of the blue
mottled clouds driven from the
northeast—a cold wind. Beyond, the
waste of broad, muddy fields
brown with dried weeds, standing and fallen

patches of standing water
the scattering of tall trees

All along the road the reddish
purplish, forked, upstanding, twiggy
stuff of bushes and small trees
with dead, brown leaves under them
leafless vines—

Lifeless in appearance, sluggish
dazed spring approaches—

They enter the new world naked,
cold, uncertain of all
save that they enter. All about them
the cold, familiar wind—

Now the grass, tomorrow
the stiff curl of wildcarrot leaf

One by one objects are defined—
It quickens: clarity, outline of leaf

But now the stark dignity of
entrance—Still, the profound change
has come upon them: rooted they
grip down and begin to awaken

WILLIAM CARLOS WILLIAMS

Questions

1. *Do the images in this poem suggest the speaker's state of mind, or do they simply attempt to present an objective description?*

2. *How does the use of images in this poem resemble "leafless vines–/Lifeless in appearance"?*
3. *How does the arrangement of images and even lines in the poem suggest the appearance of objects "one by one"?*
4. *The poem's images are at first not appealing, though they are concrete, because the things imaged ("broad, muddy fields," and so forth) are not attractive. Read the poem several times. Do you find some pleasure in this revelation of a scene by a "contagious hospital"? What is the source of your pleasure, the scene or the poetic revelation of it?*
5. *How does the last stanza suggest the relationship between the scene imaged in the poem and the language used to image it?*

DURING WIND AND RAIN

They sing their dearest songs—
He, she, all of them—yea,
Treble and tenor and bass,
   And one to play;
With the candles mooning each face. . . .
   Ah, no; the years O!
How the sick leaves reel down in throngs!

They clear the creeping moss—
Elders and juniors—aye,
Making the pathway neat
   And the garden gay;
And they build a shady seat. . . .
   Ah, no; the years, the years;
See, the white stormbirds wing across!

They are blithely breakfasting all—
Men and maidens—yea,
Under the summer tree,
   With a glimpse of the bay,
While pet fowl come to the knee. . . .
   Ah, no; the years O!
And the rotten rose is ripped from the wall.

They change to a high new house,
He, she, all of them—aye,
Clocks and carpets, and chairs
   On the lawn all day,
And brightest things that are theirs. . . .
   Ah, no; the years, the years;
Down their carved names the rain drop ploughs.

THOMAS HARDY

Questions

1. *Cite and explain the metaphor in the fifth line of this poem.*
2. *What is the subject of this poem, and what is the speaker's attitude toward the subject?*
3. *What is meant by the "carved names" mentioned in the last line? Explain the metaphor of the last four lines of the poem. How does it reveal the speaker's feelings toward the passage of time?*

ENTERING ARKANSAS

The tree frogs' song wells up through dark wet air
chorus on chorus green and undulant
around the stone of my silence;

over head a motel sign hisses
and blinks a red electric VACANCY;
from down the rock-road I hear

a steady velvet roar of air conditioners
leeched to high porched tin roofed houses
staggered like bad teeth down the hill.

I imagine the sleepers on damp beds in the darkness
I hear wave on wave the voices of their dreams
heave through the sea of leaves around me

I see the dreams themselves
scatter suddenly like clouds of bats from caves,
shapes featherless and thin

against the mirror of a low full moon
white as patience, whose radiance
floods southward

over the plots of defoliated cotton plants and sunken rice land

whose silence consumes the sleepers emptied of dreams
and the dreams searching for voices
and the abandoned town

until I hear only the scream of roots reaching out
blind, beginning again.

RICHARD MESSER

Questions

1. What senses are appealed to in the first stanza? How does the phrase "green and undulant" prepare for the images of the fourth stanza?
2. Explain the simile of "houses/staggered like bad teeth down the hill."
3. Cite and explain the simile in the fifth stanza. How effective is it?

TO AUTUMN

Season of mists and mellow fruitfulness,
    Close bosom-friend of the maturing sun;
Conspiring with him how to load and bless
    With fruit the vines that round the thatch-eves run;
To bend with apples the moss'd cottage-trees,
    And fill all fruit with ripeness to the core;
        to swell the gourd, and plump the hazel shells
With a sweet kernel; to set budding more,
    And still more, later flowers for the bees,
    Until they think warm days will never cease,
        For Summer has o'er-brimm'd their clammy cells.

Who hath not seen thee oft amid thy store?
    Sometimes whoever seeks abroad may find
Thee sitting careless on a granary floor,
    Thy hair soft-lifted by the winnowing wind;
Or on a half-reap'd furrow sound asleep,
    Drows'd with the fume of poppies, while thy hook
        Spares the next swath and all its twined flowers:
And sometimes like a gleaner thou dost keep
    Steady thy laden head across a brook;
    Or by a cyder-press, with patient look,
        Thou watchest the last oozings hours by hours.

Where are the songs of Spring? Ay, where are they?
    Think not of them, thou hast thy music too,—
While barred clouds bloom the soft-dying day,
    And touch the stubble-plains with rosy hue;
Then in a wailful choir the small gnats mourn
    Among the river sallows, borne aloft
        Or sinking as the light wind lives or dies;
And full-grown lambs loud bleat from hilly bourn;
    Hedge-crickets sing; and now with treble soft
The red-breast whistles from a garden-croft;
    And gathering swallows twitter in the skies.

JOHN KEATS

Questions

1. *Which images in the first stanza reveal Autumn's quality of "mellow fruitful-ness"? To what senses do these images appeal: "moss'd cottage-trees," "sweet kernel," "clammy cells"?*
2. *In stanza one Autumn is compared to a person, the "bosom-friend" of the sun. How is this comparison extended in stanza two?*
3. *How is the idea of an "Indian Summer" suggested by the description of the person-Autumn in stanza two? What senses are appealed to in the following: "hair soft-lifted," "Drows'd with the fume of poppies," "thy laden head," and "the last oozings hours by hours"?*
4. *What sense is appealed to in the final stanza? What words suggest the difference between the music of Spring and the music of Autumn?*
5. *Compare the use of images in this poem with the use of them in Williams' poem "Spring and All." Do both poems use images to suggest an emotional mood, to encourage a certain emotional response to the concrete scene they image? Which poem is more appealing to you?*

THE DARKLING THRUSH

I leant upon a coppice gate
   When Frost was specter-gray,
And Winter's dregs made desolate
   The weakening eye of day.
The tangled bine-stems scored the sky
   Like strings of broken lyres,
And all mankind that haunted nigh
   Had sought their household fires.

The land's sharp features seemed to be
   The Century's corpse outleant,
His crypt the cloudy canopy,
   The wind his death-lament.
The ancient pulse of germ and birth
   Was shrunken hard and dry,
And every spirit upon earth
   Seemed fervorless as I.

At once a voice arose among
   The bleak twigs overhead
In a full-hearted evensong
   Of joy illimited;
An aged thrush, frail, gaunt, and small,
   In blast-beruffled plume,
Had chosen thus to fling his soul
   Upon the growing gloom.

So little cause for carolings
   Of such ecstatic sound
Was written on terrestrial things
   Afar or nigh around,
That I could think there trembled through
   His happy good-night air
Some blessed Hope, whereof he knew
   And I was unaware.

December 1900.

THOMAS HARDY

1. *What is the speaker's attitude toward the landscape in the first two stanzas? Explain the comparison between the land and the "Century's corpse" in the second stanza: how is the "crypt" a "cloudy canopy," and how is "The wind his death-lament"?*
2. *With what does the darkling thrush oppose the depressing landscape? What is suggested by the bird's "blast-beruffled plume"?*
3. *Does the song of the bird inspire the speaker, or does it simply confuse him?*

from AS YOU LIKE IT

All the world's a stage,
And all the men and women merely players.
They have their exits and their entrances,
And one man in his time plays many parts,
His acts being seven ages. At first, the infant,
Mewling and puking in the nurse's arms.
Then the whining schoolboy, with his satchel
And shining morning face, creeping like snail
Unwillingly to school. And then the lover,
Sighing like furnace, with a woeful ballad
Made to his mistress' eyebrow. Then a soldier,
Full of strange oaths and bearded like the pard,
Jealous in honor, sudden and quick in quarrel,
Seeking the bubble reputation
Even in the cannon's mouth. And then the justice,
In fair round belly with good capon lined,
With eyes severe and beard of formal cut,
Full of wise saws and modern instances;
And so he plays his part. The sixth age shifts
Into the lean and slippered pantaloon,
With spectacles on nose and pouch on side;
His youthful hose, well saved, a world too wide
For his shrunk shank, and his big manly voice,
Turning again toward childish treble, pipes
And whistles in his sound. Last scene of all,
That ends this strange eventful history,
Is second childishness and mere oblivion,
Sans teeth, sans eyes, sans taste, sans everything.

WILLIAM SHAKESPEARE

Questions

1. *Explain the comparison between the "world" and a "stage" as it is drawn in the first five lines.*
2. *Point out the images appealing to the sense of sound in the descriptions of the seven ages of man. Why would sound be an especially important sense in poetry that is meant to be spoken by an actor? (This is a speech from Shakespeare's play* As You Like It.*)*
3. *Explain these similes: "creeping like snail," "Sighing like furnace," "bearded like the pard." (A "pard" is a "leopard.")*
4. *Explain this metaphor: "the bubble reputation."*
5. *Create an extended comparison of your own between life and something else. Use vivid images, as Shakespeare does, to make the comparison come alive.*

THE SILKEN TENT

She is as in a field a silken tent
At midday when a sunny summer breeze
Has dried the dew and all its ropes relent,
So that in guys it gently sways at ease,
And its supporting central cedar pole,
That is its pinnacle to heavenward
And signifies the sureness of the soul,
Seems to owe naught to any single cord,
But strictly held by none, is loosely bound
By countless silken ties of love and thought
To everything on earth the compass round,
And only by one's going slightly taut
In the capriciousness of summer air
Is of the slightest bondage made aware.

ROBERT FROST

Questions

1. *Explain the points of comparison between a woman and a "silken tent." What are "guys"? With what word later in the poem does "guys" rhyme?*
2. *To what is the woman's soul compared? What are the qualities which support her soul? To what are these qualities compared?*

3. How does the inverted word order in the first and last lines (and elsewhere) suggest the flowing quality of the silken tent?
4. What sounds in the phrase "a sunny summer breeze" contribute to this sense of silk flowing?
5. Does the effectiveness of the poem depend upon the originality of the comparison, or upon something else? Explain.

THE HARLEM DANCER

Applauding youths laughed with young prostitutes
And watched her perfect, half-clothed body sway;
Her voice was like the sound of blended flutes
Blown by black players upon a picnic day.
She sang and danced on gracefully and calm,
The light gauze hanging loose about her form;
To me she seemed a proudly-swaying palm
Grown lovelier for passing through a storm.
Upon her swarthy neck black shiny curls
Luxuriant fell; and tossing coins in praise,
The wine-flushed, bold-eyed boys, and even the girls,
Devoured her shape with eager, passionate gaze;
But looking at her falsely-smiling face,
I knew her self was not in that strange place.

CLAUDE McKAY

Questions

1. Explain the effectiveness of the simile in lines 3 and 4. To what sense does it appeal?
2. How is the dancer like a "palm"? Would the comparison be as effective without the extension of it provided by line 8?
3. How can a "gaze" appear to "devour" something?
4. What is the difference between the dancer's "shape" and her "self"? What is the difference between the poet's "looking" and his "knowing"?
5. Compare the relationship between appearance ("shape") and reality ("self") in this poem with the same relationship in Frost's "The Silken Tent."

DOVER BEACH

The sea is calm tonight.
The tide is full, the moon lies fair
Upon the straits; on the French coast the light
Gleams and is gone; the cliffs of England stand,
Glimmering and vast, out in the tranquil bay.
Come to the window, sweet is the night-air!
Only, from the long line of spray
Where the sea meets the moon-blanched land,
Listen! you hear the grating roar
Of pebbles which the waves draw back, and fling,
At their return, up the high strand,
Begin, and cease, and then again begin,
With tremulous cadence slow, and bring
The eternal note of sadness in.

Sophocles long ago
Heard it on the AEgean, and it brought
Into his mind the turbid ebb and flow
Of human misery; we
Find also in the sound a thought,
Hearing it by this distant northern sea.

The Sea of Faith
Was once, too, at the full, and round earth's shore
Lay like the folds of a bright girdle furled.
But now I only hear
Its melancholy, long, withdrawing roar,
Retreating, to the breath
Of the night-wind, down the vast edges drear
And naked shingles of the world.

Ah, love, let us be true
To one another! for the world, which seems
To lie before us like a land of dreams,
So various, so beautiful, so new,
Hath really neither joy, nor love, nor light,
Nor certitude, nor peace, nor help for pain;
And we are here as on a darkling plain
Swept with confused alarms of struggle and flight,
Where ignorant armies clash by night.

MATTHEW ARNOLD

Questions

1. What senses are appealed to by the images in the first stanza? What effect is achieved by placing "slow" after, rather than before, the words "tremulous cadence"?
2. Which line in stanza two reveals that the activity of the senses has led to the activity of the mind?
3. Explain the metaphor "Sea of Faith" as it is developed in stanza three. Is the imagery in that stanza merely sensory, as in stanza one, or has the third stanza's initial metaphor changed the significance of the images?
4. Explain the comparison in the last three lines of the poem. How does the activity imaged as "confused alarms of struggle and flight" relate to the activity of "the grating roar of pebbles" on Dover Beach?
5. The speaker has looked upon a particular, concrete scene and generalized about it. How do his metaphors reflect this process of generalization? (Note especially "the eternal note of sadness," "the turbid ebb and flow/Of human misery," "The Sea of Faith," and "a land of dreams.")

FERN HILL

Now as I was young and easy under the apple boughs
About the lilting house and happy as the grass was green,
   The night above the dingle starry,
    Time let me hail and climb
   Golden in the heydays of his eyes,
And honored among wagons I was prince of the apple towns
And once below a time I lordly had the trees and leaves
    Trail with daisies and barley
   Down the rivers of the windfall light.

And as I was green and carefree, famous among the barns
About the happy yard and singing as the farm was home,
   In the sun that is young once only,
    Time let me play and be
   Golden in the mercy of his means,
And green and golden I was huntsman and herdsman, the calves
Sang to my horn, the foxes on the hills barked clear and cold,
    And the sabbath rang slowly
   In the pebbles of the holy streams.

All the sun long it was running, it was lovely, the hay
Fields high as the house, the tunes from the chimneys, it was air
  And playing, lovely and watery
    And fire green as grass.
  And nightly under the simple stars
As I rode to sleep the owls were bearing the farm away,
All the moon long I heard, blessed among stables, the nightjars
  Flying with the ricks, and the horses
    Flashing into the dark.

And then to awake, and the farm, like a wanderer white
With the dew, come back, the cock on his shoulder: it was all
  Shining, it was Adam and maiden,
    The sky gathered again
  And the sun grew round that very day.
So it must have been after the birth of the simple light
In the first, spinning place, the spellbound horses walking warm
  Out of the whinnying green stable
    On to the fields of praise.

And honored among foxes and pheasants by the gay house
Under the new made clouds and happy as the heart was long,
  In the sun born over and over,
    I ran my heedless ways,
  My wishes raced through the house high hay
And nothing I cared, at my sky blue trades, that time allows
In all his tuneful turning so few and such morning songs
  Before the children green and golden
    Follow him out of grace,

Nothing I cared, in the lamb white days, that time would take me
Up to the swallow thronged loft by the shadow of my hand,
  In the moon that is always rising,
    Nor that riding to sleep
  I should hear him fly with the high fields   Time –Him
And wake to the farm forever fled from the childless land.
Oh as I was young and easy in the mercy of his means,
    Time held me green and dying
  Though I sang in my chains like the sea.

DYLAN THOMAS

Questions

1. *The poet's recording of "Fern Hill" should be heard for its musicality. But the importance of music to the poem is not limited to its sounds and rhythms. Explain the following: "the lilting house," "the calves/Sang to my horn," "the sabbath rang slowly/In the pebbles of the holy streams," "in all his tuneful turning," "Though I sang in my chains like the sea."*
2. *Point out the references in the poem to "the children green and golden." How can a child be "green and golden"?*
3. *In the second stanza the speaker refers to "the sun that is young once only." In the fifth stanza he speaks of "the sun born over and over." Explain the seeming contradiction between these two lines.*
4. *What is the significance of the change from "green and golden" to "green and dying"? Does the child or the adult see himself as "dying"? What is the "childless land"?*
5. *What is the relationship of the speaker to time? Does he lament the loss of innocence, "grace," and childhood, or does he accept it as part of an inevitable process? Is there any sense of affirmation in the last line? Has the speaker ceased to sing? Compare the speaker's attitude toward life with that of the speaker of "Dover Beach."*

Bibliography: Dylan Thomas

Aivaz, David. "The Poetry of Dylan Thomas." *Hudson Review* 8 (1955):382–404.
Arrowsmith, William. "The Wisdom of Poetry." *Hudson Review* 6 (1954):597–604.
Brinnin, John Malcolm. *A Casebook on Dylan Thomas.* New York: Macmillan Publishing Co., 1960.
———. *Dylan Thomas in America.* Boston: Little, Brown & Co., 1955.
Davis, William V. "Several Comments on 'A Refusal to Mourn the Death, by Fire, of a Child in London'." *Concerning Poetry* 6 (1969):45–48.
Evans, Oliver. "The Making of a Poem (I): Dylan Thomas' 'Do not go gentle into that good night'." *English Miscellany* 6 (1955):163–73.
Jenkins, Jack L. "How Green Is 'Fern Hill'?" *English Journal* 55 (1966):1180–82.
Maud, Ralph. *Entrances to Dylan Thomas' Poetry.* Pittsburgh: University of Pittsburgh Press, 1963.
Murphy, Michael W. "Thomas' 'Do Not Go Gentle Into That Good Night'." *Explicator* 28 (1970):Item 55.
———. "Dylan Thomas: 'A Refusal to Mourn the Death, by Fire, of a Child in London'." *Festschriften* 96 (1967):252–61.

Parshall, Peter F. "Thomas' 'The Force that Through the Green Fuse Drives the Flower'." *Explicator* 29 (1971):Item 65.

Tindall, William Y. *A Reader's Guide to Dylan Thomas.* New York: Farrar, Straus and Giroux, 1962.

Topics for Writing

1. Compare and contrast the uses of image and metaphor to describe nature in Keats' "To Autumn" and Thomas' "Fern Hill." What aspects of nature do the different poems focus on?
2. Using either Frost's "The Silken Tent" or the selection from Shakespeare's *As You Like It* as a model, write your own poem using images and metaphors based on one extended comparison. You might choose:
   a. A city is a zoo.
   b. A diary (wallet, scrapbook) is a pirate's ship.
   c. Love is a trip.
3. Using either Swenson's "Working on Wall Street" or McKay's "The Harlem Dancer" as a model, write your own poem using images and metaphors revealing one particular experience. You might choose:
   a. A particular city street during a 24-hour period.
   b. The changes of the sky during a 24-hour period.
   c. Getting dressed to go on a date.
4. Write a 500-word essay on the relationship of faith and fatalism in Arnold's "Dover Beach." Show how the images and metaphors reveal this relationship.

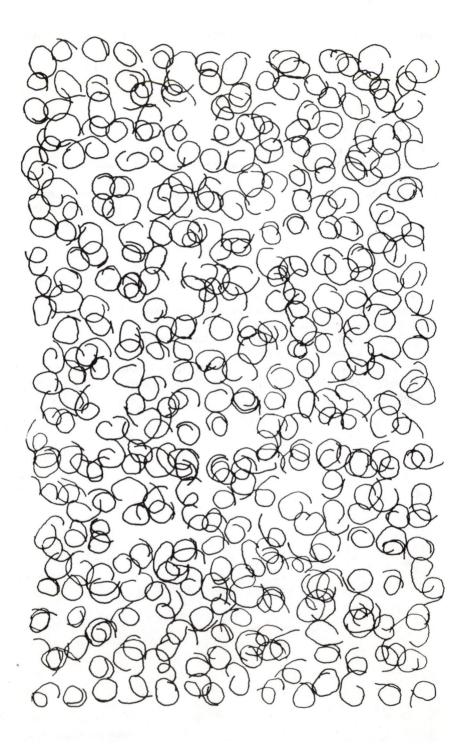

4 Metonymy, Synecdoche, Personification, Allusion

A good poem is always more than the sum of its parts. Nevertheless, once the reader has a sense of a poem's wholeness, its integrity and completeness, he begins to wonder what specific devices of language were used in the poem to achieve that wholeness. He wants to know what contribution the poem's parts make to the whole.

This chapter offers working definitions of four devices of language that occur in many poems. Of course, like images and metaphors, these devices occur in everyday speech as well. You have used all of them yourself, though you may not have been aware of doing so. By paying attention to the ways in which these devices contribute to the life of the poems in this chapter, you will become aware of the ways in which they can contribute to the life of your own speech and writing.

Metonymy is the use of the name of one thing to stand for another with which it is commonly associated. In "you can't fight City Hall," the term "City Hall" stands for the mayor, councilmen, and so forth, who have offices in the city hall. Similarly, the "crown" stands for the king and his authority, and the "flag" stands for the country over which it flies. In Stafford's "One Home" (p. 30) the phrase "black hats" is a metonymy for the people of authority who wear the hats.

Explain the following examples of metonymy:

a. "from the cradle to the grave"

b. "I've read all of Whitman"

c. "I offered my heart, but she asked for my soul"

Synecdoche is the use of a part to signify a whole thing. In the phrase "all hands on deck," the word "hands" stands for the sailors. Similarly, in "lend me your ears" the word "ears" refers to the listeners' complete attention, of which hearing is only a part; and in "he asked for her hand in marriage" the word "hand" is a synecdoche for the whole woman.

Explain the following examples of synecdoche:

a. "many mouths to feed"

b. "two dollars a head"

c. "a fleet of fifty sails"

Synecdoche and metonymy are closely related figures of speech. It is not so important to be able to distinguish between the two; but it is important to recognize their effects. Both devices particularize experience by making the general or abstract become individual and concrete. Both give the language of poetry emotional intensity which other, more generalized forms of writing or speaking lack. Both figures of speech urge the reader's imagination to its own activity, demanding that the reader see and recreate *for himself* the relationship between the parts and the whole. Synecdoche and metonymy are devices by which a poet can enliven and strengthen his poem. As the poet William Blake noted: "To Generalize is to be an Idiot./To Particularize is the Alone Distinction of Merit."

Personification is the giving of human qualities to abstractions or inanimate objects. It is a way of comparing something to a human being. In Keat's poem "To Autumn" (p. 59) the season of autumn is personified as a human being, sometimes "sitting" on a floor, sometimes "sound asleep." We might personify a tree, as in "The tree wept at the axe's cruelty." Or we might personify an automobile, as in "Your car has bad breath."

Explain the following personifications:

a. "the laughing brook"

b. "the snarling bus"

c. "money talks"

The effect of personification is to make the thing personified more human, and hence more familiar to humans. Some anthropolotists believe that the earliest human cultures gave human attributes to the elements of nature because people were afraid of forces they couldn't understand. Thinking the sea or sky became gentle or angry, just as humans did, perhaps made those forces seem more understandable, if not more controllable. At any rate, the human tendency to personify things has always been with us, and poets have always recognized and used this tendency in their language.

Allusion is a reference to a person, place, or event that the reader could be expected to know. An allusion makes an implied comparison between what is being spoken of and the reference which is being invoked. If we say "he has the patience of Job," we are likening someone's patience to that of the character Job in the Bible. In "she is another Helen of Troy," we are comparing some woman to the legendary beauty who caused the Trojan War. When the government named the space shots "Apollo," "Gemini," and "Mercury," they were alluding to figures from mythology who were associated with the heavenly bodies. The effectiveness of allusion depends upon the reader's recognition of both the reference and the basis of the comparison between the reference and the thing under consideration.

Explain the following allusions:

a. "He was a Superman on the football field, but a Clark Kent at the party."

b. "Watergate may turn out to be Nixon's Waterloo."

c. "Barbara's failure to keep her mouth shut proved to be her Achilles' heel."

THE GLORIES OF OUR BLOOD AND STATE

The glories of our blood and state
  Are shadows, not substantial things;
There is no armor against fate;
  Death lays his icy hand on kings:
      Scepter and crown
      Must tumble down,
And in the dust be equal made
With the poor crooked scythe and spade.

Some men with swords may reap the field,
  And plant fresh laurels where they kill;
But their strong nerves at last must yield;
  They tame but one another still:
      Early or late,
      They stoop to fate,
And must give up their murmuring breath,
When they, pale captives, creep to death.

The garlands wither on your brow,
   Then boast no more your mighty deeds;
Upon death's purple altar now,
   See where the victor-victim bleeds:
      Your heads must come
      To the cold tomb;
Only the actions of the just
Smell sweet and blossom in their dust.

JAMES SHIRLEY

Questions

1. *What do "blood" and "state" stand for? Is this use of metonymy effective?*
2. *What figure of speech is used in line 4?*
3. *What kinds of people are associated with the "Scepter and crown" and the "scythe and spade"? How does the mention of "scythe and spade" subtly allude to death? Who is the Grim Reaper?*
4. *For what is "murmuring breath" in line 15 a synecdoche? Why are the warriors called "pale captives" of death? How can a soldier be a "victor-victim" with regard to death?*
5. *What is the difference between the "glories of our blood and state" and the "actions of the just"? Which has ultimate power over death? Why?*

SINCE THERE'S NO HELP

Since there's no help, come let us kiss and part;
Nay, I have done, you get no more of me,
And I am glad, yea, glad with all my heart
That thus so cleanly I myself can free;
Shake hands forever, cancel all our vows,
And when we meet at any time again,
Be it not seen in either of our brows
That we one jot of former love retain.
Now at the last gasp of Love's latest breath,
When, his pulse failing, Passion speechless lies,
When Faith is kneeling by his bed of death,
And Innocence is closing up his eyes,
Now, if thou wouldst, when all have given him over,
From death to life thou mightst him yet recover.

MICHAEL DRAYTON

Questions

1. *What is the difference between the speaker's attitude toward the relationship in the first eight lines and the last six?*
2. *How do lines 3 and 4 contrast with the last two lines of the poem?*
3. *Explain the deathbed scene in the last six lines. Are Love and Passion related in this personification? How?*
4. *Why is Faith personified as "kneeling" by the deathbed of Love? Why is Innocence "closing up his eyes"?*
5. *In what ways do the personifications enliven and intensify the speaker's feelings about the death of love? Can you think of another effective way of writing about the last moments of a love affair?*

ASTROPHEL AND STELLA

Sonnet 31

With how sad steps, O Moon! thou climb'st the skies!
How silently, and with how wan a face!
What! may it be, that even in heavenly place
That busy archer his sharp arrows tries?
Sure, if that long-with-love-acquainted eyes
Can judge of love, thou feel'st a lover's case;
I read it in thy looks; thy languish'd grace,
To me that feel the like, thy state descries.
Then, even of fellowship, O Moon, tell me,
Is constant love deem'd there but want of wit?
Are beauties there as proud as here they be?
Do they above love to be loved, and yet
    Those lovers scorn whom that love doth possess?
    Do they call virtue there ungratefulness?

ASTROPHEL AND STELLA

Sonnet 39

Come, Sleep! O Sleep, the certain knot of peace,
The baiting-place of wit, the balm of woe,
The poor man's wealth, the prisoner's release,
The indifferent judge between the high and low;
With shield of proof shield me from out the press
Of those fierce darts Despair at me doth throw:

Oh, make in me those civil wars to cease;
I will good tribute pay, if thou do so.
Take thou of me smooth pillows, sweetest bed,
A chamber deaf to noise and blind to light,
A rosy garland and a weary head:
And if these things, as being thine by right,
   Move not thy heavy grace, thou shalt in me,
   Livelier than elsewhere, Stella's image see.

PHILIP SIDNEY

Questions

1. *These two poems, taken from a* sonnet sequence *(cf. Chapter 8), both utilize the device of personification to achieve their effects. What aspects of a person are attributed to the moon in the first three lines of the poem?*
2. *Explain the allusion in the fourth line. Who is the "busy archer" that might be responsible for the moon's lovesickness?*
3. *In the second sonnet Sleep is described with a series of metaphors in the first four lines, and then is personified as a soldier who might protect the lover from the "fierce darts" of "Despair." Explain the metaphors in the first four lines.*
4. *How will Sleep see in the speaker the lively image of his beloved Stella?*

TO HIS COY MISTRESS

   Had we but world enough, and time,
This coyness, lady, were no crime.
We would sit down, and think which way
To walk, and pass our long love's day.
Thou by the Indian Ganges' side
Shouldst rubies find: I by the tide
Of Humber would complain. I would
Love you ten years before the Flood,
And you should if you please refuse
Till the conversion of the Jews.
My vegetable love should grow
Vaster than empires, and more slow;
An hundred years should go to praise
Thine eyes, and on thy forehead gaze;
Two hundred to adore each breast,

But thirty thousand to the rest.
An age at least to every part,
And the last age should show your heart.
For, lady, you deserve this state,
Nor would I love at lower rate.

  But at my back I always hear
Time's wingéd chariot hurrying near;
And yonder all before us lie
Deserts of vast eternity.
Thy beauty shall no more be found,
Nor, in thy marble vault, shall sound
My echoing song; then worms shall try
That long preserved virginity,
And your quaint honor turn to dust,
And into ashes all my lust:
The grave's a fine and private place,
But none, I think, do there embrace.

  Now therefore, while the youthful hue
Sits on thy skin like morning dew,
And while thy willing soul transpires
At every pore with instant fires,
Now let us sport us while we may,
And now, like am'rous birds of prey,
Rather at once our time devour
Than languish in his slow-chapped pow'r.
Let us roll all our strength and all
Our sweetness up into one ball,
And tear our pleasures with rough strife
Thorough the iron gates of life.
Thus, though we cannot make our sun
Stand still, yet we will make him run.

ANDREW MARVELL

Questions

1. *The speaker's argument (one you may have heard or used) is composed of three parts, corresponding to the three sections of the poem. Using one sentence for each part, paraphrase the argument.*
2. *In the first section how do the allusions to places in time and space, places ridiculously far apart, support the speaker's argument that lovers don't have "world*

enough, and time"? How distant is the "Indian Ganges" from the "Humber" (a little river in Marvell's home town in England)? How many years separate the "Flood" from "the conversion of the Jews," according to general Christian belief?

3. How are the references to time and space combined in the phrase "Deserts of vast eternity"?
4. What is the relationship between the woman's "beauty" and the speaker's "echoing song"?
5. Explain the last two lines of the poem. For what is "our sun" a metonymy?

LOVE

Love bade me welcome; yet my soul drew back,
   Guilty of dust and sin.
But quick-eyed Love, observing me grow slack
   From my first entrance in,
Drew nearer to me, sweetly questioning
   If I lacked anything.

"A guest," I answered, "worthy to be here."
   Love said, "You shall be he."
"I, the unkind, ungrateful? Ah my dear,
   I cannot look on Thee."
Love took my hand, and smiling, did reply,
   "Who made the eyes but I?"

"Truth, Lord, but I have marred them; let my shame
   Go where it doth deserve."
"And know you not," says Love, "who bore the blame?"
   "My dear, then I will serve."
"You must sit down," says Love, "and taste my meat."
   So I did sit and eat.

GEORGE HERBERT

Questions

1. In this poetic conversation between Love and a potential lover, personification is used quite effectively. Select specific details which indicate that the speaker is being invited to sit at the banquet of Love.
2. What is meant by "dust" in the second line? What is "dust" a metonymy for? Why would it be incompatible with an ideal love?

3. *How does Love explain away the speaker's presumed "shame" for his eyes? Why would someone seeking an ideal love feel ashamed at being attracted by the physical beauties his eyes see?*
4. *What is meant by "meat" in the second-to-last line? Is "meat" a metonymy? What is the meaning of the last line of the poem?*

ON HIS TWENTY-THIRD YEAR

How soon hath Time, the subtle thief of youth,
    Stolen on his wing my three and twentieth year!
    My hasting days fly on with full career,
    But my late spring no bud or blossom shew'th.
Perhaps my semblance might deceive the truth,
    That I to manhood am arriv'd so near,
    And inward ripeness doth much less appear,
    That some more timely-happy spirits indu'th.
Yet be it less or more, or soon or slow,
    It shall be still in strictest measure even,
    To that same lot, however mean, or high,
Toward which Time leads me, and the will of Heaven;
    All is, if I have grace to use it so,
    As ever in my great Taskmaster's eye.

JOHN MILTON

Questions

1. *How does the personification in the first two lines vivify the old cliché that "time flies"?*
2. *Explain the personification in the last line of the poem.*

ON THE DEATH OF DR. ROBERT LEVET

Condemn'd to hope's delusive mine,
    As on we toil from day to day,
By sudden blasts, or slow decline,
    Or social comforts drop away.

Well tried through many a varying year,
   See Levet to the grave descend;
Officious, innocent, sincere,
   Of ev'ry friendless name the friend.

Yet still he fills affection's eye,
   Obscurely wise, and coarsely kind;
Nor, letter'd arrogance, deny
   Thy praise to merit unrefin'd.

When fainting nature call'd for aid,
   And hov'ring death prepar'd the blow,
His vig'rous remedy display'd
   The power of art without the show.

In misery's darkest caverns known,
   His useful care was ever nigh.
Where hopeless anguish pour'd his groan,
   And lonely want retir'd to die.

No summons mock'd by chill delay,
   No petty gain disdain'd by pride,
The modest wants of ev'ry day
   The toil of ev'ry day supplied.

His virtues walk'd their narrow round,
   Nor made a pause, nor left a void;
And sure th' Eternal Master found
   The single talent well employ'd.

The busy day, the peaceful night,
   Unfelt, uncounted, glided by;
His frame was firm, his powers were bright,
   Tho' now his eightieth year was nigh.

Then with no throbbing fiery pain,
   No cold gradations of decay,
Death broke at once the vital chain,
   And freed his soul the nearest way.

SAMUEL JOHNSON

Questions

1. *This elegy for Dr. Robert Levet uses a number of personifications to achieve its effects. Explain the following:*
   a. *"hope's delusive mine"*
   b. *"affection's eye"*
   c. *"Where hopeless anguish pour'd his groan,*
      And lonely want retir'd to die."
2. *What kind of death did Levet have, according to the last stanza of the poem?*

COLD WATER FLAT

Come to conquer
this living Labyrinth of rock,
young Theseus of Dubuque
finds he is mazed without a minotaur,
without his Ariadne in the dark.

He dreams beyond
his steelwalled fear to fields grown
vertical with corn
and hope. Home to this heroic end:
imprisoned in the city of alone;

here smog obscures
his visionary victor's world
and streetsounds dulled
with rain reverberate in airshaft hours
where braver conquerors have been felled.

Amazed at night,
stalking the seven maids no sword
can save, he is devoured
in passageways of reinforced concrete,
trapped by his beast, and overpowered

in sleepless dead-
end dreams. How now, Theseus? How send
word home you are confined
with neither wings nor lover's thread
in the city that a murderer designed?

PHILIP BOOTH

Questions

1. The poet uses an extended allusion to the myth of Theseus and the Labyrinth. Using a dictionary or a book on mythology, explain the allusions to Theseus, Labyrinth, minotaur, and Ariadne.
2. What is the effect of describing the young man in New York as a "Theseus of Dubuque"? Where is Dubuque? Why does The New Yorker magazine claim it is not written for "the little old lady from Dubuque"?
3. To what does "visionary victor's world" refer? How does it contrast with the "city of alone"?
4. What effect is achieved by breaking the word "dead-end" in the last stanza? Explain the allusions to "wings" and the "lover's threat."
5. Is the use of allusion to contrast the "heroic" myth of Theseus with the commonplace story of the newcomer in the city effective? Suggest a way other than allusion which effectively would represent the contrast between youthful dreams of succeeding in New York and the reality of a cold-water flat.

LINES ON A PAID MILITIA

The country rings around with loud alarms,
And raw in fields the rude militia swarms;
Mouths without hands; maintained at vast expense,
In peace a charge, in war a weak defense:
Stout once a month they march, a blustering band,
And ever, but in times of need, at hand.
This was the morn when, issuing on the guard,
Drawn up in rank and file they stood prepared
Of seeming arms to make a short essay,
Then hasten to be drunk, the business of the day.

JOHN DRYDEN

tions

at is meant by a "rude" militia (line 2)? In what ways are these soldiers less
desirable as defenders of the country?
and explain the example of synecdoche in the third line. Is it effective?

ing Poetry

THE HAND THAT SIGNED THE PAPER FELLED A CITY

The hand that signed the paper felled a city;
Five sovereign fingers taxed the breath,
Doubled the globe of dead and halved a country;
These five kings did a king to death.

The mighty hand leads to a sloping shoulder,
The finger joints are cramped with chalk;
A goose's quill has put an end to murder
That put an end to talk.

The hand that signed the treaty bred a fever,
And famine grew, and locusts came;
Great is the hand that holds dominion over
Man by a scribbled name.

The five kings count the dead but do not soften
The crusted wound nor stroke the brow;
A hand rules pity as a hand rules heaven;
Hands have no tears to flow.

DYLAN THOMAS

Questions

1. *Explain the figure of speech in the first line of this poem. What does the hand stand for? Why are its five fingers called "sovereign" in the second line? Explain the fourth line of the poem.*
2. *In the last stanza Thomas makes effective use of the contrast between "hand" as a synecdoche for a king and "hand" as a literal feeling and comforting human limb. How does this contrast illustrate the callousness of the governor for those being governed? Explain the last line of the poem.*

BOOM!

SEES BOOM IN RELIGION, TOO

Atlantic City, June 23, 1957 (AP).—President Eisenhower's pastor said tonight that Americans are living in a period of "unprecedented religious activity" caused partially by paid vacations, the eight-hour day and modern conveniences.

"These fruits of material progress," said the Rev. Edward L. R. Elson of the National Presbyterian Church, Washington, "have provided the leisure, the energy, and the means for a level of human and spiritual values never before reached."

Here at the Vespasian-Carlton, it's just one
religious activity after another; the sky
is constantly being crossed by cruciform
airplanes, in which nobody disbelieves
for a second, and the tide, the tide
of spiritual progress and prosperity
miraculously keeps rising, to a level
never before attained. The churches are full,
the beaches are full, and the filling-stations
are full, God's great ocean is full
of paid vacationers praying an eight-hour day
to the human and spiritual values, the fruits,
the means for the level, the unprecedented level,
the leisure, the energy, and the means, Lord,
and the modern conveniences, which also are full.
Never before, O Lord, have the prayers and praises
from belfry and phonebooth, from ballpark and barbecue
the sacrifices, so endlessly ascended.
It was not thus when Job in Palestine
sat in the dust and cried, cried bitterly;
when Damien kissed the lepers on their wounds
it was not thus; it was not thus
when Francis worked a fourteen-hour day
strictly for the birds; when Dante took
a week's vacation without pay and it rained
part of the time, O Lord, it was not thus.

But now the gears mesh and the tires burn
and the ice chatters in the shaker and the priest
in the pulpit, and Thy Name, O Lord,
is kept before the public, while the fruits
ripen and religion booms and the level rises
and every modern convenience runneth over,
that it may never be with us as it hath been
with Athens and Karnak and Nagasaki,
nor Thy sun for one instant refrain from shining
on the rainbow Buick by the breezeway
or the Chris Craft with the uplift life raft;
that we may continue to be the just folks we are,
plain people with ordinary superliners and
disposable diaperliners, people of the stop'n'shop
'n'pray as you go, of hotel, motel, boatel,
the humble pilgrims of no deposit no return
and please adjust thy clothing, who will give to Thee,
if Thee will keep us going, our annual
Miss Universe, for Thy Name's Sake, Amen.

HOWARD NEMEROV

Questions

1. The newspaper clipping suggests that material progress leads to spiritual progress. Does the poet agree with this judgment?
2. Characterize the tone of the poem. Cite specific instances where the poet mocks the association of material and spiritual success.
3. Explain the allusions to "Job," "Damien," "Francis" ("strictly for the birds"), and "Dante." Do these allusions prove or disprove the judgment of the newspaper article?
4. Explain the allusions to "Athens," "Karnak," and "Nagasaki." How do they contrast with the civilizations of "the just folks we are"?
5. How does the phrase "people of the stop'n'shop/'n'pray as you go, of hotel, motel, boatel" ridicule the association of commerce and religion? Does the babble of language in this phrase also suggest the confusion of values in modern society?

IN CALIFORNIA THERE ARE TWO HUNDRED AND FIFTY-SIX RELIGIONS

I
In California there are
Two hundred and fifty six religions,
And I guess I belonged
To the two hundred fifty fifth;
At least it was odd
Or seems odd in retrospect
Or will seem odd to you, when I tell you
We didn't eat meat or drink alcoholic beverages
Or smoke.
You say that's not odd in California?
Then how about not wearing red and black,
Not BELIEVING in red and black,
Because colors have vibratory rates,
And black and red have low vibratory rates,
Cosmically speaking;

Black not being a color at all and red being
On the short end of the spectrum.

II
Everyone knows that black is the color of death
And we didn't believe in death,
And red is the color of blood and therefore—
No, not life, but anger, danger.
(You know a bull is angered by a red cape,
Despite the fact he is colorblind and bleeding.)
Like those of any faith, I needed all faith,
And you would laugh, not having faith,
Were I to tell you about the Cosmos
And the Creation
Because you heard it differently.
Most people like their myths to be familiar,
Or to have attained a respectable age;

No one wants to be caught, in this day and age,
On the short end of the spectrum.

RICHARD E. ALBERT

Questions

1. *Explain the allusions to the "Cosmos" and the "Creation" in this poem. How does the speaker suggest that those terms have different meanings for different people?*
2. *Describe the speaker's attitude toward religion in this poem. How does it compare with that of the speaker in Nemerov's "Boom!"?*

ON THE VANITY OF EARTHLY GREATNESS

The tusks that clashed in mighty brawls
Of mastodons, are billiard balls.

The sword of Charlemagne the Just
Is ferric oxide, known as rust.

The grizzly bear whose potent hug
Was feared by all, is now a rug.

Great Caesar's dead and on the shelf,
And I don't feel so well myself!

ARTHUR GUITERMAN

Question

The humor of this poem comes from the speaker's reduction of things once mighty to a lesser rank of existence. How do the allusions to Caesar and Charlemagne work in this reduction process?

MOVING

Bookshelves empty, tables lampless, walls
bare, the house is a rubble of moving—
foothills of boxes, trunks
under clouds of ceiling.

My friends
said good-bye hours ago, when June twilight
hung on the hills. Now, in late dark
muggy for stars, moths whir at the yellow porch light,
ping screens. By the one dim floor lamp
among the shadowy undoings of my life,
in a limbo between having gone and having gone,
I sit like a caretaker of my doom.
Not an ashtray or a spoon.
In the real dawn, I will be going.

My friends are sleeping, turned toward
tomorrows without me—will still be sleeping
when I begin to drive the familiar streets and roads
in which sun will come only after me.
If I called them now, in this hollow
past midnight, anything I said would
be from the future.

Alone in the present,
I wait, smoking (a tin can for ashes).
Bugs thwack on the screens. Beyond love
I am a projectile into the future—
still hours, days away.
Time has stopped at the speed I am going, landmarks
appear strangely in new light,
clouds whirling past me, into the past.

The phone has been disconnected.

ROBERT WALLACE

Questions

1. *Explain the comparison between the house and a "rubble" as developed in the first stanza.*
2. *Compare the treatment of time in this poem with the treatment of the same subject in Shirley's "The Glories of Our Blood and State" or in Guiterman's "On the Vanity of Earthly Greatness (p. 87)." What does the speaker mean by "Time has stopped at the speed I am going"?*

A VALEDICTORY TO STANDARD OIL OF INDIANA

In the darkness east of Chicago, the sky burns over the
  plumbers' nightmares
Red and blue, and my hometown lies there loaded with
  gasoline.
Registers ring like gas-pumps, pumps like pinballs, pinballs like
  broken alarm clocks,
And it's time for morning, but nothing's going to work.
From cat-cracker to candle-shop, from grease-works along the
  pipeline,
Over storage tanks like kings on a checkerboard ready to jump
  the county,
The word goes out: With refined regrets
We suggest you sleep all day in your houses shaped like lunch
  buckets
And don't show up at the automated gates.
Something else will tap the gauges without yawning
And check the valves at the feet of the cooling-towers without
  complaining.
Standard Oil is canning my high school classmates
And the ones who fell out of junior high or slipped in the grades.
What should they do, gassed up in their Tempests and Comets,
  raring to go
Somewhere with their wives scowling in front and kids stuffed
  in the back,
Past drive-ins jammed like car-lots, trying to find the beaches
But blocked by freights for hours, stopped dead in their tracks
Where the rails, as thick as thieves along the lakefront,
Lower their crossing gates to shut the frontier? What can they
  think about
As they stare at the side of boxcars for a sign,
And Lake Michigan drains slowly into Lake Huron,
The mills level the Dunes, and the eels go sailing through the
  trout,
And mosquitoes inherit the evening, while toads no bigger than
  horseflies
Hop crazily after them over the lawns and sidewalks, and the
  rainbows fall
Flat in the oil they came from? There are two towns now,
One dark, one going to be dark, divided by cyclone fences;
One pampered and cared for like pillboxes and cathedrals,

The other vanishing overnight in the dumps and swamps like a
   struck sideshow.
As the Laureate of the Class of '44—which doesn't know it has
   one—
I offer this poem, not from hustings or barricades
Or the rickety stage where George Rogers Clark stood glued to
   the wall,
But from another way out, like Barnum's "This Way to the
   Egress,"
Which moved the suckers when they'd seen enough. Get out of
   town.

DAVID WAGONER

Questions

1. *What is meant by "the plumbers' nightmares" in the first line of the poem? Is this
   an effective metaphor?*
2. *Select details from the first twelve lines of the poem that illustrate the process of
   automation that is pervading both town and refinery. What are two possible
   meanings of "canning" in line 12?*
3. *Explain the allusions to George Rogers Clark and Barnum in the last three lines of
   the poem. How is the entrapment of the refinery workers suggested by the fact that
   Clark is "glued to the wall"? What is an "Egress"?*

Gray's "Elegy" is one of the most famous poems in the English language.
For 200 years it has been a source of pleasure and enlightenment to readers of
all ages and stations in life. It is a poem that will reward a close reading.

Following the poem are a number of questions that are designed to focus
attention on especially important elements in the poem. Gray makes exten-
sive use of the language devices discussed in this chapter: metonymy, synec-
doche, personification, and allusion. An understanding of the poet's use of
these and other devices will increase the reader's appreciation of the poem.

The questions are followed by a brief bibliography of short and easily
accessible articles on the poem. The "Elegy" has been fortunate in its critics,
and you would be well advised to examine one or more of these articles. After
you have formulated your own reaction to the "Elegy," you might like to
compare it with the reactions of various scholars. A more demanding but
perhaps more interesting exercise would be to compare one scholarly reaction
with another.

ELEGY

Written in a Country Churchyard

The curfew tolls the knell of parting day,
   The lowing herd wind slowly o'er the lea,
The plowman homeward plods his weary way,
   And leaves the world to darkness and to me.   4

Now fades the glimmering landscape on the sight,
   And all the air a solemn stillness holds,
Save where the beetle wheels his droning flight,
   And drowsy tinklings lull the distant folds;   8

Save that from yonder ivy-mantled tower
   The moping owl does to the moon complain
Of such, as wandering near her secret bower,
   Molest her ancient solitary reign.   12

Beneath those rugged elms, that yew-tree's shade,
   Where heaves the turf in many a mouldering heap,
Each in his narrow cell for ever laid,
   The rude forefathers of the hamlet sleep.   16

The breezy call of incense-breathing Morn,
   The swallow twittering from the straw-built shed,
The cock's shrill clarion, or the echoing horn,
   No more shall rouse them from their lowly bed.   20

For them no more the blazing hearth shall burn,
   Or busy housewife ply her evening care:
No children run to lisp their sire's return,
   Or climb his knees the envied kiss to share.   24

Oft did the harvest to their sickle yield,
   Their furrow oft the stubborn glebe has broke;
How jocund did they drive their team afield!
   How bowed the woods beneath their sturdy stroke!   28

Let not Ambition mock their useful toil,
 Their homely joys, and destiny obscure;
Nor Grandeur hear with a disdainful smile
 The short and simple annals of the poor.   32

The boast of heraldry, the pomp of power,
 And all that beauty, all that wealth e'er gave,
Awaits alike the inevitable hour.
 The paths of glory lead but to the grave.   36

Nor you, ye proud, impute to these the fault,
 If Memory o'er their tomb no trophies raise,
Where through the long-drawn aisle and fretted vault
 The pealing anthem swells the note of praise.   40

Can storied urn or animated bust
 Back to its mansion call the fleeting breath?
Can honor's voice provoke the silent dust,
 Or flattery sooth the dull cold ear of death?   44

Perhaps in this neglected spot is laid
 Some heart once pregnant with celestial fire;
Hands, that the rod of empire might have swayed,
 Or waked to ecstasy the living lyre.   48

But Knowledge to their eyes her ample page
 Rich with the spoils of time did ne'er unroll;
Chill Penury repressed their noble rage,
 And froze the genial current of the soul.   52

Full many a gem of purest ray serene,
 The dark unfathomed caves of ocean bear:
Full many a flower is born to blush unseen,
 And waste its sweetness on the desert air.   56

Some village Hampden, that with dauntless breast
 The little tyrant of his fields withstood;
Some mute inglorious Milton here may rest,
 Some Cromwell guiltless of his country's blood.   60

Th' applause of listening senates to command,
 The threats of pain and ruin to despise,
To scatter plenty o'er a smiling land,
 And read their history in a nation's eyes   64

Their lot forbade: nor circumscribed alone
   Their growing virtues, but their crimes confined;
Forbade to wade through slaughter to a throne,
   And shut the gates of mercy on mankind,   68

The struggling pangs of conscious truth to hide,
   To quench the blushes of ingenuous shame,
Or heap the shrine of Luxury and Pride
   With incense kindled at the Muse's flame.   72

Far from the madding crowd's ignoble strife,
   Their sober wishes never learned to stray;
Along the cool sequestered vale of life
   They kept the noiseless tenor of their way.   76

Yet ev'n these bones from insult to protect
   Some frail memorial still erected nigh,
With uncouth rhymes and shapeless sculpture decked,
   Implores the passing tribute of a sigh.   80

Their name, their years, spelt by th' unlettered Muse,
   The place of fame and elegy supply:
And many a holy text around she strews,
   That teach the rustic moralist to die.   84

For who to dumb Forgetfulness a prey,
   This pleasing anxious being e'er resigned,
Left the warm precincts of the cheerful day,
   Nor cast one longing lingering look behind?   88

On some fond breast the parting soul relies,
   Some pious drops the closing eye requires;
Ev'n from the tomb the voice of Nature cries,
   Ev'n in our ashes live their wonted fires.   92

For thee, who mindful of the unhonored dead
   Dost in these lines their artless tale relate;
If chance, by lonely contemplation led,
   Some kindred spirit shall inquire thy fate,   96

Haply some hoary-headed swain may say,
   "Oft have we seen him at the peep of dawn
Brushing with hasty steps the dews away
   To meet the sun upon the upland lawn.   100

"There at the foot of yonder nodding beech
    That wreathes its old fantastic roots so high,
His listless length at noontide would he stretch.
    And pore upon the brook that babbles by.   104

"Hard by yon wood, now smiling as in scorn,
    Mutt'ring his wayward fancies he would rove,
Now drooping, woeful wan, like one forlorn,
    Or crazed with care, or crossed in hopeless love.   108

"One morn I missed him on the customed hill,
    Along the heath and near his favorite tree;
Another came; nor yet beside the rill,
    Nor up the lawn, nor at the wood was he;   112

"The next with dirges due in sad array
    Slow through the churchway path we saw him borne.
Approach and read (for thou canst read) the lay,
    Graved on the stone beneath yon aged thorn."   116

The Epitaph

Here rests his head upon the lap of Earth
    A youth to Fortune and to Fame unknown,
Fair Science frowned not on his humble birth,
    And Melancholy marked him for her own.   120

Large was his bounty, and his soul sincere,
    Heaven did a recompense as largely send:
He gave to Misery all he had, a tear,
    He gained from Heaven ('twas all he wished) a friend.   124

No farther seek his merits to disclose,
    Or draw his frailties from their dread abode
(There they alike in trembling hope repose),
    The bosom of his Father and his God.   128

THOMAS GRAY

Questions

1. *Cite specific images which reveal the time of day and the location of the speaker of the poem, the "me" of line 4.*
2. *Select specific images which reveal the kind of life which the people buried in the country graveyard led. Describe the speaker's attitude toward these people and their life style.*

3. Discuss the relationship of money and education which is suggested in lines 49–52. What is meant by the "spoils of time" in line 50?
4. What are some of the advantages of poetry, as suggested in lines 66–76? What specific "crime" is suggested in lines 71–72? Why would this be particularly offensive to the speaker of the poem?
5. Discuss the speaker's reaction to the "uncouth rhymes and shapeless sculpture" (line 79) which decorate the graves of the poor. Is he a snob, a sentimentalist, or a realist?
6. Explain and discuss lines 85–92. Is it true that everyone, rich or poor, wants to be remembered after death? What other kinds of immortality are there?
7. Who is the "thee" of line 93? Is it the same person as the "me" of line 4, the speaker of the poem? If so, who is speaking to him? What is meant by "these lines" (line 94): the poem itself or some inscription carved on the gravestones?
8. What kind of person is described by the "hoary-headed swain" in lines 98–116? Is he a simple farmboy, or do his activities indicate an exceptional spirit? Why does he "pore upon the brook that babbles by" (line 104)?
9. Who is the "youth to Fortune and to Fame unknown" (line 118) for whom the Epitaph is written? Is he the "thee" of line 93, and the "me" of line 4? If no one in the village can read or write, who wrote the Epitaph? Is the Epitaph-writer the "friend" (line 124) the youth finally "gained"?
10. In what does the youth's "hope" for immortality lie, according to the Epitaph?
11. In what ways does the use of personification contribute to the poem? Examine specifically the personifications in lines 17, 29, 31, 38, 43, 85, 91. Do you see a pattern in the choice of human qualities by which the abstract concepts are personified?
12. Explain the following uses of metonymy in the poem: "the rod of empire" (line 47), "the living lyre" (line 48), "slaughter" (line 67). How do they make the poem more vivid?
13. Line 92, "Ev'n in our ashes live their wonted fires," is an allusion to an earlier poem. The reference was put in a footnote by Gray when he wrote the "Elegy." Keeping lines 91–92 in mind, why do you think Gray alluded to the voice of a dead poet at this point in the "Elegy"?
14. Explain the examples of synecdoche in lines 42 and 44. Is the part chosen to represent the whole in these examples similar to the concrete qualities used in most of the personifications?
15. How do the sounds of the language in the first five stanzas contribute to the sense of those stanzas, reflecting the scene which the poet images for us?

Bibliography: Thomas Gray

Brady, Frank. "Structure and Meaning in Gray's Elegy." In From Sensibility to Romanticism: Essays Presented to Frederick A. Pottle, edited by Frederick W. Hilles and Harold Bloom. New York: Oxford University Press, 1965.

Brooks, Cleanth. The Well-Wrought Urn: Studies in the Structure of Poetry. New York: Harcourt, Brace & World, 1947.

Ellis, Frank H. "Gray's *Elegy:* The Biographical Problem in Literary Criticism." *PMLA* 66 (1951):971–1008.

Glazier, Lyle. "Gray's *Elegy:* The Skull Beneath the Skin." *University of Kansas City Review* 19 (1963):174–80.

Greene, Richard Leighton. "Gray's 'Elegy Written in a Country Churchyard', 31–32." *Explicator* 24 (1966):Item 47.

Kuist, James M. "The Conclusion of Gray's *Elegy.*" *South Atlantic Quarterly* 70 (1971):203–14.

Reichard, Hugo M. "The Elegist Who Sang for All He Was Worth." *Dalhousie Review* 51 (1971):24–30.

Shankar, D. A. "Cleanth Brooks and the *Elegy Written in a Country Church-Yard.*" *Literary Criterion* 9 (1970):77–80.

Shepherd, Odell. "A Youth to Fortune and to Fame Unknown." *Modern Philology* 20 (1923):347–73.

Starr, Herbert W., ed. *Twentieth Century Interpretations of Gray's Elegy.* Englewood Cliffs, N.J.: Prentice-Hall, 1968.

Watson-Smyth, Peter. "The Origins of the Elegy." *Ariel: A Review of International English Literature* 1 (1970):39–47.

Topics for Writing

1. Write a 200-word passage of prose structured around an extended personification. You might use:
   a. Fortune is a woman ("Lady Luck").
   b. War is a glutton at the banquet of life.
   c. Love is an unexpected but welcomed guest.
2. Select five allusions from the newspaper, television, or conversation, and explain them.
3. Read the article on Gray's "Elegy" by Frank H. Ellis, and summarize his argument against a biographical interpretation of the poem. Then compare it with the article by Odell Shepherd.
4. Compare the article on the "Elegy" by Frank Brady with the one by Cleanth Brooks. Which is closer to your reaction to the poem? Which taught you the most?

5 Paradox and Irony

Paradox and irony demonstrate perhaps better than any other poetic devices the truth of the statement that language (and poetry) has a life greater than the sum of the dictonary definitions of words. You may have heard someone remark that "the Constitution is a living document," by which they mean that the laws and definitions of the Constitution are flexible enough to change with the times, that the truths of the Constitution are just as useful in our modern context as they were 200 years ago. Language, like the living Constitution, adapts itself to changing contexts; and the user of language, like the interpreter of the Constitution, must be able to perceive and understand the meanings of words as they change and grow in different contexts, whether in different poems or in other forms of language usage.

Consider the words "lost" and "found." In most contexts these words convey opposing meanings: to "lose" something is the opposite of to "find" something. Yet one of the best known statements of the Bible is, "To find yourself you must lose yourself." What does this literal contradiction mean? In the context of the Bible and Christian thought the statement means that a person must lose his worldly ambitions in order to find his spiritual heritage. But what if someone said, "To find your watch you must lose your watch." This sentence makes literal sense as a statement about logical sequence, since only lost objects can be found. But if the sentence is taken figuratively, as the Biblical statement must be taken, it seems ridiculous. The words "lost" and "found" are the same, but the context has changed; and the reader can understand the language only if he understands the context.

Poets and other users of language have long realized that paradox is an important means of displaying the life of language. *Paradox* is a statement which *seems* to be a contradiction, but which in a given context *really* is true. The Bible, for instance, often makes use of paradox, perhaps because it often contrasts the values of one context (this world) with another (the next). "One must die in order to be truly born." "Blessed are they that mourn, for they shall be comforted." "Blessed are the poor, for they shall inherit the kingdom." The modern world, of course, offers plenty of paradoxes: "The more thermonuclear weapons each side has, the less likely it is that there will be a war;" "If the government overspends its income, the country will be more prosperous." Presidents have been elected by convincing the voters of the truth of such paradoxes.

Irony is similar to paradox, since it depends for its effect upon the reader's recognition of the difference between the literal meaning of a statement and the intended meaning. *Irony* is a way of speaking or writing in which there is a tension or opposition between what is expressed and what is implied. In the simplest examples of *verbal irony,* what is said is the exact opposite of what is meant. If you say to the person who has just spilled soup in your lap, "Thank you," or "You are too graceful for words," you are using a simple form of verbal irony, saying the exact opposite of what you mean. But often the tension or opposition between what is said and what is intended is more complex. If a policeman gives you a ticket for driving without a headlight, you might say, "Thank you," and mean 1) that you are *not* appreciative of the ticket, 2) that you are still aware that it is good that the policeman is doing his job of protecting motorists from traffic hazards (like you), and 3) that you are thankful that he has alerted you to your headlight problem before you crashed into a pole. If your "Thank you" expresses only the first of these meanings, then it is a simple ironic statement, expressing only the opposite of what it means. But all three of the meanings could exist simultaneously in the statement, and in that case the irony would be more complex, since your "Thank you" would convey at least two opposing meanings at once (Thanks, but No Thanks). To appreciate the richness of the complexity and ambiguity that irony can convey, first you must appreciate the complexity and ambiguity that life itself affords. You must realize that it is possible for two opposing statements or truths both to be true. Your own experience will eventually show this to be possible, if it hasn't already.

Dramatic irony occurs in a situation in which a person says or does something which suggests more than the person intends or realizes. The irony results from the tension between what the person *thinks* he is doing or saying and what the audience *knows* him to be doing or saying. Dramatic irony depends upon the audience's knowing more than the speaker. In Sophocles' *Oedipus Rex,* for instance, the king is determined to find and banish the person who has brought bad luck to his kingdom; but as the play progresses the audience realizes that it is the king himself who is the offender. Hence, every time the king repeats his determination to punish the offender, the audience perceives that the king is really, and unknowingly, threatening himself. Dramatic irony is used not only in plays but also in dramatic poems in which a character-speaker says something which ironically means more than he intends it to mean. In Robert Browning's "My Last Duchess" the Duke believes himself to be a good and even great man who made the mistake of marrying a stupid child-woman (the woman who, now dead, was his last duchess); but as he describes what he considers her faults and his virtues, he ironically convinces the reader that the woman was generous, lovely, and good, and that he was, and still is, stupid, pompous, and selfish.

A third kind of irony is *irony of fate,* and it results from the tension between what the audience expects and what actually happens. The "of fate" suggests that the cause of the difference is chance, luck, or fate. If a man is lynched in front of the courthouse (symbol of due process under law), then the situation, caused by chance, is ironic. If a seemingly happy man unexpectedly commits suicide (as in "Richard Cory"), the irony is one "of fate" rather than verbal or dramatic. This kind of irony is commonly used in both poems and novels; when used skillfully it is very effective, but it is easily overused, with the result that the irony is not so much "of fate" as of the contriving writer. Irony of fate must be both believable and unexpected; it fails when it is too exaggerated or too obvious.

Irony, then, is an important way in which language can convey the complexities of situations and of our understanding of and reaction to them. Life is not a series of simple choices between black and white, right and wrong; most often it is lived in the gray areas between these extremes. Irony is the device of language which allows the skillful writer or speaker to explore these areas, and the reader must be equally skillful at appreciating irony if he is to share this exploration with the poet.

TO AN ATHLETE DYING YOUNG

The time you won your town the race
We chaired you through the market-place;
Man and boy stood cheering by,
And home we brought you shoulder-high.

To-day, the road all runners come,
Shoulder-high we bring you home,
And set you at your threshold down,
Townsman of a stiller town.

Smart lad, to slip betimes away
From fields where glory does not stay
And early though the laurel grows
It withers quicker than the rose.

Eyes the shady night has shut
Cannot see the record cut,
And silence sounds no worse than cheers
After earth has stopped the ears:

Now you will not swell the rout
Of lads that wore their honours out,
Runners whom renown outran
And the name died before the man.

So set, before its echoes fade,
The fleet foot on the sill of shade,
And hold to the low lintel up
The still-defended challenge-cup.

And round that early-laurelled head
Will flock to gaze the strengthless dead.
And find unwithered on its curls
The garland briefer than a girl's.

A. E. HOUSMAN

Questions

1. *Explain the paradox expressed in the third stanza. In what sense is the athlete a "smart lad"?*
2. *What is the "road all runners come" mentioned in the second stanza? What is the "stiller town"?*
3. *How does the fourth stanza explain the paradox around which the poem is structured?*
4. *What is suggested by the following: the "laurel," the "rose," the "garland"?*
5. *What is meant by "the garland briefer than a girl's," in the last line of the poem? Is it true that fame dies even sooner than beauty?*

DEATH BE NOT PROUD

Death be not proud, though some have called thee
Mighty and dreadful, for thou art not so;
For those whom thou think'st thou dost overthrow
Die not, poor Death, nor yet canst thou kill me.
From rest and sleep, which but thy pictures be,
Much pleasure; then from thee much more must flow,
And soonest our best men with thee do go,
Rest of their bones, and soul's delivery.
Thou art slave to Fate, Chance, kings, and desperate men,
And dost with Poison, War, and Sickness dwell;
And poppy or charms can make us sleep as well,
And better than thy stroke; why swell'st thou then?
One short sleep past, we wake eternally
And death shall be no more; Death, thou shalt die.

JOHN DONNE

Questions

1. *This poem is developed around a paradox, expressed most plainly in lines 4 and 14. Explain the paradox.*
2. *In what respect are "rest and sleep" the "pictures" of death? How does this fact lead the poet to state that death will give even more "pleasure"? Is this a logical jump?*
3. *How is death a "slave" to "Fate, Chance, kings, and desperate men"?*
4. *In what sense does Death "dwell" with "Poison, War, and Sickness"? Why should this fact make Death less "proud"?*
5. *Examine the reasons the poet gives to support his paradoxical statements that Death cannot kill him and that Death itself will die. Are they totally convincing as arguments? Does the pleasure the poem gives come from the truth of the arguments used, or from the ingenious play of the poet's mind?*

THE CONSTANT LOVER

Out upon it! I have loved
    Three whole days together;
And am like to love three more,
    If it prove fair weather.

Time shall moult away his wings,
    Ere he shall discover
In the whole wide world again
    Such a constant lover.

But the spite on 't is, no praise
    Is due at all to me:
Love with me had made no stays
    Had it any been but she.

Had it any been but she,
    And that very face,
There had been at least ere this
    A dozen dozen in her place.

SIR JOHN SUCKLING

Questions

1. *The irony in this poem comes from the difference between what the title suggests, constancy in love, and the nature of the constancy which the speaker of the poem declares he has. How long has the speaker been "the constant lover," according to the second line of the poem?*
2. *Is the speaker mocking the notion of constancy in love by bragging that he has been in love three whole days, or does he use this seemingly ridiculous definition of constancy to express his amazement and delight at being in love at all?*

TO LUCASTA, GOING TO THE WARS

Tell me not, Sweet, I am unkind,
    That from the nunnery
Of thy chaste breast and quiet mind
    To war and arms I fly.

True, a new mistress now I chase,
    The first foe in the field;
And with a stronger faith embrace
    A sword, a horse, a shield.

Yet this inconstancy is such
　　As you too shall adore;
I could not love thee, Dear, so much,
　　Loved I not honor more.

RICHARD LOVELACE

Questions

1. *What kind of relationship between the speaker and his love Lucasta is suggested in the first stanza? What specific words suggest that honor plays a part in their love?*
2. *What is the meaning of "mistress" in the second stanza? Does the word necessarily suggest a physical, illicit relationship between the lovers?*
3. *List the points of comparison between love and war in the second stanza.*
4. *Explain the paradox of Lucasta's approval of the speaker's "inconstancy."*
5. *How does the speaker's love of "honor" contribute to his love of Lucasta?*

from AUGURIES OF INNOCENCE

To see a world in a grain of sand
And a Heaven in a wild flower,
Hold Infinity in the palm of your hand
And Eternity in an hour.

A robin redbreast in a cage
Puts all Heaven in a rage.
A dove-house filled with doves and pigeons
Shudders Hell through all its regions.
A dog starved at his master's gate
Predicts the ruin of the state.
A horse misused upon the road
Calls to Heaven for human blood.
Each outcry of the hunted hare
A fibre from the brain does tear.
A skylark wounded in the wing,
A cherubim does cease to sing.
The game cock clipped and armed for fight
Does the rising sun affright.
Every wolf's and lion's howl
Raises from Hell a human soul.

The wild deer wandering here and there
Keeps the human soul from care.
The lamb misused breeds public strife
And yet forgives the butcher's knife.
The bat that flits at close of eve
Has left the brain that won't believe.
The owl that calls upon the night
Speaks the unbeliever's fright.
He who shall hurt the little wren
Shall never be beloved by men.
He who the ox to wrath has moved
Shall never be by woman loved.

WILLIAM BLAKE

Questions

1. *This selection of poetry begins with paradox and proceeds through a series of juxtapositions which suggest paradoxical connections between animals and humans. Explain the truth of the paradox of holding "Infinity in the palm of your hand/And Eternity in an hour."*
2. *The first three couplets suggest relationships between the particular and the general. What is the relationship here between a "robin redbreast" and "Heaven," between a "dog" and the "state"?*
3. *What is the meaning of "Auguries"? What are the "Auguries of Innocence" in this selection?*
4. *Explain the truth of the last four lines.*
5. *Describe in a few sentences the relationship of man and nature which this passage suggests. Is it simply a question of man's duty being to conserve natural resources, or is some more fundamental relationship implied?*

CRAZY JANE TALKS WITH THE BISHOP

I met the Bishop on the road
And much said he and I.
'Those breasts are flat and fallen now,
Those veins must soon be dry;
Live in a heavenly mansion,
Not in some foul sty.'

'Fair and foul are near of kin,
And fair needs foul,' I cried.
'My friends are gone, but that's a truth
Nor grave nor bed denied,
Learned in bodily lowliness
And in the heart's pride.

'A woman can be proud and stiff
When on love intent;
But Love has pitched his mansion in
The place of excrement;
For nothing can be sole or whole
That has not been rent.'

WILLIAM BUTLER YEATS

Questions

1. *Characterize the different attitudes of Crazy Jane and the Bishop toward the relationship of the physical and the spiritual.*
2. *What does the Bishop mean by a "heavenly mansion" and a "foul sty"?*
3. *Explain the metonymy of "Nor grave nor bed" which Crazy Jane uses in stanza two. How did she learn the "truth" that "fair needs foul"?*
4. *Lines 3 and 4 of the last stanza use a personification to contrast the mansion of love with the "heavenly mansion" of the Bishop. These lines also allude to the physical fact that the human genitals are very close to "the place of excrement." How does this physical fact support the metaphysical "truth" of Crazy Jane?*
5. *The last two lines present a paradox. Explain it in terms of the physical act of a woman's giving up her virginity, and also in terms of the psychological act of integrating the real and the ideal into the human. How "crazy" is Crazy Jane?*

RÉSUMÉ

Razors pain you;
Rivers are damp;
Acids stain you;
And drugs cause cramp.
Guns aren't lawful;
Nooses give;
Gas smells awful;
You might as well live.

DOROTHY PARKER

1. *What is the subject of this poem?*
2. *How is the speaker's ironical attitude toward the subject reflected in the reasons that she gives for living?*

WAR IS KIND

Do not weep, maiden, for war is kind.
Because your lover threw wild hands toward the sky
And the affrighted steed ran on alone,
Do not weep.
War is kind.

Hoarse, booming drums of the regiment,
Little souls who thirst for fight,
These men were born to drill and die.
The unexplained glory flies above them,
Great is the battle-god, great, and his
      kingdom—
A field where a thousand corpses lie.

Do not weep, babe, for war is kind.
Because your father tumbled in the yellow trenches,
Raged at his breast, gulped and died,
Do not weep.
War is kind.

Swift blazing flag of the regiment,
Eagle with crest of red and gold,
These men were born to drill and die.
Point for them the virtue of slaughter,
Make plain to them the excellence of killing
And a field where a thousand corpses lie.

Mother whose heart hung humble as a button
On the bright splendid shroud of your son,
Do not weep.
War is kind.

STEPHEN CRANE

1. The phrase "war is kind" is clearly ironic. Does it gain in ironic intensity from being repeated throughout the poem?
2. Cite and explain two instances of irony in the second stanza.
3. Describe the ironic implications of the phrase "the virtue of slaughter" in the fourth stanza.
4. Summarize the ironic contrasts between a man's roles as lover, father, and son and his role as soldier.
5. Compare and contrast the attitude of the speaker toward war in this poem with that of the speaker in Lovelace's "To Lucasta, Going to the Wars." Which poem is more pleasing? Why?

KARMA

Christmas was in the air and all was well
With him, but for a few confusing flaws
In divers of God's images. Because
A friend of his would neither buy nor sell,
Was he to answer for the axe that fell?
He pondered; and the reason for it was,
Partly, a slowly freezing Santa Claus
Upon the corner, with his beard and bell.

Acknowledging an improvident surprise,
He magnified a fancy that he wished
The friend whom he had wrecked were here again.
Not sure of that, he found a compromise;
And from the fulness of his heart he fished
A dime for Jesus who had died for men.

EDWIN ARLINGTON ROBINSON

Questions

1. Explain the irony of the first three lines of the poem.
2. What is the speaker's attitude toward the subject of the poem? How is irony used in the last two lines of the poem?
3. What is the meaning of "Karma"? Why is it the title of this poem?

DUST

Agatha Morley
All her life
Grumbled at dust
Like a good wife.

Dust on a table,
Dust on a chair,
Dust on a mantel
She couldn't bear.

She forgave faults
In man and child
But a dusty shelf
Would set her wild.

She bore with sin
Without protest,
But dust thoughts preyed
Upon her rest.

Agatha Morley
Is sleeping sound
Six feet under
The mouldy ground.

Six feet under
The earth she lies
With dust at her feet
And dust in her eyes.

SYDNEY KING RUSSELL

Questions

1. *This poem is built around one basic irony. What is it?*
2. *How is the speaker's attitude toward Agatha Morley conveyed in his listing of the various things she would rather put up with than the dreaded dust?*

AND DEATH SHALL HAVE NO DOMINION

And death shall have no dominion.
Dead men naked they shall be one
With the man in the wind and the west moon;
When their bones are picked clean and the clean bones gone,
They shall have stars at elbow and foot;
Though they go mad they shall be sane,
Though they sink through the sea they shall rise again;
Though lovers be lost love shall not;
And death shall have no dominion.

And death shall have no dominion.
Under the windings of the sea
They lying long shall not die windily;
Twisting on racks when sinews give way,
Strapped to a wheel, yet they shall not break;
Faith in their hands shall snap in two,
And the unicorn evils run them through;
Split all ends up they shan't crack;
And death shall have no dominion.

And death shall have no dominion.
No more may gulls cry at their ears
Or waves break loud on the seashores;
Where blew a flower may a flower no more
Lift its head to the blows of the rain;
Though they be mad and dead as nails,
Heads of the characters hammer through daisies;
Break in the sun till the sun breaks down,
And death shall have no dominion.

DYLAN THOMAS

Questions

1. *This poem is based on a paradox, that the dead shall still be living. How is this seeming contradiction resolved in terms of the poem?*
2. *Explain the paradox of "Strapped to a wheel, yet they shall not break . . . . Split all ends up they shan't crack."*

SAFE IN THEIR ALABASTER CHAMBERS

Safe in their Alabaster Chambers—
Untouched by Morning
And untouched by Noon—
Sleep the meek members of the Resurrection—
Rafter of satin,
And Roof of stone.

Light laughs the breeze
In her Castle above them—
Babbles the Bee in a stolid Ear,
Pipe the Sweet Birds in ignorant cadence—
Ah, what sagacity perished here!

OF GOD WE ASK ONE FAVOR

Of God we ask one favor,
That we may be forgiven—
For what, he is presumed to know:
The crime from us is hidden.
Immured the whole of life
Within a magic prison,
We reprimand the happiness
That too competes with heaven.

EMILY DICKINSON

Questions

1. *Many readers assume that Emily Dickinson is a superficial, if delightful, poetess. These poems reveal how important irony is in her work. How do the following details contribute to the ironic contrast between the dead believers and the natural world above their graves: "Safe," "the meek members," "Roof of stone," "Babbles the Bee in a stolid Ear," and "ignorant cadences"?*
2. *From what are the dead believers "Safe"? What threats are offered by "Morning" and "Noon," by the laughing "breeze"?*

3. *Explain the contrast between the Birds' "ignorant cadence" and the dead believers' "sagacity." Does the poet mean what she says, or is she being ironic?*
4. *What is the "crime" mentioned in the poem "Of God We Ask One Favor"? What is the "happiness That too competes with heaven"?*
5. *Explain the irony of the phrase "magic prison." Compare the "Alabaster Chambers," the "Castle," and the "magic prison." What is Dickinson's attitude toward these types of homes? Which is most pleasant? Which is most permanent?*

THE CHIMNEY SWEEPER

When my mother died I was very young,
And my father sold me while yet my tongue
Could scarcely cry "'weep! 'weep! 'weep! 'weep!"
So your chimneys I sweep, and in soot I sleep.

There's little Tom Dacre, who cried when his head,
That curled like a lamb's back, was shaved: so I said
"Hush, Tom! never mind it, for, when your head's bare,
You know that the soot cannot spoil your white hair."

And so he was quiet, and that very night,
As Tom was asleeping, he had such a sight!
That thousands of sweepers, Dick, Joe, Ned, and Jack,
Were all of them locked up in coffins of black.

And by came an Angel who had a bright key,
And he opened the coffins and set them all free;
Then down a green plain leaping, laughing, they run,
And wash in a river, and shine in the sun.

Then naked and white, all their bags left behind,
They rise upon clouds and sport in the wind;
And the Angel told Tom, if he'd be a good boy,
He'd have God for his father, and never want joy.

And so Tom awoke, and we rose in the dark,
And got with our bags and our brushes to work.
Though the morning was cold, Tom was happy and warm;
So if all do their duty they need not fear harm.

WILLIAM BLAKE

Questions

1. *Select details from the poem which reveal the contrast between the everyday life of the chimney sweepers and the dream-vision of the heaven of chimney sweepers.*
2. *What is the speaker's attitude toward the situation of the chimney sweepers? Is the last line of the poem ironical, or straightforward?*
3. *How does the nursery-rhyme language of the poem make an ironical contrast with its subject?*

FLORIDA ROAD WORKER

I'm makin' a road
For the cars to fly by on,
Makin' a road
Through the palmetto thicket
For light and civilization
To travel on.

Sure,
A road helps everybody!
Rich folks ride—
And I get to see 'em ride.

I'm makin' a road
For the rich to sweep over
In their big cars
And leave me standin' here.

I ain't never seen nobody
Ride so fine before.
Hey, Buddy! Look!
I'm makin' a road.

LANGSTON HUGHES

Questions

1. *What is the attitude of the speaker of the poem? Who is the speaker? What is his "occupation"?*
2. *Explain the irony of "Rich folks ride–/And I get to see 'em ride."*
3. *Characterize the speaker's attitude at the conclusion of the poem. Is he angry, or laughing?*

MY LAST DUCHESS

That's my last Duchess painted on the wall,
Looking as if she were alive. I call
That piece a wonder, now; Fra Pandolf's hands
Worked busily a day, and there she stands.
Will't please you sit and look at her? I said
"Fra Pandolf" by design, for never read
Strangers like you that pictured countenance,
The depth and passion of its earnest glance,
But to myself they turned (since none puts by
The curtain I have drawn for you, but I)
And seemed as they would ask me, if they durst,
How such a glance came there; so, not the first
Are you to turn and ask thus. Sir, 'twas not
Her husband's presence only, called that spot
Of joy into the Duchess' cheek; perhaps
Fra Pandolf chanced to say, "Her mantle laps
Over my lady's wrist too much," or, "Paint
Must never hope to reproduce the faint
Half-flush that dies along her throat." Such stuff
Was courtesy, she thought, and cause enough
For calling up that spot of joy. She had
A heart—how shall I say?—too soon made glad,
Too easily impressed; she liked whate'er
She looked on, and her looks went everywhere.
Sir, 'twas all one! My favor at her breast,
The dropping of the daylight in the West,
The bough of cherries some officious fool
Broke in the orchard for her, the white mule
She rode with round the terrace—all and each
Would draw from her alike the approving speech,
Or blush, at least. She thanked men—good! but thanked
Somehow—I know not how—as if she ranked
My gift of a nine-hundred-years-old name
With anybody's gift. Who'd stoop to blame
This sort of trifling? Even had you skill
In speech—which I have not—to make your will
Quite clear to such an one, and say, "Just this
Or that in you disgusts me; here you miss,
Or there exceed the mark"—and if she let
Herself be lessoned so, nor plainly set

Her wits to yours, forsooth, and made excuse—
E'en then would be some stooping; and I choose
Never to stoop. Oh, sir, she smiled, no doubt,
Whene'er I passed her; but who passed without
Much the same smile? This grew; I gave commands;
Then all smiles stopped together. There she stands
As if alive. Will't please you rise? We'll meet
The company below, then. I repeat,
The Count your master's known munificence
Is ample warrant that no just pretense
Of mine for dowry will be disallowed;
Though his fair daughter's self, as I avowed
At starting, is my object. Nay, we'll go
Together down, sir. Notice Neptune, though,
Taming a sea-horse, thought a rarity,
Which Claus of Innsbruck cast in bronze for me!

ROBERT BROWNING

Questions

1. *This poem is a monologue by a Duke on his "Last Duchess," and it concerns not only the characters of the Duke and the Duchess, but also the relationship which existed between the two. To whom is the Duke speaking, and why is he telling his listener about his "Last Duchess"?*
2. *Select lines in which the Duke, in explaining the character of his Last Duchess, ironically reveals his own character.*
3. *Explain the difference between the Duke's opinion of himself and the reader's opinion of him.*
4. *Characterize the Duchess, using lines from the poem to support your characterization.*
5. *Explain the contrast between the painting of the Duchess and the sculpture mentioned at the poem's conclusion. How do the two different works of art reflect the two different approaches to life of the Duke and his "Last Duchess"?*

Bibliography: Robert Browning

Carrington, C. E. "'My Last Duchess'." *London Times Literary Supplement* 6 November 1969, p. 1288.

Cox, Ollie. "The 'Spot of Joy' in 'My Last Duchess'." *College Language Association Journal* 12 (1968):70–76.

Drew, Philip, ed. *Robert Browning: A Collection of Critical Essays.* Boston: Houghton Mifflin Co., 1966.

———. *The Poetry of Browning: A Critical Introduction.* New York: Barnes & Noble, 1970.

Fleissner, R. F. "Browning's Last Lost Duchess: A Purview." *Victorian Poetry* 5 (1967):217–19.

———. "'My Last Duchess'." *London Times Literary Supplement* 4 December 1969, p. 1405.

Jones, A. R. "Robert Browning and the Dramatic Monologue: The Impersonal Art." *Critical Quarterly* 9 (1968):301–28.

King, Roma A., Jr. *The Focusing Artifice: The Poetry of Robert Browning.* Athens, Ohio: Ohio University Press, 1968.

Litzinger, Boyd, and Smalley, Donald, eds. *Browning: The Critical Heritage.* New York: Barnes & Noble, 1970.

Melchiori, Barbara. *Browning's Poetry of Reticence.* New York: Barnes & Noble, 1968.

Raymond, William O. *The Infinite Moment and Other Essays in Robert Browning.* Toronto: University of Toronto Press, 1965.

Shaw, W. David. "Browning's Duke as Theatrical Producer." *Victorian Newsletter* No. 29 (1966):18–22.

Solimine, Joseph, Jr. "Browning's 'My Last Duchess'." *Explicator* 26 (1967):Item 11.

Tracy, Clarence. *Browning's Mind and Art.* New York: Barnes & Noble, 1970.

Vondersmith, Bernard J. "*My Last Duchess* and *The Love Song of J. Alfred Prufrock*: A Method of Counterbalance." *Contemporary Education* 43 (1971):106–10.

Topics for Writing

1. Write a 500-word essay comparing and contrasting the paradoxical relationship of life and death in the poems of Housman ("To an Athlete Dying Young") and Donne ("Death Be Not Proud").

2. Write a 500-word essay comparing and contrasting the presentation of the paradoxical relationship between body and spirit in the poems of Blake (from "Auguries of Innocence" and "The Chimney Sweeper") and Yeats ("Crazy Jane and the Bishop").

3. Using Crane's poem ("War Is Kind") as a model, write your own poem ironically treating a subject of your choice. You might begin with:
   a. Money buys happiness.
   b. School is fun.
   c. Life is boring.

4. Using Browning's "My Last Duchess" as a model, write a poem in which one person's speech about another ironically reveals the speaker's character. You might choose:
   a. a new bride describing her wedding ceremony
   b. a divorcée describing her (his) ex-spouse
   c. a parent describing a son or daughter

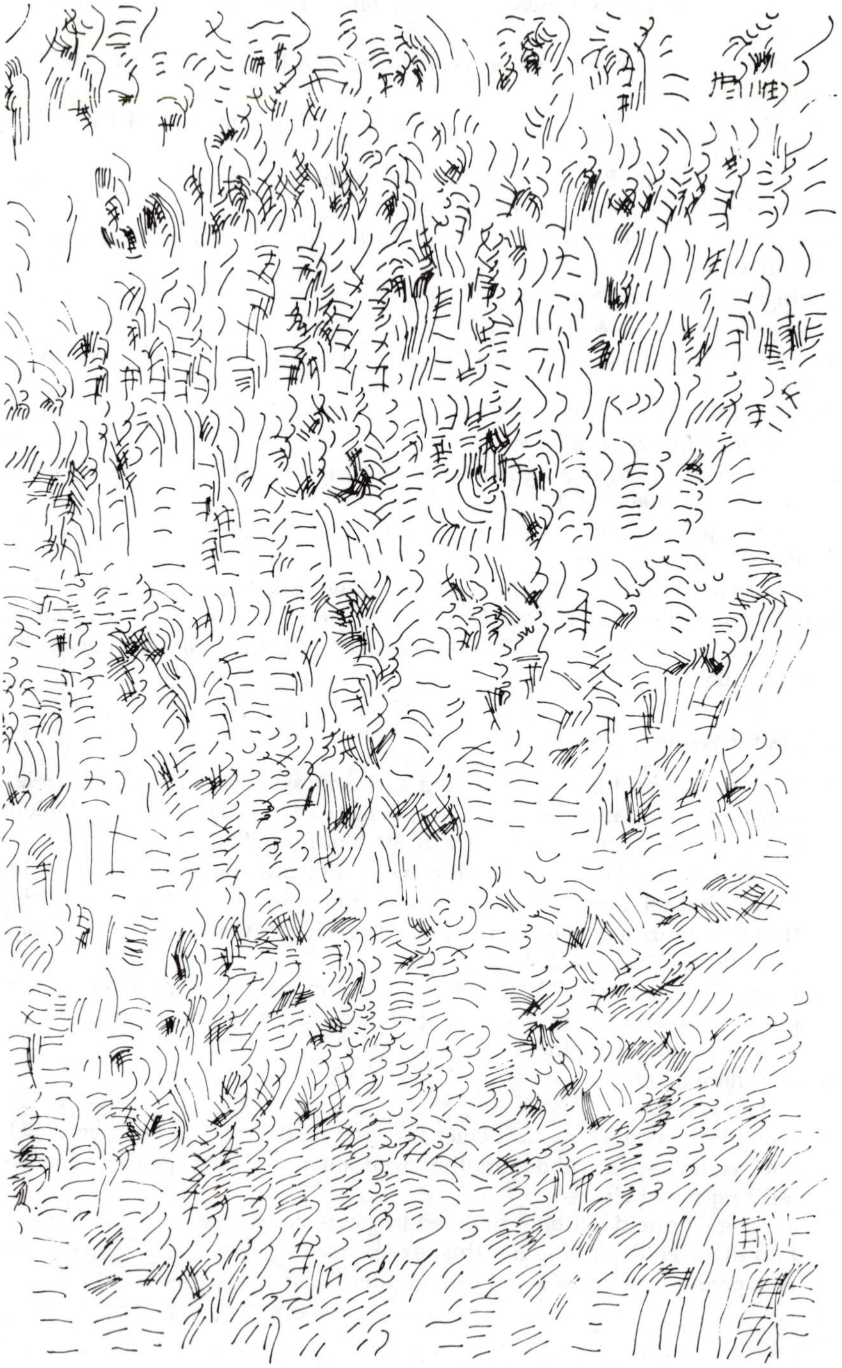

6 Symbolism

One of the most important techniques by which poets say one thing and suggest much more is symbolism. In general, a *symbol* is something concrete which in a given context can convey something abstract as well as its literal meaning.

There are a number of *conventional symbols* which a particular culture or country immediately recognizes as suggestive of a whole set of meanings. The cross, for instance, suggests not only the actual cross on which Jesus Christ was crucified, but it also symbolizes the Christian religion and various aspects of that religion, such as redemption, the necessity of suffering, and sacrifice. Other conventional symbols are the flag, the peace sign, and the crown. All these conventional symbols use a concrete thing to suggest abstractions (patriotism, peace, and power) to those people who recognize them as symbols. However, if you had never seen the cross or the peace sign, you would not grasp their symbolism. In America, for instance, a hitchhiker sticks out his thumb; in Europe he holds out his hand, palm downwards, and flaps it as though he were dribbling a basketball. Many wasted hours can be spent on life's highways and byways by one who doesn't know the conventional symbols.

Another kind of symbol which poets use is the *natural symbol*, which is something concrete that in a particular context (a poem, or novel, and so forth) develops into something symbolic as well. The natural symbol is called natural not because it is a tree or river or some other concrete aspect of nature, but because it grows from the concrete into the symbolic in the particular context in which it is used. Bridges and towers, for instance, have been used as natural symbols by some major twentieth-century poets. A natural symbol is different from a conventional symbol in that it is understandable only in terms of the context in which it exists. A poet can use the cross as a symbol without developing it especially for his particular poem, because people may be assumed to recognize some of the symbolic aspects of the cross. But if he wants to use a bridge or tower symbolically, he must provide a context in which his symbol can take on symbolic meanings, can grow from the concrete to the symbolic. In Frost's "Stopping By Woods on a Snowy Evening" the journey ("miles to go before I sleep") becomes a natural symbol in the context of the poem, because the poet associates that journey with the journey of life. (At least he allows the reader to see that abstraction as one of several possible associations and expansions.) But the journey is not a conventional symbol (though it is often used symbolically); all poems and novels that present a journey do not necessarily use it symbolically. In perceiving a symbol, you must always perceive it in the context in which it exists, not only to decide if it is really a symbol but also to decide exactly what it symbolizes.

Both conventional and natural symbols depend upon a relationship between something concrete and something abstract, whether the cross and Christianity or a journey and life. But some symbols tend to look through the concrete to the abstraction, hence placing greater importance on the abstraction. These symbols approach the condition of *allegory*, a technique which used to be quite popular in stories and poems whose main purpose was to give a dramatic rendering of the lessons of philosophical and religious doctrines. In such allegories, characters were given names like Everyman, Vice, and Grace, and the actions of these characters suggested that they were not well-rounded personalities but stereotypes: they acted in the story only in the way that the concepts signified by their names operated in the philosophy or religion which the story dramatized. Because their concrete presentation didn't matter much, they were really signs rather than symbols. A symbol always utilizes the concrete element in a meaningful way, and thus is different from an allegory. But in some symbols the concrete element has been seen so often that it has lost most of its power to strike the reader as concrete, unless the poet revitalizes it in some way. For instance, when you see a cross on top of a church, do you think of the actual cross on which Jesus was crucified, or do you think of the abstraction of Christianity in general? Probably the latter. Similarly, in some allegories the characters who stand for readily identifiable aspects of some larger doctrine are nevertheless so elaborately presented that they take on some of the suggestibility and concrete presence of a symbol. Thus the distinction between the definitions of symbol and allegory may be clear, but the practice of these two modes presents examples in which the distinctions blur.

What students should appreciate about the use of symbolism in poetry is the shifting relationship between the concrete and the abstract which different examples of symbolism provide. The first three poems of this chapter, all by William Blake, illustrate some of the possibilities. The first poem, "The Sick Rose," is extremely powerful in both its concrete presence and its symbolic suggestibility. The rose and the worm are symbolic of more than a literal rose and a literal worm, but their symbolism, like that of the journey in Frost's poem, is open-ended. Both rose and worm appeal to the reader as concrete images as well as symbols, so that they are not mere allegorical figures. Furthermore, any attempt to turn the relationship of rose and worm into some doctrinal code (such as, the worm kills the rose as evil kills goodness) is frustrated: not only is it impossible to assign specific, and therefore limiting, terms to the symbols, but it also is difficult to determine whether the poem says that it is bad that the worm kills the rose, or that it is unavoidable but still tragic, or that it is inevitable and thus good. Allegorical doctrines, on the other hand, are usually logical and definite in the relationships they establish (when logic fails in doctrine, mystery is invoked, as with the Trinity, the Virgin Birth, and the Resurrection). After reading this poem, with its ambiguous relationship of worm and rose, look again at the relationship of "fair and foul" in Yeats' "Crazy Jane Talks with the Bishop" on pages 106–7. Yeats, by the way, was a great admirer of Blake.

The second of Blake's poems, "Ah Sunflower," is a symbolic poem which uses certain allegorical symbols. The "Youth" and the "Virgin" are types, yet their concrete element is present in the phrases by which they are described. The Sunflower, on the other hand, is a full-blown symbol which develops naturally in the context of the poem. Its concrete aspect is important, since the reader has to know what a sunflower looks like to appreciate all the details of the poem. But what abstraction does the Sunflower symbolize? Possibly a yearning for a naturally glorious eternity, to be achieved in "that sweet golden clime" which the poem mentions. The Sunflower is symbolic for the speaker of the poem; his reflection on it makes it symbolic, and as the reader perceives the speaker's reflection, the Sunflower becomes symbolic for the reader too. Blake has written other poems in which he uses what are termed *private symbols,* symbols whose ultimate meaning cannot be known by simply reading the poem. But in "Ah Sunflower" the symbolism is not private, since the reader can understand the symbolism of the Sunflower by reading the poem closely.

It might be added that a fuller appreciation of Blake's symbolism is available to the reader who is familiar with a number of his poems. Blake has written a series of poems entitled "The Songs of Innocence and Experience, Showing the Two Contrary States of the Human Soul." In these poems he uses many different symbols to convey the same "Two Contrary States."

In the third poem, "The Tiger," Blake uses a pair of opposing conventional symbols, the "Tiger" suggestive of experience, Satan, and evil, and the

"Lamb" suggestive of innocence, Christ, and good. But he revitalizes these symbols, here mainly that of the Tiger (he wrote a companion poem called "The Lamb"), and he endows them with a significance and presence that depends more on the context of his poem than on any prior context such as Christianity. He revitalizes the conventional symbol of the Tiger by particularizing it with specific images and by presenting his own specific and powerful reaction to the creature's symbolic possibilities. The poem begins with a conventional symbol whose meanings are fairly well known and relatively limited and, by elaborating on the concrete element, goes on to generate new symbolic meanings. Unlike allegory, in which the concrete is controlled by the abstraction, the symbol of the Tiger creates new abstractions by focusing on the concrete. Also, by revitalizing a conventional symbol like the Tiger instead of choosing to develop a previously unknown natural symbol, Blake is able to tap the energies that lie frozen under the surface of all overused conventional symbols and use that energy for his own purposes. The effect is perhaps similar to that of writing a rock musical about Jesus and calling him a "Superstar": by changing the concrete element, the poet can revitalize the old abstractions and claim the emotional appeal that they used to have. In this poem, of course, much of the Tiger's symbolic power comes from its association with God, from the reader's growing awareness throughout the poem that no matter how difficult it is to comprehend the creation of the fearsome Tiger, that is still only half as difficult as comprehending the awesomeness of "He" who created the Tiger *and* the Lamb.

The different relationships between the concrete and the abstract in the symbols of Blake's poems should illustrate some of the problems of dealing with symbolism. Remember the initial definition of a symbol, something concrete which can stand for something abstract as well. Just as an allegory, which presents abstractions while denying their concrete basis, is not symbolism, so too simple images and metaphors, which present concrete figures that do not suggest any abstractions, are not symbols. Since there are far more poems that use images and metaphors rather than allegories, the student's real problem is how to determine if an image is a symbol. This can be done best by considering the image in the context of the whole poem, which of course means reading the poem very closely. But the test for determining the presence of a symbol is this: there should be other lines and images in the poem that encourage you to perceive a symbolic meaning in a particular image, and you should be able to specify what they are and how they suggest the presence of symbolism in the image. The abstract meanings of symbols are evident in the poem, not merely in your own head. Things that are symbols in one context are not necessarily symbols in another, and the proper context is the poem, not your own fancy. As Sigmund Freud, an inveterate smoker of cigars and the popularizer of the phallic symbol, reportedly told a symbol-hunting woman, "This may be a phallic symbol, madam, but it is definitely a good cigar." Unless you can cite positive evidence from the context of the poem, it is best to assume that an image is descriptive and not symbolic.

As it is a mistake to read symbolic meanings into any concrete object, it is also a mistake to be too eager to pin down the meanings of any bonafide symbol to one or two specific abstractions. One of the main reasons poets use symbols is that they are speaking about things which can't be pinned down precisely and finally. A really effective symbol will often vibrate with meanings, and it would be wrong to stop the vibrations by selecting one wave length and discarding the others. Symbolism, then, is important not merely because it allows a poet to present many meanings at once, like a kind of shorthand; it is most important because it allows him to present the *effect* of the complexity and simultaneity of a world whose richness and powerful presence cannot be explained by a mere listing of meanings, one by one, however long.

THE SICK ROSE

O rose, thou art sick.
The invisible worm
That flies in the night
In the howling storm

Has found out thy bed
Of crimson joy,
And his dark secret love
Does thy life destroy.

WILLIAM BLAKE

AH SUNFLOWER

Ah Sunflower! weary of time,
Who countest the steps of the Sun,
Seeking after that sweet golden clime
Where the traveler's journey is done,

Where the Youth pined away with desire,
And the pale Virgin shrouded in snow,
Arise from their graves and aspire,
Where my Sunflower wishes to go.

WILLIAM BLAKE

THE TIGER

Tiger, Tiger, burning bright
In the forests of the night,
What immortal hand or eye
Could frame thy fearful symmetry?

In what distant deeps or skies
Burnt the fire of thine eyes?
On what wings dare he aspire?
What the hand dare seize the fire?

And what shoulder and what art,
Could twist the sinews of thy heart?
And when thy heart began to beat,
What dread hand, and what dread feet?

What the hammer? What the chain?
In what furnace was thy brain?
What the anvil? What dread grasp
Dare its deadly terrors clasp?

When the stars threw down their spears
And watered heaven with their tears,
Did he smile his work to see?
Did he who made the Lamb make thee?

Tiger, Tiger, burning bright
In the forests of the night,
What immortal hand or eye
Dare frame thy fearful symmetry?

WILLIAM BLAKE

Questions

1. In "The Sick Rose" the "invisible worm" discovers the rose's "bed/Of crimson joy" and, paradoxically, threatens its life with "his dark secret love." Can you specify exactly what the "worm" and the "rose" stand for? Should you try to? How do the unspecifiable but symbolic meanings of the "worm" and the "rose" increase the power of the poem's representation of the paradoxical relationship of love and death?
2. Select specific phrases which describe the "sweet golden clime" of eternity that the "Sunflower" symbolizes. How does the actual appearance of a sunflower suggest to the poet that it "countest the steps of the Sun"? How are the "youth" and the "Virgin" trapped in time? How will the vitality of the Sunflower's "sweet golden clime" resurrect them? Explain the difference between the initial phrase "Ah Sunflower" and the final "my Sunflower." Does the Sunflower symbolize something in the poet himself?
3. In "The Tiger" what possible things could the "Tiger" and the "Lamb" symbolize? How is the power of the Tiger emphasized by the questions about its creator and the means by which it was created? Characterize the tone of the speaker (notice he never asks "Why," only "How" and "What"). Explain the significance of the shift from "Could" in the first stanza to "Dare" in the last.

TO THE VIRGINS, TO MAKE MUCH OF TIME

Gather ye rosebuds while ye may:
    Old Time is still a-flying,
And this same flower that smiles to-day
    To-morrow will be dying.

The glorious lamp of heaven, the sun,
    The higher he's a-getting,
The sooner will his race be run,
    And nearer he's to setting.

That age is best which is the first,
    When youth and blood are warmer;
But, being spent, the worse, and worst
    Times, still succeed the former.

Then be not coy, but use your time,
    And while ye may, go marry:
For having lost but once your prime,
    You may for ever tarry.

ROBERT HERRICK

Questions

1. *What is the subject of this poem? Is the speaker's attitude serious or lighthearted?*
2. *What is symbolized by the "rosebuds" in the first line of the poem? How does the third stanza explain some of its symbolism?*

THE RANCHER

Hard old gray eyes, no pity
in him after years branding cattle—
a cruel man with cows & men

he drove both hard & once
when he was 70 tried to kill
a young puncher for smiling at his

old wife, sat down & cried in fury
because his grown sons took his
ivoryhandled .45 away, held

his head in his arms & didn't
ever come back to the dance.
After awhile his wife went slowly

out into the clear night
saying how late it is getting
now isn't it? without

pity for his eyes, him showing
nothing the next morning
barking at the hands to get

popping, the sun already up,
coffee on the fire & him
stifflegged, hard pot hanging

over the saddlehorn, he led
fall's last drive
across the hazy range.

KEITH WILSON

1. *What is the subject of the poem?*
2. *Why does the rancher's wife go to him "without/pity for his eyes"?*
3. *How does the poem encourage the reader to read the last two lines symbolically? What is suggested by "fall's last drive"?*

DREAM-LAND

By a route obscure and lonely,
Haunted by ill angels only,
Where an Eidolon, named NIGHT,
On a black throne reigns upright,
I have reached these lands but newly
From an ultimate dim Thule—
From a wild weird clime that lieth, sublime,
Out of SPACE—out of TIME.

Bottomless vales and boundless floods,
And chasms, and caves, and Titan woods,
With forms that no man can discover
For the tears that drip all over;
Mountains toppling evermore
Into seas without a shore;
Seas that restlessly aspire,
Surging, unto skies of fire;
Lakes that endlessly outspread
Their lone waters—lone and dead,—
Their still waters—still and chilly
With the snows of the lolling lily.

By the lakes that thus outspread
Their lone waters, lone and dead,—
Their sad waters, sad and chilly
With the snows of the lolling lily,—
By the mountains—near the river
Murmuring lowly, murmuring ever,—
By the grey woods,—by the swamp
Where the toad and the newt encamp,—
By the dismal tarns and pools
Where dwell the Ghouls,—
By each spot the most unholy—
In each nook most melancholy,—

There the traveller meets, aghast,
Sheeted Memories of the Past—
Shrouded forms that start and sigh
As they pass the wanderer by—
White-robed forms of friends long given,
In agony, to the Earth—and Heaven.

For the heart whose woes are legion
'Tis a peaceful, soothing region—
For the spirit that walks in shadow
'Tis—oh 'tis an Eldorado!
But the traveller, travelling through it,
May not—dare not openly view it;
Never its mysteries are exposed
To the weak human eye unclosed;
So wills its King, who hath forbid
The uplifting of the fringed lid;
And thus the sad Soul that here passes
Beholds it but through darkened glasses.

By a route obscure and lonely,
Haunted by ill angels only,
Where an Eidolon, named NIGHT,
On a black throne reigns upright,
I have wandered home but newly
From this ultimate dim Thule.

EDGAR ALLAN POE

Questions

1. *What details in the first stanza explain how the speaker travelled from "Dream-Land," the "ultimate dim Thule," back to reality? What two meanings of "sublime" might apply to this land "Out of Space–out of Time"?*
2. *Select details in the second stanza which suggest the breakdown of usual time and space relationships.*
3. *What emotional responses to "Dream-Land" are evoked by the description of the setting in the third stanza? What are "Ghouls"?*
4. *What effect does "Dream-Land" have on the heart and on the spirit? Why can its "mysteries" never be seen by the "human eye unclosed"?*
5. *How does this inability to see clearly the landscape of "Dream-Land" contribute to its symbolic power over the dreamer?*

ELDORADO

Gaily bedight,
A gallant knight,
In sunshine and in shadow,
Had journeyed long,
Singing a song,
In search of Eldorado.

But he grew old—
This knight so bold—
And o'er his heart a shadow
Fell as he found
No spot of ground
That looked like Eldorado.

And, as his strength
Failed him at length,
He met a pilgrim shadow—
"Shadow," said he,
"Where can it be—
This land of Eldorado?"

"Over the Mountains
Of the Moon,
Down the Valley of the Shadow,
Ride, boldly ride,"
The shade replied,—
"If you seek for Eldorado!"

EDGAR ALLAN POE

Questions

1. *Relate the symbolic importance of "Eldorado" in this poem to its use in "Dream-Land." Where is this symbolic place "located" in stanza four?*
2. *What is the effect of imaging the seeker of Eldorado as a "gallant knight"? What do knights usually seek for?*
3. *What is Eldorado?*

THE HOST OF THE AIR

O'Driscoll drove with a song
The wild duck and the drake
From the tall and the tufted reeds
Of the drear Hart Lake.

And he saw how the reeds grew dark
At the coming of night-tide,
And dreamed of the long dim hair
Of Bridget his bride.

He heard while he sang and dreamed
A piper piping away,
And never was piping so sad,
And never was piping so gay.

And he saw young men and young girls
Who danced on a level place,
And Bridget his bride among them,
With a sad and a gay face.

The dancers crowded about him
And many a sweet thing said,
And a young man brought him red wine
And a young girl white bread.

But Bridget drew him by the sleeve
Away from the merry bands,
To old men playing at cards
With a twinkling of ancient hands.

The bread and the wine had a doom,
For these were the host of the air;
He sat and played in a dream
Of her long dim hair.

He played with the merry old men
And thought not of evil chance,
Until one bore Bridget his bride
Away from the merry dance.

He bore her away in his arms,
The handsomest young man there,
And his neck and his breast and his arms
Were drowned in her long dim hair.

O'Driscoll scattered the cards
And out of his dream awoke:
Old men and young men and young girls
Were gone like a drifting smoke;

But he heard high up in the air
A piper piping away,
And never was piping so sad,
And never was piping so gay.

WILLIAM BUTLER YEATS

Questions

1. *Like Poe's "Dream-Land," this poem presents a symbolic situation whose definitions and specific meanings elude yet haunt the reader. Where, for instance, does O'Driscoll leave reality and enter the world of the dream?*
2. *What detail in the poem associates the "piping" with the face of "Bridget"?*
3. *In certain religious services, the "host" is bread and wine that the priest symbolically changes into the body and blood of Christ. What is the "host of the air" in this poem? Who serves it to O'Driscoll? What is the "doom" which it carries?*
4. *What is suggested by the change from "merry bands" of young people to "merry old men" and then to the "handsomest young man there"? What part has "evil chance" played in O'Driscoll's loss of Bridget? What part has Bridget played?*
5. *In what ways has O'Driscoll been changed by his dream? Describe your response to the last two lines. Is it the same as your response to the first use of those lines in stanza three?*

MAGGIE AND MILLY AND MOLLY AND MAY

maggie and milly and molly and may
went down to the beach(to play one day)

and maggie discovered a shell that sang
so sweetly she couldn't remember her troubles,and

milly befriended a stranded star
whose rays five languid fingers were;

and molly was chased by a horrible thing
which raced sideways while blowing bubbles:and

may came home with a smooth round stone
as small as a world and as large as alone.

For whatever we lose(like a you or a me)
it's always ourselves we find in the sea

E E CUMMINGS

Questions

1. *In what ways does this poem use symbolism to achieve its effects?*
2. *Characterize the individual girls according to what they found at the beach. Which is the romantic escapist, which is the potential hysteric?*
3. *Explain the paradox of a stone "as small as a world and as large as alone."*
4. *What is the difference between "a you or a me" and "ourselves"?*
5. *How does the poet make the beach scene symbolic of life itself? In what way does the putting of "to play one day" in parenthesis contribute to this movement from the specific to the symbolic?*

THE ABORTION

Somebody who should have been born
is gone.

Just as the earth puckered its mouth,
each bud puffing out from its knot,
I changed my shoes, and then drove south.

Up past the Blue Mountains, where
Pennsylvania humps on endlessly,
wearing, like a crayoned cat, its green hair,

its roads sunken in like a gray washboard;
where, in truth, the ground cracks evilly,
a dark socket from which the coal has poured,

Somebody who should have been born
is gone.

the grass as bristly and stout as chives,
and me wondering when the ground would break,
and me wondering how anything fragile survives;

up in Pennsylvania, I met a little man,
not Rumpelstiltskin, at all, at all . . .
he took the fullness that love began.

Returning north, even the sky grew thin
like a high window looking nowhere.
The road was as flat as a sheet of tin.

Somebody who should have been born
is gone.

Yes, woman, such logic will lead
to loss without death. Or say what you meant,
you coward . . . this baby that I bleed.

ANNE SEXTON

Questions

1. *Select specific details which suggest a symbolic connection between the landscape and the speaker of the poem. Note especially "each bud puffing out from its knot,"*

"Pennsylvania humps on endlessly," and "a dark socket from which the coal has poured."

2. How do the following details suggest the state of mind of the speaker: "the Blue Mountains," "like a crayoned cat," and "I met a little man,/not Rumpelstiltskin, at all, at all"?

3. Describe the effect of counterpointing the recurring sentence "Somebody who should have been born/is gone," with the description of the journey. How is the tension of this counterpoint resolved in the last stanza?

4. Explain the significance of the stanza beginning "Returning north . . ." How does it reflect the state of the woman's mind and body?

5. How is the change in the woman's attitude reflected in the change from "the fullness that love began" to "this baby that I bleed"?

THE MOON AND THE YEW TREE

This is the light of the mind, cold and planetary,
The trees of the mind are black. The light is blue.
The grasses unload their griefs on my feet as if I were God,
Prickling my ankles and murmuring of their humility.
Fumey, spiritous mists inhabit this place
Separated from my house by a row of headstones.
I simply cannot see where there is to get to.

The moon is no door. It is a face in its own right,
White as a knuckle and terribly upset.
It drags the sea after it like a dark crime; it is quiet
With the O-gape of complete despair. I live here.
Twice on Sunday, the bells startle the sky—
Eight great tongues affirming the Resurrection.
At the end, they soberly bong out their names.

The yew tree points up. It has a Gothic shape.
The eyes lift after it and find the moon.
The moon is my mother. She is not sweet like Mary.
Her blue garments unloose small bats and owls.
How I would like to believe in tenderness—
The face of the effigy, gentled by candles,
Bending, on me in particular, its mild eyes.

I have fallen a long way. Clouds are flowering
Blue and mystical over the face of the stars.
Inside the church, the saints will be all blue,
Floating on their delicate feet over the cold pews,
Their hands and faces stiff with holiness.
The moon sees nothing of this. She is bald and wild.
And the message of the yew tree is blackness—blackness and
   silence.

SYLVIA PLATH

Questions

1. *This poem presents a landscape which is symbolic of the speaker's state of mind. Select specific passages which suggest what the moon and the yew tree symbolize.*
2. *What separates "this place" of moon and yew tree from the speaker's "house"? What is suggested by her statement that she "cannot see where there is to get to," by the "the O-gape of complete despair"?*
3. *In relation to the woman, how does the moon drag the sea "like a dark crime"?*
4. *Select details which suggest the difference between the moon and "Mary."*
5. *Explain the symbolic difference between the message of the church bells and the message of the yew tree.*

THE ROAD NOT TAKEN

Two roads diverged in a yellow wood,
And sorry I could not travel both
And be one traveler, long I stood
And looked down one as far as I could
To where it bent in the undergrowth;

Then took the other, as just as fair,
And having perhaps the better claim,
Because it was grassy and wanted wear;
Though as for that, the passing there
Had worn them really about the same,

And both that morning equally lay
In leaves no step had trodden black.
Oh, I kept the first for another day!
Yet knowing how way leads on to way,
I doubted if I should ever come back.

I shall be telling this with a sigh
Somewhere ages and ages hence:
Two roads diverged in a wood, and I—
I took the one less traveled by,
And that has made all the difference.

ROBERT FROST

Questions

1. *This poem by Frost illustrates some of the difficulties involved in specifying exactly what a symbol symbolizes. Is there any detail in the poem which specifies what either of the two roads symbolize?*
2. *Does stanza two suggest that there is a radical difference between the appearance of the two roads? Does it explain why the traveler took one rather than the other?*
3. *Do the roads symbolize specific choices (such as being a poet or getting married), or do they symbolize Choice itself? Why is the title "The Road Not Taken" rather than "The Road Taken"? Would either title serve equally well?*

CHERRYLOG ROAD

Off Highway 106
At Cherrylog Road I entered
The '34 Ford without wheels,
Smothered in kudzu,
With a seat pulled out to run
Corn whiskey down from the hills,

And then from the other side
Crept into an Essex
With a rumble seat of red leather
And then out again, aboard
A blue Chevrolet, releasing
The rust from its other color,

Reared up on three building blocks.
None had the same body heat;
I changed with them inward, toward
The weedy heart of the junkyard,
For I knew that Doris Holbrook
Would escape from her father at noon

And would come from the farm
To seek parts owned by the sun
Among the abandoned chassis,
Sitting in each in turn
As I did, leaning forward
As in a wild stock-car race

In the parking lot of the dead.
Time after time, I climbed in
And out the other side, like
An envoy or movie star
Met at the station by crickets.
A radiator cap raised its head,

Become a real toad or a kingsnake
As I neared the hub of the yard,
Passing through many states,
Many lives, to reach
Some grandmother's long Pierce-Arrow
Sending platters of blindness forth

From its nickel hubcaps
And spilling its tender upholstery
On sleepy roaches,
The glass panel in between
Lady and colored driver
Not all the way broken out,

The back-seat phone
Still on its hook.
I got in as though to exclaim,
"Let us go to the orphan asylum,
John; I have some old toys
For children who say their prayers."

I popped with sweat as I thought
I heard Doris Holbrook scrape
Like a mouse in the southern-state sun
That was eating the paint in blisters
From a hundred car tops and hoods.
She was tapping like code,

Loosening the screws,
Carrying off headlights,
Sparkplugs, bumpers,
Cracked mirrors and gear-knobs,
Getting ready, already,
To go back with something to show

Other than her lips' new trembling
I would hold to me soon, soon,
Where I sat in the ripped back seat
Talking over the interphone,
Praying for Doris Holbrook
To come from her father's farm

And to get back there
With no trace of me on her face
To be seen by her red-haired father
Who would change, in the squalling barn,
Her back's pale skin with a strop,
Then lay for me

In a bootlegger's roasting car
With a string-triggered 12-gauge shotgun
To blast the breath from the air.
Not cut by the jagged windshields,
Through the acres of wrecks she came
With a wrench in her hand,

Through dust where the blacksnake dies
Of boredom, and the beetle knows
The compost has no more life.
Someone outside would have seen
The oldest car's door inexplicably
Close from within:

I held her and held her and held her,
Convoyed at terrific speed
By the stalled, dreaming traffic around us,
So the blacksnake, stiff
With inaction, curved back
Into life, and hunted the mouse

With deadly overexcitement,
The beetles reclaimed their field
As we clung, glued together,
With the hooks of the seat springs
Working through to catch us red-handed
Amidst the gray breathless batting

That burst from the seat at our backs.
We left by separate doors
Into the changed, other bodies
Of cars, she down Cherrylog Road
And I to my motorcycle
Parked like the soul of the junkyard

Restored, a bicycle fleshed
With power, and tore off
Up Highway 106, continually
Drunk on the wind in my mouth,
Wringing the handlebar for speed,
Wild to be wreckage forever.

JAMES DICKEY

Questions

1. *How do the following details suggest that the speaker's journey to the middle of the junkyard is symbolic as well as literal: "I changed with them inward," "the weedy heart of the junkyard," "the parking lot of the dead," "Parked like the soul of the junkyard/Restored"?*
2. *How would you characterize the speaker's attitude toward his meeting with Doris? Select details to support your opinion.*
3. *Why is Doris carrying a "wrench"? Why does she strip the cars as she moves toward her meeting with the speaker? What does her wrench have to do with the speaker's final statement that he is "Wild to be wreckage forever"?*
4. *What is the importance of nature in this junkyard of machines? How does nature (kingsnake, beetle, mouse) symbolically react to the love making of the speaker and Doris Holbrook?*
5. *Explain the reaction of the speaker in the last stanza. What is the difference between his attitude toward making love and that of Doris? Who is more possessive?*

SUNFLOWER SUTRA

I walked on the banks of the tincan banana dock and sat down under the huge shade of a Southern Pacific locomotive to look at the sunset over the box house hills and cry.

Jack Kerouac sat beside me on a busted rusty iron pole, companion, we thought the same thoughts of the soul, bleak and blue and sad-eyed, surrounded by the gnarled steel roots of trees of machinery.

The oily water on the river mirrored the red sky, sun sank on top of final Frisco peaks, no fish in that stream, no hermit in those mounts, just ourselves rheumy-eyed and hungover like old bums on the riverbank, tired and wily.

Look at the Sunflower, he said, there was a dead gray shadow against the sky, big as a man, sitting dry on top of a pile of ancient sawdust—

—I rushed up enchanted—it was my first sunflower, memories of Blake—my visions—Harlem   5

and Hells of the Eastern rivers, bridges clanking Joes Greasy Sandwiches, dead baby carriages, black treadless tires forgotten and unretreaded, the poem of the riverbank, condoms & pots, steel knives, nothing stainless, only the dank muck and the razor sharp artifacts passing into the past—

and the gray Sunflower poised against the sunset, crackly bleak and dusty with the smut and smog and smoke of olden locomotives in its eye—

corolla of bleary spikes pushed down and broken like a battered crown, seeds fallen out of its face, soon-to-be-toothless mouth of sunny air, sunrays obliterated on its hairy head like a dried wire spiderweb,

leaves stuck out like arms out of the stem, gestures from the sawdust root, broke pieces of plaster fallen out of the black twigs, a dead fly in its ear,

Unholy battered old thing you were, my sunflower O my soul, I loved you then!   10

The grime was no man's grime but death and human locomotives,

all that dress of dust, that veil of darkened railroad skin, that smog of cheek, that eyelid of black mis'ry, that sooty hand or phallus or protuberance of artificial worse-than-dirt—industrial—modern—all that civilization spotting your crazy golden crown—

and those blear thoughts of death and dusty loveless eyes and ends and withered roots below, in the home-pile of sand and sawdust, rubber dollar bills, skin of machinery, the guts and innards of the weeping coughing car, the empty lonely tincans with their rusty tongues alack, what more could I name, the smoked ashes of some cock cigar, the cunts of wheelbarrows and the milky breasts of cars, wornout asses out of chairs & sphincters of dynamos—all these entangled in your mummied roots—and you there standing before me in the sunset, all your glory in your form!

A perfect beauty of a sunflower! a perfect excellent lovely sunflower existence! a sweet natural eye to the new hip moon, woke up alive and excited grasping in the sunset shadow sunrise golden monthly breeze!

How many flies buzzed round you innocent of your grime, while you cursed the heavens of the railroad and your flower soul?   16

Poor dead flower? when did you forget you were a flower? when did you look at your skin and decide you were an impotent dirty old locomotive? the ghost of a locomotive? the specter and shade of a once powerful mad American locomotive?

You were never no locomotive, Sunflower, you were a sunflower!

And you Locomotive, you are a locomotive, forget me not!

So I grabbed up the skeleton thick sunflower and stuck it at my side like a scepter,   20

and deliver my sermon to my soul, and Jack's soul too, and anyone who'll listen,

—We're not our skin of grime, we're not our dread bleak dusty imageless locomotive, we're all beautiful golden sunflowers inside, we're blessed by our own seed & golden hairy naked accomplishment-bodies growing into mad black formal sunflowers in the sunset, spied on by our eyes under the shadow of the mad locomotive riverbank sunset Frisco hilly tincan evening sitdown vision.

ALLEN GINSBERG

Questions

1. *What is a "sutra"? Why is this poem called a sutra?*
2. *How do the long lines of this poem contribute to its "sutra" presentation of Ginsberg's "memories" and "visions"?*
3. *Select the details of lines 5–10 which prepare for the symbolic fusion of "my sunflower O my soul."*
4. *What is the significance of "all your glory in your form"? How does this statement relate to the final "sermon to my soul, and Jack's soul too, and anyone who'll listen"?*
5. *Explain the contrasting symbolism of "locomotive" and "sunflower" in the poem. How are these symbols developed throughout the poem?*

OUT OF THE CRADLE ENDLESSLY ROCKING

Out of the cradle endlessly rocking,
Out of the mockingbird's throat, the musical shuttle,
Out of the Ninth-month midnight,
Over the sterile sands and the fields beyond, where the child
    leaving his bed wandered alone, bareheaded, barefoot,
Down from the showered halo, 5
Up from the mystic play of shadows twining and twisting as
    if they were alive,
Out from the patches of briers and blackberries,
From the memories of the bird that chanted to me,
From your memories sad brother, from the fitful risings and
    fallings I heard,
From under that yellow half-moon late-risen and swollen as
    if with tears, 10
From those beginning notes of yearning and love there in the
    mist,
From the thousand responses of my heart never to cease,
From the myriad thence-aroused words,
From the word stronger and more delicious than any,
From such as now they start the scene revisiting, 15
As a flock, twittering, rising, or overhead passing,
Borne hither, ere all eludes me, hurriedly,
A man, yet by these tears a little boy again,
Throwing myself on the sand, confronting the waves,
I, chanter of pains and joys, uniter of here and hereafter, 20
Taking all hints to use them, but swiftly leaping beyond them,
A reminiscence sing.

Once Paumanok,
When the lilac scent was in the air and Fifth-month grass was
    growing,
Up this seashore in some briers, 25
Two feathered guests from Alabama, two together,
And their nest, and four light-green eggs spotted with brown,
And every day the he-bird to and fro near at hand,
And every day the she-bird crouched on her nest, silent, with
    bright eyes,
And every day I, a curious boy, never too close, never disturb-
    ing them, 30
Cautiously peering, absorbing, translating.

Shine! shine! shine!
Pour down your warmth, great sun!
While we bask, we two together.
Two together!   35
Winds blow south, or winds blow north,
Day come white, or night come black,
Home, or rivers and mountains from home,
Singing all time, minding no time,
While we two keep together.   40

Till of a sudden,
Maybe killed, unknown to her mate,
One forenoon the she-bird crouched not on the nest,
Nor returned that afternoon, nor the next,
Nor ever appeared, again.   45
And thenceforward all summer in the sound of the sea,
And at night under the full of the moon in calmer weather,
Over the hoarse surging of the sea,
Or flitting from brier to brier by day,
I saw, I heard at intervals the remaining one, the he-bird,   50
The solitary guest from Alabama.

Blow! blow! blow!
Blow up sea winds along Paumanok's shore;
I wait and I wait till you blow my mate to me.
Yes, when the stars glistened,   55
All night long on the prong of a moss-scalloped stake,
Down almost amid the slapping waves,
Sat the lone singer wonderful causing tears.
He called on his mate,
He poured forth the meanings which I of all men know.   60
Yes my brother I know,
The rest might not, but I have treasured every note,
For more than once dimly down to the beach gliding,
Silent, avoiding the moonbeams, blending myself with the
    shadows,
Recalling now the obscure shapes, the echoes, the sounds and
    sights after their sorts,   65
The white arms out in the breakers tirelessly tossing,
I, with bare feet, a child, the wind wafting my hair,
Listened long and long.
Listened to keep, to sing, now translating the notes,
Following you my brother.   70

Soothe! soothe! soothe!
Close on its wave soothes the wave behind,
And again another behind embracing and lapping, every one
   close,
But my love soothes not me, not me.
Low hangs the moon, it rose late,   75
It is lagging—O I think it is heavy with love, with love.
O madly the sea pushes upon the land,
With love, with love.
O night! do I not see my love fluttering out among the
   breakers?
What is that little black thing I see there in the white?   80

Loud! loud! loud!
Loud I call to you, my love!
High and clear I shoot my voice over the waves,
Surely you must know who is here, is here,
You must know who I am, my love.   85
Low-hanging moon!
What is that dusky spot in your brown yellow?
O it is the shape, the shape of my mate!
O moon do not keep her from me any longer.
Land! land! O land!   90
Whichever way I turn, O I think you could give me my mate
   back again if you only would,
For I am almost sure I see her dimly whichever way I look.
O rising stars!
Perhaps the one I want so much will rise, will rise with some
   of you.
O throat! O trembling throat!   95
Sound clearer through the atmosphere!
Pierce the woods, the earth,
Somewhere listening to catch you must be the one I want.

Shake out carols.
Solitary here, the night's carols!   100
Carols of lonesome love! death's carols!
Carols under that lagging, yellow, waning moon!
O under the moon where she droops almost down into the sea!
O reckless despairing carols.
But soft! sink low!   105
Soft! let me just murmur,
And do you wait a moment you husky-noised sea,
For somewhere I believe I heard my mate responding to me,
So faint, I must be still, be still to listen,
But not altogether still, for then she might not come imme-
*   diately to me.*   110

Hither my love!
Here I am! here!
With this just-sustained note I announce myself to you,
This gentle call is for you my love, for you.
Do not be decoyed elsewhere,   115
That is the whistle of the wind, it is not my voice,
That is the fluttering, the fluttering of the spray,
Those are the shadows of leaves.
O darkness! O in vain!
O I am very sick and sorrowful.   120
O brown halo in the sky near the moon, drooping upon the sea!
O troubled reflection in the sea!
O throat! O throbbing heart!
And I singing uselessly, uselessly all the night.
O past! O happy life! O songs of joy!   125
In the air, in the woods, over fields,
Loved! loved! loved! loved! loved!
But my mate no more, no more with me!
We two together no more.

The aria sinking,   130
All else continuing, the stars shining,
The winds blowing, the notes of the bird continuous echoing.
With angry moans the fierce old mother incessantly moaning.

On the sands of Paumanok's shore gray and rustling,
The yellow half-moon enlarged, sagging down, drooping, the
    face of the sea almost touching,   135
The boy ecstatic, with his bare feet the waves, with his hair
    the atmosphere dallying,
The love in the heart long pent, now loose, now at last tumul-
    tuously bursting,
The aria's meaning, the ears, the soul, swiftly depositing,
The strange tears down the cheeks coursing,
The colloquy there, the trio, each uttering,   140
The undertone, the savage old mother incessantly crying,
To the boy's soul's questions sullenly timing, some drowned
    secret hissing,
To the outsetting bard.

Demon or bird! (said the boy's soul).
Is it indeed toward your mate you sing? or is it really to me?   145
For I, that was a child, my tongue's use sleeping, now I have
    heard you,
Now in a moment I know what I am for, I awake,
And already a thousand singers, a thousand songs, clearer,
    louder and more sorrowful than yours,
A thousand warbling echoes have started to life within me,
    never to die.

O you singer solitary, singing by yourself, projecting me,   150
O solitary me listening, never more shall I cease perpetuating
    you,
Never more shall I escape, never more the reverberations,
Never more the cries of unsatisfied love be absent from me,
Never again leave me to be the peaceful child I was before
    what there in the night,
By the sea under the yellow and sagging moon,   155
The messenger there aroused, the fire, the sweet hell within,
The unknown want, the destiny of me.

O give me the clue! (it lurks in the night here somewhere),
O if I am to have so much, let me have more!
A word then (for I will conquer it),   160
The word final, superior to all,
Subtle, sent up—what is it?—I listen;
Are you whispering it, and have been all the time, you sea
    waves?
Is that it from your liquid rims and wet sands?

Whereto answering, the sea,   165
Delaying not, hurrying not,
Whispered me through the night, and very plainly before
    daybreak,
Lisped to me the low and delicious word death,
And again death, death, death, death,
Hissing melodious, neither like the bird nor like my aroused
    child's heart,   170
But edging near as privately for me rustling at my feet,
Creeping thence steadily up to my ears and laving me soft
    all over,
Death, death, death, death, death.

Which I do not forget,   175
But fuse the song of my dusky demon and brother,
That he sang to me in the moonlight on Paumanok's gray
    beach,
With the thousand responsive songs at random,
My own songs awaked from that hour,
And with them the key, the word up from the waves,   180
The word of the sweetest song and all songs,
That strong and delicious word which, creeping to my feet,
(Or like some old crone rocking the cradle, swathed in sweet
    garments, bending aside),
The sea whispered me.

WALT WHITMAN

Questions

1. *In the poem's first sentence (lines 1–22) the poet describes himself as "chanter of pains and joys, uniter of here and hereafter," and promises to use all "hints" that come from "Out of the cradle," "Down from the showered halo," "From the memories of the bird," and so forth, in creating a "reminiscence" that includes but also surpasses these "hints." How do the prepositions which begin most of the lines suggest that the poet is the singing center of a poem which symbolically unites past and present? Explain line 18, "A man, yet by these tears a little boy again."*
2. *Who are the "two feathered guests from Alabama" in line 26? Where have they made their nest? Characterize the poet as he, a boy, is "peering, absorbing, translating" the song of the he-bird to his "silent" mate.*
3. *At what time of day does the boy-poet see the he-bird singing, and when can he hear him (lines 41–51)? Why does the poet call the "love singer" his "brother"?*

How would you characterize the scene imaged in lines 52–70? Explain: "The white arms out in the breakers tirelessly tossing."

4. *The bird's song, remembered and translated by the poet, begins by representing nature as full of love. Select specific details which image the sea and the moon in terms of love. In what line begins the transition from love to death in the bird's song?*

5. *What is meant by the "aria" in line 130? Who is the "fierce old mother incessantly moaning" (line 133)? Describe what happens to the boy in lines 136–143. Who are the members of the "trio"? With what does the sea answer "the boy's soul's questions"? Why does the poet call the boy "the outsetting bard"?*

6. *Why does the boy's soul exclaim "Demon or bird!"? What possible meanings of "Demon" might apply here?*

7. *Explain how the bird has become to the boy a symbol of himself in lines 150–151, especially "never more shall I cease perpetuating you." Explain the connection between "unsatisfied love," "the fire, the sweet hell within,/The unknown want, the destiny of me." How is his destiny a "sweet hell"?*

8. *What does he want a "clue" to (line 158)? Who gives him this clue, this "word final, superior to all"? What is the word? Which member of the "trio" gives him the word, and how?*

9. *What is the relationship of the last ten lines to the rest of the poem? Of what three strains is the mature poet's song composed, according to the last ten lines? What is "the key" to this song?*

10. *Explain the meaning of the simile in the second-to-last line. Who is the mother, who is the baby, and what is the lullaby? How does this simile simultaneously complete the poem and return us to its beginning?*

Bibliography: Walt Whitman

Adams, Richard P. "Whitman: A Brief Revaluation." *Tulane Studies in English* 5(1955):111–49.

Allen, Gay Wilson. *The Solitary Singer: A Critical Biography of Walt Whitman.* New York: Macmillan Publishing Co., 1955.

Briggs, Arthur E. *Walt Whitman: Thinker and Artist.* Westport, Conn.: Greenwood Press, 1968.

Bucke, R. M. *Cosmic Consciousness.* Secaucus, N.J.: Citadel Press, 1970.

DeFalco, Joseph M. "Whitman's Changes in 'Out of the Cradle' and Poe's 'Raven'." *Walt Whitman Review* 16 (1970):22–27.

Lawrence, D. H. *Studies in Classic American Literature.* New York: Viking Press, 1923.

Lewis, R. W. B., ed. *The Presence of Walt Whitman.* New York: Columbia University Press, 1962.

Marks, Alfred H. "Whitman's Triadic Imagery." *American Literature* 23 (1951):99–126.

Miller, James E., Jr. *A Critical Guide to Leaves of Grass.* Chicago: University of Chicago Press, 1957.

Pearce, Roy Harvey, ed. *Whitman: A Collection of Critical Essays.* Englewood Cliffs, N.J.: Prentice-Hall, 1962.

Spitzer, Leo. "Explication de Texte Applied to Walt Whitman's Poem 'Out of the Cradle Endlessly Rocking'." In *A Century of Whitman Criticism,* edited by Edwin Haviland Miller. Bloomington, Ind.: Indiana University Press, 1969.

Stott, Jon C. "The Mocking-Bird in 'Out of the Cradle'." *Walt Whitman Review* 16 (1970):119–20.

Sutton, Larry. "Structural Music in Whitman's 'Out of the Cradle'." *Walt Whitman Review* 15 (1969):57–59.

Whicher, Stephen E. "Whitman's Awakening to Death—Toward a Biographical Reading of 'Out of the Cradle Endlessly Rocking'." In *A Century of Whitman Criticism,* edited by Edwin Haviland Miller. Bloomington, Ind.: Indiana University Press, 1969.

Topics for Writing

1. Write an essay comparing and contrasting the symbolic meanings and the method of presentation of the sunflower symbol in the poems of Blake ("Ah Sunflower") and Ginsberg. ("Sunflower Sutra").

2. Using either Poe's "Eldorado" or Yeats' "The Host of the Air" as a model, write a poem about a symbolic journey or encounter. Then write a brief explanation of why the usually realistic reader does not object to the elements of unreality in such symbolic poems.

3. Write an essay comparing and contrasting the ways in which the landscape is symbolic in Sexton's "The Abortion" and Plath's "The Moon and the Yew Tree."

4. Write a description of the process by which the boy in Whitman's "Out of the Cradle Endlessly Rocking" discovered his "destiny" as a poet. Be sure to consider the stages of growth of bird and sea into symbols of love and death. Then relate this process to the larger process of how the poem itself came to be created (cf. lines 1–21).

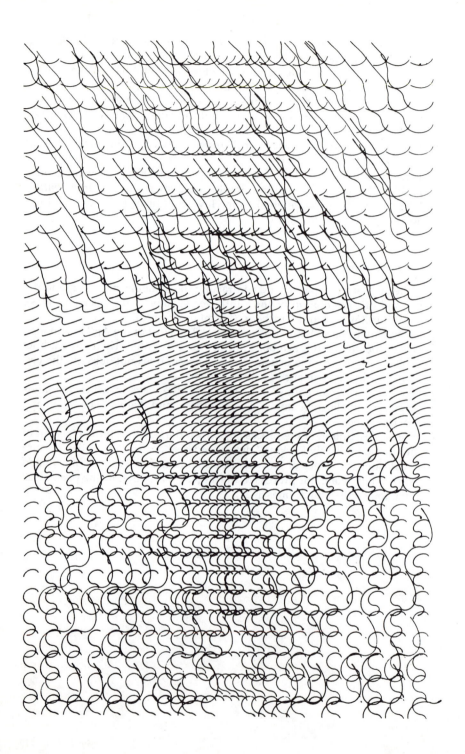

7 Rhythm and Meter

Most people are so used to considering language as a vehicle for conveying concepts and ideas that they overlook the importance of sound. Before language can communicate, express, or create anything, it first must be heard. Even when you read silently from the page of a book, language is being heard by your inner ear. And when you walk down a busy city street listening to the language of different speakers, or when you tune in to different radio and TV stations, you become aware of the great variety of sounds that people make when they speak.

The sound of language is rarely, if ever, perceived as separate from its sense. But then it is equally true that the sense is seldom perceived apart from the sound of the language that communicates it. Both sound and sense blend together in any use of language, and in poetry perhaps more than in any other language form the marriage of sound and sense prepares for the birth of a new poem into the world of words.

An appreciation of poetry, then, depends to some degree on an appreciation of the ways in which sound contributes to a poem. There are many elements which contribute to the sound of a poem, but the two most basic ones are rhythm and meter. These two terms commonly are used to describe two different ways in which the sound of poetry is perceived.

Rhythm describes the pace at which language moves. All language has rhythm, because all language (at least any series of words) moves at one pace or another. Rhythm may be smooth, jerky, staccato, fast, or slow. The pace at which you speak a particular sentence may be determined by many things, such as your emotions at the time, whom you are speaking to, and what the sentence means. Any one sentence may be spoken with different rhythms. Imagine yourself saying this sentence, "I love you now more than ever," in the following situations:

    a. You are accepting (or offering) a proposal of marriage.

    b. You are a housewife singing to a box of soap after doing the wash.

    c. You are about to kiss a bowling ball after rolling a perfect game.

The words are the same in each case, but the sentence's rhythm may be changed to reflect the change of the speaker's situation. However, it is not only the situation of the speaker, but also the form of the words themselves, that determines the rhythm of language. Some words take longer to say than others, and some series of words move faster than other series. The physical act of uttering a line of poetry is often as much a determiner of rhythm as is the sense of the line. In good poetry the pace at which you speak a line will be in harmony with the sense of the line.

Meter describes the the pattern created in a particular poem by the repetition of a basic grouping of accented syllables. There are four basic groupings in English metrical poetry, and they sound like this (*Dum* is louder than *Da* in this description): *Da Dum, Dum Da, Da Da Dum,* and *Dum Da Da.* The first two groupings have two syllables, and the last two have three syllables. For convenience, each of these groups is called a *foot.* A line of metrical poetry may consist of any number of feet, though most often one line will consist of five feet. A line of five feet is called a *pentameter,* since the prefix penta- means five (as in the Pentagon, the largest five-sided office building in the world). The foot described as *Da Dum,* the basic foot in English metrical poetry, is called *iambic.* Thus a line of poetry which consisted of five groups of *Da Dum,* in other words five iambic feet, would be called a line of *iambic pentameter.* Most of the poetry of Shakespeare, Milton, Wordsworth, Tennyson, and Frost is written in iambic pentameter. Here are five lines of iambic pentameter from these poets.

> No longer mourn for me when I am dead—Shakespeare (Sonnet 71)
> Of man's first disobedience, and the fruit—Milton (*Paradise Lost*)
> The world is too much with us; late and soon,—Wordsworth (Sonnet)
> It little profits that an idle king—Tennyson ("Ulysses")
> The land was ours before we were the land's—Frost ("The Gift Outright")

Read these lines of iambic pentameter and try to become conscious of the pattern of *Da Dum* groupings, of iambic feet consisting of a less accented syllable followed by a more accented one. Read the lines naturally, and the metrical pattern will reveal itself. Notice, however, that all the *Dum*'s are not equally accented in your reading: in the line from Shakespeare the "lon" is not so heavily stressed as the "mourn" or the "dead." In the line from

Tennyson the "li" and "that" are both *Dums,* yet neither is so heavily stressed as "king." Meter does not measure the relative stress of *all* the syllables in a line of poetry, but only the relative stress of the syllables which compose *each foot.* Hence the foot is the basic unit of meter, not the line. To discover and become conscious of the meter of any poem, then, you must discover what kind of foot is being repeated, and how often. Below is a chart which will guide you in this endeavor.

Sound	Example	Name of Foot	Name of Meter
Dă Dūm	rĕtúrn	iamb	iambic
Dūm Dă	túrnĭng	trochee	trochaic
Dă Dă Dūm	rĕsŭrréct	anapest	anapestic
Dūm Dă Dă	cúrĭoŭs	dactyl	dactylic

The basic foot of a line of metrical poetry should be described by one of the four names listed in the chart above. The length of the line (the number of feet in the line) should be described according to the following:

one foot, monometer   five feet, pentameter
two feet, dimeter   six feet, hexameter
three feet, trimeter   seven feet, heptameter
four feet, tetrameter   eight feet, octameter

The name of the foot always precedes the name of the line, as in iambic pentameter, trochaic tetrameter, and so forth. As mentioned before, most English metrical poetry is composed in iambic pentameter.

A useful way of determining the meter of a particular poem is to *scan* it. *Scansion* refers to the practice of marking each syllable of each foot of a poem with one or the other of the accent marks (˘ for *Da*, — for *Dum*), as illustrated in the chart above. Scansion is a method for determining the *kind* and the *number* of feet in a line of poetry. To do this you first should read the entire poem, allowing the meter to reveal itself to you. Then go back to the first line and begin marking the syllables according to their relative accents in your reading of the line. Do this for several lines, and then try to determine the pattern which the meter is taking. Do not be thrown off by an occasional *metrical inversion,* a foot which seems to reverse the normal pattern of accents. Look for the dominant pattern, and then read the entire poem with that pattern in mind. Do not force the pattern on the poem, reading it *Da Dum, Da Dum,* and so forth, with monotonous regularity. Remember that all *Dum's* are not equal, but are only *Dum's* because of their proximity to a *Da.* Allow the rhythm of the poem to play above the underlying meter as you read it, and you will find that the rhythm makes a pleasing counterpoint to the meter. Below is a scansion of Shakespeare's Sonnet 71. Examine it, then read it aloud, trying to be conscious of the relationship of rhythm and meter.

> No longer mourn for me when I am dead
> Than you shall hear the surly sullen bell
> Give warning to the world that I am fled
> From this vile world, with vilest worms to dwell;
> Nay, if you read this line, remember not
> The hand that writ it, for I love you so
> That I in your sweet thoughts would be forgot
> If thinking on me then should make you woe.
> Oh, if, I say, you look up on this verse
> When I perhaps compounded am with clay,
> Do not so much as my poor name rehearse,
> But let your love even with my life decay;
> Lest the wise world should look into your moan,
> And mock you with me after I am gone.

In this scansion you will notice that most of the poem is regular iambic pentameter. There are, however, some variations: the first foot of the fifth line is inverted, with the "Nay" having a greater stress than the other syllable of the foot, the twelfth line has an extra syllable (in "even") which is easily read through, and the thirteenth line begins with an inverted foot. However, the dominant pattern is clearly iambic pentameter, and it is always the dominant pattern that you should look for.

As you read the poem aloud, you will notice that some lines and phrases move faster than others, that the rhythm changes though the meter remains constant. Notice, for instance, the change of pace that occurs in the second line when you reach "the surly sullen bell," or in the fourth line at "with vilest worms." The regularity of the meter, which might seem monotonous if we considered the meter alone, is counterpointed with variations in rhythm, and the total effect is pleasing. The rhythmical variations of metrical poetry are more exciting when they are appreciated in relation to the metrical similarity which underlies them.

One of the hallmarks of twentieth-century poetry is the use of *free verse,* which is verse that is free of any metrical pattern. Many of the poems in this book are written in free verse, and the fact that they are successful indicates that meter is only one of the many devices which can contribute to a poem. All poetry has rhythm, of course; and quite often free verse really depends upon the reader's sense of a missing meter, that is, the possibility of a meter which the poet *consciously* avoids and thereby makes use of as a silent background. Quite often, too, in free verse the sense of constancy which meter contributes to poetry is supplied by using the line as a constant unit, by visually arranging the poem so that the reader is encouraged to consider each line in itself as well as in its relationship to the entire poem. In reading such free verse, it is often wise to pause slightly at the end of each line, even if there is no punctuation, so that the rhythm of the poem may play against the constancy of the line. At any rate, rhythm and meter are only tools, though very important ones, in the creation of the whole of sound and sense which is the completed poem.

from MACBETH

> To-morrow, and to-morrow, and to-morrow,
> Creeps in this petty pace from day to day,
> To the last syllable of recorded time;
> And all our yesterdays have lighted fools
> The way to dusty death. Out, out, brief candle!
> Life's but a walking shadow; a poor player
> That struts and frets his hour upon the stage
> And then is heard no more. It is a tale
> Told by an idiot, full of sound and fury,
> Signifying nothing.

WILLIAM SHAKESPEARE

Questions

1. *The basic metrical pattern of this famous passage of* blank verse *(a term used to describe iambic pentameter lines which do not rhyme the last syllables) is varied in several instances. Explain the metrical variations in line 1, line 2, line 6, and line 9.*
2. *Compare the rhythm of the first line with that of the seventh. What adjectives would you use to describe the different rhythms? Which line takes longer to say? Why?*

3. *Scan the ninth line. How do the metrical variations (the inversion of the first foot, the extra syllable at the end) suggest the sense of the line?*

4. *What emotions are being expressed by Macbeth in this passage? Cite two instances in which the rhythm of the poetry differs according to the differing emotions of the speaker.*

5. *Scan the last line of the passage. Is it iambic, or is it the reverse, trochaic? Explain how this reversal of the basic foot of the passage reflects the sense of the line? Would the reversal be as effective if the basic iambic pattern had not been established? How would you characterize the rhythm of this last line? Does it take as long to say these syllables as it did to say those of the first line of the passage? Explain the relationship of the following facts concerning the line's sound to the sense of the line: 1) the length of the line has been abbreviated, 2) the rising iambic foot has been replaced by the falling trochaic foot, and 3) the slower rhythm of the first line has been replaced by a quicker, more terse one.*

from PARADISE LOST

Of man's first disobedience, and the fruit
Of that forbidden tree whose mortal taste
Brought death into the world, and all our woe,
With loss of Eden, till one greater Man
Restore us, and regain the blissful seat,
Sing, Heav'nly Muse, that, on the secret top
Of Oreb, or Sinai, didst inspire
That shepherd who first taught the chosen seed
In the beginning how the Heav'ns and Earth
Rose out of Chaos: or, if Sion hill
Delight thee more, and Siloa's brook that flowed
Fast by the oracle of God, I thence
Invoke thy aid to my adventurous song,
That with no middle flight intends to soar
Above th' Aonian mount, while it pursues
Things unattempted yet in prose or rhyme.
And chiefly thou, O Spirit, that dost prefer
Before all temples th' upright heart and pure,
Instruct me, for thou know'st; thou from the first
Wast present, and, with mighty wings outspread,
Dovelike sat'st brooding on the vast abyss,
And mad'st it pregnant: what in me is dark

Illumine; what is low, raise and support;
That, to the height of this great argument,
I may assert Eternal Providence,
And justify the ways of God to men.

JOHN MILTON

Questions

1. *Explain how this passage fulfills the three requirements of* blank verse.
2. *How do the metrical inversions in the first feet of lines 6 and 10 reflect the sense of those lines?*
3. *Read this passage aloud. Does it sound monotonous? Does it read simply* Da Dum, Da Dum, Da Dum? *Although the iambic pentameter is quite regular in this passage, the rhythm provides innumerable variations, so that when the selection is read naturally the regularity of meter does not stand out excessively.*
4. *An important determiner of rhythm in this passage is the placement of punctuation: the reader pauses at commas, colons and periods. How many sentences does this passage consist of? Notice how the natural suspension of the reader's holding his voice until the end of the complete sentence is counterpointed with the partial resolution of suspension at the end of each line of verse. What two lines of this passage actually complete their sentences? How does the resolution of that suspension contribute to the power and statement of those lines?*
5. *Scan the first five lines of this passage. Is the meter regular? Now compare the relative stress of the* Dum's *in these lines, of the accented syllables of each iambic foot. Are they equally stressed? Is "and" in line 1 equal to "tree" in line 2 or "Man" in line 4? This should remind you that the foot, and not the line or the passage, is the basic unit of meter.*

from AN ESSAY ON CRITICISM

True ease in writing comes from art, not chance,
As those move easiest who have learned to dance.
'Tis not enough no harshness gives offense,
The sound must seem an echo to the sense:
Soft is the strain when Zephyr gently blows,
And the smooth stream in smoother numbers flows;
But when loud surges lash the sounding shore,
The hoarse, rough verse should like the torrent roar.

When Ajax strives, some rock's vast weight to throw,
The line too labors, and the words move slow;
Not so, when swift Camilla scours the plain,
Flies o'er th'unbending corn, and skims along the main.

ALEXANDER POPE

Questions

1. *What attributes of blank verse does this selection of poetry have? What attribute does it lack?*
2. *Explain the poet's argument about the relationship of sound and sense.*
3. *What metrical variation and rhythmical shift enables the sound of line 6 to echo its sense?*
4. *Scan line 10. Is the meter in this line regular iambic pentameter? If so, in what way does the poet achieve the effects of a "laboring" and "slow-moving" line?*
5. *Describe the variations in rhythm which occur in the last two lines. How do these variations reflect the sense of the three main verbs, "scours," "Flies," and "skims"?*

OZYMANDIAS

I met a traveler from an antique land
Who said: Two vast and trunkless legs of stone
Stand in the desert. . . . Near them, on the sand,
Half sunk, a shattered visage lies, whose frown,
And wrinkled lip, and sneer of cold command,
Tell that its sculptor well those passions read
Which yet survive, stamped on these lifeless things,
The hand that mocked them, and the heart that fed:
And on the pedestal these words appear:
"My name is Ozymandias, King of Kings:
Look on my works, ye Mighty, and despair!"
Nothing beside remains. Round the decay
Of that colossal wreck, boundless and bare
The lone and level sands stretch far away.

PERCY BYSSHE SHELLEY

Questions

1. *Does this poem fulfill the requirements for blank verse?*
2. *How would you describe the metrical pattern of this poem? Why can it not be* free verse?
3. *Explain how the meter of the poem instructs the reader on the correct way to pronounce the name "Ozymandias"?*
4. *Describe the variation in meter in the next-to-last line. How does it contrast with the meter of the last line of the poem?*
5. *The metrical inversion of the fourth foot in lines 12 and 13 creates a tension, since it is at odds with the basic iambic pattern of the poem, which is resolved by the return to regularity in the last line of the poem. How does this resolution of metrical tension reflect the sense of the poem? What is the emotion of the speaker at the conclusion of the poem?*

LA BELLE DAME SANS MERCI

A Ballad

O what can ail thee, knight-at-arms,
    Alone and palely loitering?
The sedge has withered from the lake,
    And no birds sing.

O what can ail thee, knight-at-arms,
    So haggard and so woe-begone?
The squirrel's granary is full,
    And the harvest's done.

I see a lily on thy brow,
    With anguish moist and fever dew,
And on thy cheeks a fading rose
    Fast withereth too.

I met a lady in the meads,
    Full beautiful—a faery's child,
Her hair was long, her foot was light,
    And her eyes were wild.

I made a garland for her head,
    And bracelets too, and fragrant zone;
She looked at me as she did love,
    And made sweet moan.

I set her on my pacing steed,
  And nothing else saw all day long,
For sidelong would she bend, and sing
  A faery's song.

She found me roots of relish sweet,
  And honey wild, and manna dew,
And sure in language strange she said,
  "I love thee true."

She took me to her elfin grot,
  And there she wept, and sighed full sore,
And there I shut her wild wild eyes
  With kisses four.

And there she lulléd me asleep,
  And there I dreamed—Ah! woe betide!
The latest dream I ever dreamed
  On the cold hill side.

I saw pale kings and princes too,
  Pale warriors, death-pale were they all;
They cried—"La Belle Dame sans Merci
  Hath thee in thrall!"

I saw their starved lips in the gloam,
  With horrid warning gapéd wide,
And I awoke and found me here,
  On the cold hill's side.

And this is why I sojourn here,
  Alone and palely loitering,
Though the sedge has withered from the lake,
  And no birds sing.

JOHN KEATS

Questions

1. *This poem is a literary ballad, written by a specific author using the ballad form. It is structured around the question-response pattern. Where does the speaker's question end and the knight's response begin?*
2. *How has the meaning of the last three lines of the first stanza been added to by the knight's narrative when he repeats them in the last three lines of the poem?*

3. *What is the meaning of the title of the poem?*
4. *Scan the poem. What is its meter?*

from MORTE d'ARTHUR

And slowly answered Arthur from the barge:
"The old order changeth, yielding place to new,
And God fulfills himself in many ways,
Lest one good custom should corrupt the world.
Comfort thyself: what comfort is in me?
I have lived my life, and that which I have done
May He within Himself make pure! but thou,
If thou shouldst never see my face again,
Pray for my soul. More things are wrought by prayer
Than this world dreams of. Wherefore, let thy voice
Rise like a fountain for me night and day.
For what are men better than sheep or goats
That nourish a blind life within the brain,
If, knowing God, they lift not hands of prayer
Both for themselves and those who call them friend?
For so the whole round earth is every way
Bound by gold chains about the feet of God.
But now farewell. I am going a long way
With these thou seest—if indeed I go—
For all my mind is clouded with a doubt—
To the island-valley of Avilion;
Where falls not hail, or rain, or any snow,
Nor ever wind blows loudly, but it lies
Deep-meadowed, happy, fair with orchard lawns
And bowery hollows crowned with summer sea,
Where I will heal me of my grievous wound."
So said he, and the barge with oar and sail
Moved from the brink, like some full-breasted swan
That, fluting a wild carol ere her death,
Ruffles her pure cold plume, and takes the flood
With swarthy webs. Long stood Sir Bedivere
Revolving many memories, till the hull
Looked one black dot against the verge of dawn,
And on the mere the wailing died away.

ALFRED, LORD TENNYSON

Questions

1. *Is this selection of poetry written in blank verse? Why or why not?*
2. *Cite three metrical inversions in Arthur's speech and justify them in terms of the sense of the lines in which they occur.*
3. *Tennyson is justly praised for the music of his poetry, which he achieves through pleasing use of assonance (the repetition of similar vowel sounds), consonance (the repetition of similar consonant sounds), and rhythm. Examine the five lines from "Where falls not . . ." to ". . . my grievous wound." Describe the rhythm of these lines, and explain the contributions made to the rhythm by the use of sounds of varying length (length refers to the time it takes you to say the syllable, so that variations in length affect the pace of the saying of the line).*
4. *What is the relationship between the rhythm of the last two lines of this selection and the sense of those lines? In what ways, and to what ends, is "one black dot" different from "the wailing died away"?*
5. *Compare and contrast the different means by which Milton and Tennyson create rhythmical variation against a background of metrical regularity in their poetry.*

DO NOT GO GENTLE INTO THAT GOOD NIGHT

Do not go gentle into that good night,
Old age should burn and rave at close of day;
Rage, rage against the dying of the light.

Though wise men at their end know dark is right,
Because their words had forked no lightning they
Do not go gentle into that good night.

Good men, the last wave by, crying how bright
Their frail deeds might have danced in a green bay,
Rage, rage against the dying of the light.

Wild men who caught and sang the sun in flight,
And learn, too late, they grieved it on its way,
Do not go gentle into that good night.

Grave men, near death, who see with blinding sight
Blind eyes could blaze like meteors and be gay,
Rage, rage against the dying of the light.

And you, my father, there on the sad height,
Curse, bless, me now with your fierce tears, I pray.
Do not go gentle into that good night.
Rage, rage against the dying of the light.

DYLAN THOMAS

Questions

1. *Describe the dominant meter of this poem. Is it blank verse?*
2. *How regular is the meter of the poem? In what way does the regularity of the meter interact with the rhythmical variations that express the speaker's emotions?*
3. *How does the interaction of rhythm and meter in this poem reflect the sense of the poem?*
4. *The principle of repetition-with-variation is very important in this poem. How frequently are the two end rhymes in the first stanza repeated ("night" and "day" rhymes)? How frequently are entire lines of the poem repeated? Are the lines spoken with the same rhythm each time they are repeated? What factor influences the change in rhythm at each new occurance of these lines?*
5. *Read the poem aloud. Describe the emotions of the speaker, and the ways in which these emotions shift during the poem. Explain how the rhythms of the language echo these shifts of emotion.*

THE QUARRY

O what is that sound which so thrills the ear
   Down in the valley drumming, drumming?
Only the scarlet soldiers, dear,
   The soldiers coming.

O what is that light I see flashing so clear
   Over the distance brightly, brightly?
Only the sun on their weapons, dear,
   As they step lightly.

O what are they doing with all that gear,
   What are they doing this morning, this morning?
Only their usual maneuvers, dear,
   Or perhaps a warning.

O why have they left the road down there,
   Why are they suddenly wheeling, wheeling?
Perhaps a change in their orders, dear.
   Why are you kneeling?

O haven't they stopped for the doctor's care,
   Haven't they reined their horses, their horses?
Why, they are none of them wounded, dear,
   None of these forces.

O is it the parson they want, with white hair,
   Is it the parson, is it, is it?
No, they are passing his gateway, dear,
   Without a visit.

O it must be the farmer who lives so near.
   It must be the farmer so cunning, so cunning?
They have passed the farmyard already, dear,
   And now they are running.

O where are you going? Stay with me here!
   Were the vows you swore, deceiving, deceiving?
No, I promised to love you, dear,
   But I must be leaving.

O it's broken the lock and splintered the door,
   O it's the gate where they're turning, turning;
Their boots are heavy on the floor
   And their eyes are burning.

W. H. AUDEN

Questions

1. *What different meters are used in this poem? What is the effect of shortening the line length as each stanza draws to a close?*
2. *What is the subject of the poem?*
3. *How does the meaning of the word "dear" shift as the poem progresses? Is "dear" used ironically?*

THE DANCE

In Breughel's great picture, The Kermess,
the dancers go round, they go round and
around, the squeal and the blare and the
tweedle of bagpipes, a bugle and fiddles
tipping their bellies (round as the thick-
sided glasses whose wash they impound)
their hips and their bellies off balance
to turn them. Kicking and rolling about
the Fair Grounds, swinging their butts, those
shanks must be sound to bear up under such
rollicking measures, prance as they dance
in Breughel's great picture, The Kermess.

WILLIAM CARLOS WILLIAMS

Questions

1. *After reading the poem aloud, read it substituting the* **Da Dum** *sounds for the syllables. What is the dominant* **Da Dum** *grouping in the poem, and what is the name of the metrical foot which describes this basic grouping?*
2. *What kind of dance movement does this basic metrical foot suggest? Is it the box step?*
3. *One of the ways in which Williams achieves the effect of continual motion is by carrying one metrical foot over from one line to the next, so that the reader is urged to continue reading* through *the end of the line. Describe this effect as it occurs in lines 2–3.*
4. *Point out the prevalent verb form through which the poet chooses to convey the poem's "rollicking measures."*
5. *How do the first and last lines, taken together, suggest the circular and continual motion of the dance?*

VARIATIONS FOR TWO PIANOS

For Thomas Higgins, pianist

There is no music now in all Arkansas.
Higgins is gone, taking both his pianos.

Movers dismantled the instruments, away
Sped the vans. The first detour untuned the strings.

There is no music now in all Arkansas.

Up Main Street, past the cold shopfronts of Conway,
The Brash, self-important brick of the college,

Higgins is gone, taking both his pianos.

Warm evenings, the windows open, he would play
Something of Mozart's for his pupils, the birds,

There is no music now in all Arkansas.

How shall the mockingbird mend her trill, the jay
His eccentric attack, lacking a teacher?

Higgins is gone, taking both his pianos.
There is no music now in all Arkansas.

DONALD JUSTICE

Questions

1. *How is the title of this poem reflected in the variable recurrence of the first two lines of the poem?*
2. *Read the poem aloud. Notice the different rhythms and sounds in their musicality. What, for instance, is the rhythm of "in all Arkansas"? How fast can you say "The first detour untuned the strings"?*
3. *Who were Higgins' pupils in Arkansas?*

THE WAKING

I wake to sleep, and take my waking slow.
I feel my fate in what I cannot fear.
I learn by going where I have to go.

We think by feeling. What is there to know?
I hear my being dance from ear to ear.
I wake to sleep, and take my waking slow.

Of those so close beside me, which are you?
God bless the Ground! I shall walk softly there,
And learn by going where I have to go.

Light takes the Tree; but who can tell us how?
The lowly worm climbs up a winding stair;
I wake to sleep, and take my waking slow.

Great Nature has another thing to do
To you and me; so take the lively air,
And, lovely, learn by going where to go.

This shaking keeps me steady. I should know.
What falls away is always. And is near.
I wake to sleep, and take my waking slow.
I learn by going where I have to go.

THEODORE ROETHKE

Questions

1. *How do the rhythm and meter of this poem contribute to its meaning?*
2. *Explain the central paradox of the poem, "I wake to sleep." How does this paradox suggest a relationship between life and death? What is that relationship?*
3. *What is the "Ground" in the third stanza?*
4. *Explain the second line of the last stanza.*
5. *Is the meter regular? What is the meter? How is the regularity of meter kept from being monotonous by the rhythm of the lines?*

IN A PROMINENT BAR IN SECAUCUS ONE DAY

**To the tune of "The Old Orange Flute" or
the tune of "Sweet Betsy from Pike"**

In a prominent bar in Secaucus one day
Rose a lady in skunk with a topheavy sway,
Raised a knobby red finger—all turned from their beer—
While with eyes bright as snowcrust she sang high and clear:

"Now who of you'd think from an eyeload of me
That I once was a lady as proud as could be?
Oh I'd never sit down by a tumbledown drunk
If it wasn't, my dears, for the high cost of junk.

"All the gents used to swear that the white of my calf
Beat the down of a swan by a length and a half.
In the kerchief of linen I caught to my nose
Ah, there never fell snot, but a little gold rose.

"I had seven gold teeth and a toothpick of gold,
My Virginia cheroot was a leaf of it rolled
And I'd light it each time with a thousand in cash—
Why the bums used to fight if I flicked them an ash.

"Once the toast of the Biltmore, the belle of the Taft,
I would drink bottle beer at the Drake, never draft,
And dine at the Astor on Salisbury steak
With a clean tablecloth for each bite I did take.

"In a car like the Roxy I'd roll to the track,
A steel-guitar trio, a bar in the back,
And the wheels made no noise, they turned over so fast,
Still it took you ten minutes to see me go past.

"When the horses bowed down to me that I might choose,
I bet on them all, for I hated to lose.
Now I'm saddled each night for my butter and eggs
And the broken threads race down the backs of my legs.

"Let you hold in mind, girls, that your beauty must pass
Like a lovely white clover that rusts with its grass.
Keep your bottoms off barstools and marry you young
Or be left—an old barrel with many a bung.

"For when time takes you out for a spin in his car
You'll be hard-pressed to stop him from going too far
And be left by the roadside, for all your good deeds,
Two toadstools for tits and a face full of weeds."

All the house raised a cheer, but the man at the bar
Made a phonecall and up pulled a red patrol car
And she blew us a kiss as they copped her away
From that prominent bar in Secaucus, N.J.

X. J. KENNEDY

Questions

1. *What is the dominant metrical foot of this poem? How many feet are there is each line? The poem, then, is written in:*
2. *Sing the poem, if the tunes the poet mentions are familiar to you. Do you notice any differences between the rhythm of the song and the rhythm of the poem as it is read?*
3. *In poems with a regular metrical pattern like this one, the poet is able to achieve different effects by comparing and contrasting words that occupy similar positions in the line (say, at the end of lines or in the middle of lines) and the foot (in the accented position). The metrical location provides the unity, and the meaning provides the contrast. Describe this process as it applies to "snot" and "rose" in the third stanza, "young" and "bung" in stanza eight, and "deeds" and "weeds" in stanza nine.*
4. *In what way are the meter and rhythm appropriate to the emotions and condition of the speaker?*
5. *Explain the relationship of sound and sense in this poem.*

REFLECTIONS DENTAL

How pure, how beautiful, how fine
Do teeth on television shine!
No flutist flutes, no dancer twirls,
But comes equipped with matching pearls.
Gleeful announcers all are born
With sets like rows of hybrid corn.
Clowns, critics, clergy, commentators,
Ventriloquists and roller skaters,
M.C.s who beat their palms together,
The girl who diagrams the weather,
The crooner crooning for his supper—
All flash white treasures, lower and upper.
With miles of smiles the airwaves teem,
And each an orthodontist's dream.

'Twould please my eye as gold a miser's—
One charmer with uncapped incisors.

PHILLIS McGINLEY

Questions

1. *What is the meter of this poem? Notice the variations in rhythm, as between the seventh and eighth line.*
2. *How are the following like teeth: "matching pearls," "rows of hybrid corn," and "white treasures"?*
3. *What is an "orthodontist"?*

CHEERS

The frogs and the serpents each had a football team,
and I heard their cheer leaders in my dream:

"Bilgewater, bilgewater," called the frog,
"Bilgewater, bilgewater,
Sis, boom, bog!
Roll 'em off the log,
Slog 'em in the sog,
Swamp'em, swamp'em,
Muck mire quash!"

"Sisyphus, Sisyphus," hissed the snake,
"Sibilant, syllabub,
Syllable-loo-ba-lay.
Scylla and Charybdis,
Sumac, asphodel,
How do you spell Success?
With an S-S-S!"

EVE MERRIAM

Questions

1. *How do the cheers of the frog and snake cheerleaders reflect the sounds of those creatures?*

2. *The cheers of the snake incorporate words like "Sisyphus" and "Scylla and Charybdis," which are names of people and places in classical mythology. Are these words allusions, or are they used strictly for their sounds?*

"BUFFALO BILL'S"

Buffalo Bill's
defunct
      who used to
      ride a watersmooth-silver
                  stallion
and break onetwothreefourfive pigeonsjustlikethat
                            Jesus

he was a handsome man
                  and what i want to know is
how do you like your blueeyed boy
Mister Death

    E E CUMMINGS

Questions

1. *What is the dominant metrical foot in this poem? Is it written in blank verse? Is it written in free verse?*
2. *How does the spacing of the lines influence the rhythm of your reading of the poem?*
3. *What is the effect of the separation of "stallion" from its adjective "watersmooth-silver" on the rhythm of the line?*
4. *What is the effect of putting "Jesus" at the end of, and below, the long line in which it appears? Would a different effect result from putting "Jesus" in front of "he was a handsome man"?*
5. *How would you describe the emotion of the speaker of the poem? How does the rhythm of the poem, especially in the last two lines, convey this emotion?*

THE LANGUAGE

      Locate *I*
      love you some-
      where in

      teeth and
      eyes, bite
      it but

take care not
to hurt, you
want so

much so
little. Words
say everything,

I
love you
again,

then what
is emptiness
for. To

fill, fill.
I heard words
and words full

of holes
aching. Speech
is a mouth.

ROBERT CREELEY

Questions

1. *What is the meter of this poem? Is it free verse?*
2. *How do you read a poem like this out loud? Should you stop at the end of each line, or pause slightly, or ignore the line endings and pause according to punctuation and sense?*
3. *What is the meaning of the last sentence of the poem?*

POEM FOR BLACK BOYS

(With Special Love To James)

Where are your heroes, my little Black ones
You are the indian you so disdainfully shoot
Not the big bad sheriff on his faggoty white horse

You should play run-away-slave
or Mau Mau
These are more in line with your history

Ask your mothers for a Rap Brown gun
Santa just may comply if you wish hard enough
Ask for CULLURD instead of Monopoly
DO NOT SIT IN DO NOT FOLLOW KING
GO DIRECTLY TO STREETS
This is a game you can win

As you sit there with your all understanding eyes
You know the truth of what I'm saying
Play Back-to-Black
Grow a natural and practice vandalism
Those are useful games (some say a skill is even learned)

There is a new game I must tell you of
Its called Catch The Leader Lying
(and knowing your sense of the absurd you will enjoy
this)

Also a company called Revolution has just issued a
special kit for little boys called Burn Baby
I'm told it has full instructions on how to siphon gas
and fill a bottle

Then our old friend Hide and Seek becomes valid
Because we have much to seek and ourselves to hide
from a lecherous dog

And this poem I give is worth much more than any
nickle bag
or ten cent toy
And you will understand all too soon
That you, my children of battle, are your heroes
You must invent your own games and teach us old ones
how to play

NIKKI GIOVANNI

Questions

1. *Is this poem written in blank verse or free verse? Does a particular metrical foot provide the basic metrical pattern?*
2. *What fact about the lines of this poem make it different from all the other poems in this book? What effect does this difference have on the unity and coherence of the poem? How does it affect the reading of the poem?*
3. *Explain the allusions to "Mau Mau," "Rap Brown" and "CULLURD." How do they contribute to the subject of the poem?*
4. *What are the emotions and attitudes of the speaker of the poem? How do they affect the poem's rhythm? How is the tone of the speaker reflected in the fact that the lines all end at the same place rather than begin there?*
5. *Although this poem is designated as being "for Black Boys," does the conclusion of the poem transcend this limited audience and appeal to all people? How does the sense of the last two lines reflect the freedom of the poem's form?*

Bibliography: Black Aesthetic

Aubert, Alvin. "Black American Poetry: Its Language and the Folk Tradition." *Black Academy Review: Quarterly of the Black World* 2 (1971):71–80.

Bakish, David. *Richard Wright.* New York: Frederick Ungar Publishing Co., 1973.

Baldwin, James, and Giovanni, Nikki. *A Dialogue.* Philadelphia: J. B. Lippincott Co., 1972.

Bigsby, C. W. E., ed. *The Black American Writer: Volume 2, Poetry and Drama.* Baltimore: Penguin Books, 1969.

Emmanuel, James. *Langston Hughes.* New York: Twayne Publishers, 1967.

Fabre, Michel. "The Poetry of Richard Wright." *Studies in Black Literature* 1 (1970):10–22.

Ferguson, Blanche E. *Countee Cullen and the Negro Renaissance.* New York: Dodd, Mead & Co., 1966.

Gayle, Addison, Jr. *The Black Aesthetic.* New York: Doubleday & Co., 1971.

———. *Claude McKay: The Black Poet at War.* Detroit: Broadside Press, 1972.

———. "Cultural Strangulation: Black Literature and the White Aesthetic." *Negro Digest* 18 (1969):32–39.

Hill, Herbert, ed. *Anger and Beyond: The Negro Writer in the United States.* New York: Harper & Row Publishers, 1966.

Kent, George. "The Poetry of Gwendolyn Brooks, Part I." *Black World* 20 (1971):30–43.

———. "The Poetry of Gwendolyn Brooks, Part II." *Black World* 20 (1971):36.

Margolies, Edward. *Native Sons: A Critical Study of Twentieth-Century Negro-American Authors.* Philadelphia: J. B. Lippincott Co., 1968.

O'Daniel, Therman B., ed. *Langston Hughes, Black Genius: A Critical Evaluation.* New York: William Morrow & Co., 1972.

Palmer, R. Roderick. "The Poetry of Three Revolutionists: Don L. Lee, Sonia

Sanchez, and Nikki Giovanni." *College Language Association Journal* 15 (1971):25–36.

Perry, Margaret. *A Bio-Bibliography of Countee Cullen.* Westport, Conn.: Greenwood Press, 1971.

Stavros, George. "An Inteview with Gwendolyn Brooks." *Contemporary Literature* 11 (1970):1–20.

Turner, Darwin T. *Black American Literature: Poetry.* Columbus, Ohio: Charles E. Merrill Publishing Co., 1969.

Wagner, Jean. *Black Poets of the United States: Racial and Religious Feeling in Poetry From P. L. Dunbar to L. Hughes (1890–1940).* Urbana, Ill.: University of Illinois Press, 1973.

Topics for Writing

1. Using the selections from Shakespeare (Sonnet 71, from *Macbeth*) or Milton (from *Paradise Lost*) as a model, write ten lines of blank verse. Keep the meter as regular as possible, but use rhythmical variation to avoid the monotonous repetition of *Da Dum, Da Dum.*

2. Using the selections from Cummings or Giovanni ("Poem for Black boys") as a model, write a poem in free verse, preferably on the same general subject as your poem in blank verse. Then write a paragraph describing the difference in your own attitudes when beginning a poem in metered and non-metered poetry. With which form do you feel more comfortable, and why?

3. Take a brief newspaper story, or another selection of prose, and rearrange it into a poetic form (the result may not be poetry, but it shouldn't be prose either). You might cut the sentences, or stretch them, into ten-syllable lengths; or you might break the sentences into phrases which have enough unity to occupy an entire line by themselves, as in free verse.

4. Select a poem from some other section of this book and scan it. Then write a short essay explaining the relationship of the poem's meter (if any) and rhythm to its sense. Justify or attack the poet's use of metrical inversions, rhythmical variations, and word sounds. Be specific.

8 The Pattern of Poetry

One source of our enjoyment of a work of art is our perception of and participation in its design, its pattern. The pattern of a poem results from the organization of the elements of structure and meaning into a unified and coherent whole; the creation of such a pattern is the work of imaginative genius. A poet does not sit down and say to himself, "Today I'll write a poem with five symbols, four stanzas, and three paradoxes." Rather, he uses these elements of structure and meaning to give a satisfying pattern to his imaginative vision, and he uses these elements only insofar as they seem absolutely necessary to the vision's final shape in language. Similarly, the reader does not respond favorably to a poem because it uses five symbols and three paradoxes, but because the work forms a pleasing whole and thus appeals to his own imagination. Poetry is the language of the poet's genius speaking to your own genius.

Although the source of a poem's fundamental pattern is the creative imagination, many of the formal effects of that pattern can be recognized and described. Similarly, though each poem is to some degree unique in itself, each poem is also part of the poetic tradition, having at least some things in common with a number of other poems. Literary critics have developed many terms to describe similarities among different poems, terms which are often used to group poems by subject (elegies, epics, tragedies) and form (odes, ballads, sonnets). Terms such as these can be useful as long as you keep in mind that they are really descriptions of things that have already been done: there is no guarantee that terms which describe the past are going to be useful in the future, in literary criticism or anything else. Furthermore, an understanding of these terms, while contributing to your appreciation of poetry, is not going to substitute for an imaginative acceptance of the poem itself.

At the end of this book is a glossary of terms, many of which define different kinds of patterns possible in poetry. You may want to read through this glossary, using it to determine the names of the kinds of poems this book includes. This chapter, however, considers a limited number of these patterns, in the hope that you will begin to understand and appreciate the importance of pattern to poetry.

Poetry probably began as song. One of the earliest forms of poetry is the ballad, which is a song that tells a story. Since folk ballads were passed on from singer to singer and generation to generation by word of mouth before they were finally written down, they tended to share certain features which made oral transmission possible. They were short enough to be remembered easily, and they often employed a *refrain,* a passage repeated at regular intervals. They frequently employed a device known as *incremental repetition,* which means repetition with an addition, an increment, or increase. In other words, the first stanza establishes a pattern which the second stanza repeats but adds a variation to, a change which advances the story of the whole ballad. This pattern of repetition with variation not only enabled both singer and audience to remember the story, but it also pleased them both by creating a suspense which only the next stanza could resolve.

The power of the ballad form is evident in the fact that it remains as pleasing to modern audiences as it was to our ancestors. Poets still use the ballad form in creating *literary ballads,* a term which distinguishes these poems from the folk ballads whose authors are really the folk rather than a particular poet. And the basic ballad form, with some modifications, is used frequently in popular songs. In this chapter "Lord Randal" and "Sir Patrick Spens" are folk ballads, while "Ballad of Birmingham" and "Down in Dallas" are literary ballads.

Another important form which many poets employ is the *sonnet.* A sonnet is a fourteen-line poem of iambic pentameter which utilizes one of two particular rhyme schemes. An *Italian sonnet* is composed of two parts: an *octave* (the first eight lines), which generally states a problem or situation, and a *sestet* (the last six lines), which resolves the problem or responds satisfactorily to the situation presented in the octave. The rhyme scheme of the octave is **abbaabba**: the first, fourth, fifth, and eighth lines rhyme with each other, and then the second, third, sixth, and seventh rhyme with each other. The rhyme scheme of the sestet is most often **cdecde.**

An *English sonnet* is composed of three *quatrains* (groups of four lines) and a *couplet* (two lines which rhyme). The English sonnet sometimes follows the

Italian pattern of presenting a problem and resolving it, and sometimes it presents a problem in the first quatrain and then repeats it with some expansion and variation in the next two quatrains. But the final couplet of the English sonnet always answers in some satisfactorily conclusive way the problem or situation presented in the three quatrains. The rhyme scheme of the English sonnet is **abab cdcd efef gg.** You might note that the difference between the Italian and English sonnet patterns is reflected in the difference in rhyme schemes, the Italian octave utilizing similar rhymes to make it felt as a unit, while the English quatrains employ rhymes which set the quatrains apart from each other.

Compared to the ballad, the sonnet is a very sophisticated form (sophisticated means more complex, not necessarily better), and it poses a challenge which has been accepted by many poets. The tight form of the Italian sonnet lends itself to dramatic contrasts and resolutions, generated by the tension between the octave and sestet. The English sonnet is perhaps more suitable to the development of situations by progressive stages, a development which cleverly may be reversed or summarized by the concluding couplet. But both types of sonnets reveal a pattern of tension and resolution; in this way they differ in their closed forms from other short lyric poems that are based on the expansiveness of an intense personal emotion rather than on the statement and resolution of a problem. Some poets have written a series of sonnets on a single subject (usually a love affair), and these are called *sonnet sequences*. William Shakespeare, Edmund Spenser, George Meredith, Elizabeth Barrett Browning, and John Berryman all have written sonnet sequences. In this chapter an example of the Italian sonnet is John Keats' poem "On First Looking into Chapman's Homer"; the English sonnet is represented by Shakespeare's "That Time of Year."

The term *lyric* describes many types of poetry, including the sonnet, the elegy, the ode, and the dramatic monologue (all of these terms are defined in the glossary). Originally the term lyric referred to words sung to the accompaniment of a lyre, an ancient musical instrument. A lyric does not have a narrative story line, as a ballad does. Rather, a lyric is (generally) a short poem that expresses the speaker's feelings and thoughts on a particular subject, whether it be love, death, or automobiles. The pattern of a lyric poem depends upon the expression of the speaker's feelings and thoughts, and hence that pattern varies from poem to poem, from poet to poet. Although it is difficult, even impossible, to define the lyric pattern in any but general terms, it is clear that lyric poems all issue from a common lyric impulse, a desire to utter forth personal feelings and thoughts. The suitability of the poetic form chosen to convey these personal feelings and thoughts is judged by its appropriateness to the feelings and thoughts revealed, not by its adherence to some external standard, such as the ballad's plot development or the sonnet's rhyme scheme. Since the lyric pattern is the most popular one in the twentieth century, this chapter presents a number of lyric poems.

LORD RANDAL

"O where hae ye been, Lord Randal, my son?
O where hae ye been, my handsome young man?"
"I hae been to the wild wood; mother, make my bed soon,
For I'm weary wi' hunting, and fain wald lie down."

"Where gat ye your dinner, Lord Randal, my son?
Where gat ye your dinner, my handsome young man?"
"I dined wi' my true-love; mother, make my bed soon,
For I'm weary wi' hunting, and fain wald lie down."

"What gat ye to your dinner, Lord Randal, my son?
What gat ye to your dinner, my handsome young man?"
"I gat eels boiled in broo; mother, make my bed soon,
For I'm weary wi' hunting, and fain wald lie down."

"What became of your bloodhounds, Lord Randal, my son?
What became of your bloodhounds, my handsome young man?"
"O they swelled and they died; mother, make my bed soon,
For I'm weary wi' hunting, and fain wald lie down."

"O I fear ye are poisoned, Lord Randal, my son!
O I fear ye are poisoned, my handsome young man!"
"O yes! I am poisoned; mother, make my bed soon,
For I'm sick at the heart, and I fain wald lie down."

ANONYMOUS

Questions

1. *What is the basic story of this ballad?*
2. *Select the new detail which each stanza adds to the story line. In particular, how does the new information of the fourth stanza contribute to the story of Lord Randal?*

3. *Lord Randal's response to his mother's questions is in the form of two lines, the first variable and the second repeated. The second line, the* **refrain,** *is constant until the end of the poem. Explain the significance and the effect of the variation in the refrain at the ballad's conclusion.*
4. *The basic stanza pattern of question and answer, and the basic pattern of word order, are repeated with changes that add to the meaning (incremental repetition). In the first stanza what is suggested by Lord Randal's request that his mother "make my bed soon"? Is there another level of significance to "bed" in this phrase in the last stanza?*
5. *How does the question-response pattern contribute to the increasing tension of this ballad? Does it make a difference that the questioner is Lord Randal's mother? The meter and the stanza pattern, among other things, impose a regularity on the ballad that contrasts with the increase in emotional intensity. In reading the poem aloud, how would you indicate the tension between emotional development and metrical regularity?*

SIR PATRICK SPENS

The king sits in Dumferling toune,
   Drinking the blude-reid wine:
"O whar will I get guid sailor,
   To sail this ship of mine?"

Up and spake an eldern knicht,
   Sat at the king's richt knee:
"Sir Patrick Spens is the best sailor
   That sails upon the sea."

The king has written a braid letter
   And signed it wi' his hand,
And sent it to Sir Patrick Spens,
   Was walking on the sand.

The first line that Sir Patrick read,
   A loud lauch lauched he;
The next line that Sir Patrick read,
   The tear blinded his ee.

"O wha is this has done this deed,
   This il deed done to me,
To send me out this time o' the year,
   To sail upon the sea?

"Make haste make haste, my merry men all,
  Our guid ship sails the morn."
"O say na sae, my master dear,
  For I fear a deadly storm.

"Late, late yestre'en I saw the new moon
  Wi' the auld moon in her arm,
And I fear, I fear, my dear mastér,
  That we will come to harm."

O our Scots nobles were richt laith
  To weet their cork-heeled shoon,
But lang owre a' the play were played
  Their hats they swam aboon.

O lang, lang, may their ladies sit,
  Wi' their fans into their hand,
Or ere they see Sir Patrick Spens
  Come sailing to the land.

O lang, lang, may the ladies stand
  Wi' their gold kems in their hair,
Waiting for their ain dear lords,
  For they'll see them na mair.

Half o'er, half o'er to Aberdour
  It's fifty fadom deep,
And there lies guid Sir Patrick Spens
  Wi' the Scots lords at his feet.

ANONYMOUS

Questions

1. *What is the basic story of this ballad? To what class of society does the speaker belong? About what class is he singing? Of what social class is Sir Patrick Spens a member?*
2. *Does the ballad explain why the king wanted to send out a ship in bad weather, or whether the king went on the ship with the "Scots lords"? Is this information necessary?*
3. *Why does Sir Patrick first laugh and then cry when he reads the king's order? What is suggested by the fact that the king is drinking blood-red wine?*
4. *How is the attitude of the speaker toward the Scots lords and ladies revealed in stanzas eight, nine, and ten? What details suggest the richness of the royalty? How do the last two lines of these stanzas suggest the futility of such richness?*

5. *The ballad ends by reversing the relationship that existed between Sir Patrick and the nobles at the beginning of the story. How has Sir Patrick put "the Scots lords at his feet"? Is Sir Patrick a kind of lower-class hero in this ballad? If so, what does the end of the story suggest about the fate of the lower classes?*

BALLAD OF BIRMINGHAM

Mother dear may I go downtown
Instead of out to play
And march the streets of Birmingham
In a freedom march today?

No baby no, you may not go
For the dogs are fierce and wild,
And clubs and hoses, guns and jails
Aren't good for a little child.

But mother I won't be alone,
Other children will go with me
And march the streets of Birmingham
To make our people free.

No baby no, you may not go
I fear the guns will fire,
But you may go to church instead and sing in the
    children's choir.

She's combed and brushed her night dark hair
And bathed rose petal sweet,
And drawn white gloves on small brown hands,
White shoes on her feet.

Her mother smiled to know her child
Was in that sacred place,
But that smile was the last
Smile to come to her face.

For when she heard the explosion
Her eyes grew wet and wild,
She raced through the streets of Birmingham
Yelling for her child.

She dug in bits of glass and brick,
Then pulled out a shoe
Oh here is the shoe my baby wore
But baby where are you?

DUDLEY RANDALL

Questions

1. *In this* literary ballad *how effective is the question-response pattern? Does the child actually talk like a child might? Does it make any difference?*
2. *What contribution to the story do the details in stanza five make? How does stanza five increase the effectiveness and forcefulness of the last stanza?*
3. *This poem, like "Sir Patrick Spens," uses an ironic reversal to achieve its effects. How are the "streets of Birmingham" contrasted with the "children's choir" in the beginning, and how is this relationship reversed?*
4. *What do the details in stanza two suggest? Are they explained, or is it assumed the reader will understand them? Did you find similar examples of unexplained references in "Sir Patrick Spens"?*
5. *What is the basic story of the Birmingham murders? Compare this ballad account with a newspaper report of the explosion. Which is more moving? Which is more informative?*

DOWN IN DALLAS

Down in Dallas, down in Dallas,
Where the shadow of blood lies black,
Little Oswald nailed Jack Kennedy up
With the nail of a rifle crack.

The big bright Cadillacs stomped on their brakes,
The street fell unearthly still
While, smoke on its chin, that slithering gun
Coiled back from its window sill.

In a white chrome room on a table top
They tried all a scalpel knows,
But they couldn't spell stop to that drop-by-drop
Till it bloomed to a rigid rose.

Out on the altar, out on the altar
Christ blossoms in bread and wine,
But each asphalt stone where his blood dropped down
Is burst to a cactus spine.

Oh down in Dallas, down in Dallas
Where a desert wind walks by night,
He stood and they bound him foot and hand
To the cross of a rifle sight.

X. J. KENNEDY

Questions

1. *What is the basic story of this literary ballad? What specific details of the actual events of the murder of President Kennedy does the poem use?*
2. *This ballad, unlike the others in this chapter, does not depend merely on the development of a story line. In fact, the poem begins in the past tense, with the story's conclusion revealed in the first stanza. How do you account for the poem's success?*
3. *Select and explain the details which associate the killing of Kennedy with the crucifixion of Christ. How do these allusions culminate in the last line of the poem?*
4. *Examine the flower imagery in the third and fourth stanzas. How is the difference between the effects of Christ's death and the effects of Kennedy's death contrasted in the words "blossoms" and "burst to a cactus spine"? Explain the metaphor of the "rigid rose."*
5. *How has the poet used details of the setting (Dallas, the desert, and so forth) to suggest his attitude toward the incident?*

ON FIRST LOOKING INTO CHAPMAN'S HOMER

Much have I traveled in the realms of gold,
And many goodly states and kingdoms seen;
Round many western islands have I been
Which bards in fealty to Apollo hold.
Oft of one wide expanse had I been told
That deep-browed Homer ruled as his demesne;
Yet did I never breathe its pure serene
Till I heard Chapman speak out loud and bold:
Then felt I like some watcher of the skies

When a new planet swims into his ken;
Or like stout Cortez when with eagle eyes
He stared at the Pacific—and all his men
Looked at each other with a wild surmise—
Silent, upon a peak in Darien.

JOHN KEATS

Questions

1. *Describe the pattern of this sonnet. What is the meter, and what is the rhyme scheme? Is it an English or an Italian sonnet?*
2. *What are the "realms of gold" in which the speaker has traveled? What is the "demesne" of "deep-browed Homer"? What does "Chapman' have to do with Homer's "demesne"?*
3. *In one sentence paraphrase the octave of this sonnet. Describe the attitude of the speaker in this octave.*
4. *The contrast between octave and sestet in this sonnet may be roughly described as a before-and-after contrast. How do the comparisons used by the speaker in the sestet heighten the contrast in his feelings after reading Chapman's translation of Homer? How is this heightening process brought to a climax in the last line of the poem? Does the final silence signify boredom or awe?*
5. *It has been pointed out that Keats has his facts wrong in this poem: Cortez did not discover the Pacific, and Darien is not the place from which the Pacific was first seen (by Balboa). Does this make any difference to the reader of the poem? What does this example of poetic license suggest about the relationship of art and empirical fact?*

SONNET 73

That time of year thou mayst in me behold
When yellow leaves, or none, or few, do hang
Upon those boughs which shake against the cold,
Bare ruined choirs, where late the sweet birds sang.
In me thou see'st the twilight of such day
As after sunset fadeth in the west;
Which by and by black night doth take away,
Death's second self, that seals up all in rest.
In me thou see'st the glowing of such fire,
That on the ashes of his youth doth lie,
As the deathbed whereon it must expire,

Consumed with that which it was nourished by.
This thou perceiv'st, which makes thy love more strong,
To love that well which thou must leave ere long.

WILLIAM SHAKESPEARE

Questions

1. *Describe the pattern of this sonnet. What kind of meter is used? What is the rhyme scheme?*
2. *How many sentences are used in the poem? Do they correspond to the structural units which make up an English sonnet (three quatrains and a couplet)?*
3. *The three quatrains give examples of things "which thou must leave ere long" (I'm like the season of late fall, I'm like twilight, I'm like the dying embers of a fire). Is the poem's pattern, then, based on contrast and resolution or on development by example? How is this pattern satisfactorily concluded by the couplet?*
4. *Explain the following: the metaphor of a tree's "boughs" as "Bare ruined choirs, where late the sweet birds sang," the metaphor of "black night" as "Death's second self," the paradox of a fire "Consumed with that which it was nourished by."*
5. *How is the speaker's attitude toward his situation, as developed in the three quatrains, modified by the couplet?*

DEER HUNT

Because the warden is a cousin, my
mountain friends hunt in summer when the deer
cherish each rattler-ridden spring, and I
have waited hours by a pool in fear
that manhood would require I shoot or that
the steady drip of the hill would dull my ear
to a snake whispering near the log I sat
upon, and listened to the yelping cheer
of dogs and men resounding ridge to ridge.
I flinched at every lonely rifle crack,
my knuckles whitening where I gripped the edge
of age and clung, like retching, sinking back,
then gripping once again the monstrous gun—
since I, to be a man, had taken one.

JUDSON JEROME

1. *What kind of sonnet pattern does this poem utilize?*
2. *What is the attitude of the speaker toward the "Deer Hunt"?*
3. *Explain the irony of the last line.*

THE BELLS

1

       Hear the sledges with the bells—
          Silver bells!
What a world of merriment their melody foretells!
      How they tinkle, tinkle, tinkle,
        In the icy air of night!
      While the stars that oversprinkle
      All the heavens, seem to twinkle
        With a crystalline delight;
      Keeping time, time, time,
      In a sort of runic rhyme,
To the tintinnabulation that so musically wells
    From the bells, bells, bells, bells,
       Bells, bells, bells—
From the jingling and the tinkling of the bells.

2

       Hear the mellow wedding bells—
          Golden bells!
What a world of happiness their harmony foretells!
      Through the balmy air of night
      How they ring out their delight!—
       From the molten-golden notes,
         And all in tune,
       What a liquid ditty floats
    To the turtledove that listens, while she gloats
        On the moon!
      Oh, from out the sounding cells,
What a gush of euphony voluminously wells!
       How it swells!
       How it dwells
      On the Future!—how it tells
      Of the rapture that impels
    To the swinging and the ringing
       Of the bells, bells, bells—
      Of the bells, bells, bells, bells,
       Bells, bells, bells—
To the rhyming and the chiming of the bells!

3

    Hear the loud alarum bells—
        Brazen bells!
What a tale of terror, now, their turbulency tells!
  In the startled ear of night
  How they scream out their affright!
    Too much horrified to speak,
    They can only shriek, shriek,
      Out of tune,
In a clamorous appealing to the mercy of the fire,
In a mad expostulation with the deaf and frantic fire,
      Leaping higher, higher, higher,
      With a desperate desire,
    And a resolute endeavor
    Now—now to sit, or never,
By the side of the pale-faced moon.
    Oh, the bells, bells, bells!
    What a tale their terror tells
      Of Despair!
  How they clang, and clash, and roar!
  What a horror they outpour
On the bosom of the palpitating air!
    Yet the ear, it fully knows,
      By the twanging
      And the clanging,
   How the danger ebbs and flows;
Yet the ear distinctly tells,
      In the jangling
      And wrangling,
  How the danger sinks and swells,
By the sinking or the swelling in the anger of the bells—
      Of the bells,—
  Of the bells, bells, bells, bells,
   Bells, bells, bells—
In the clamor and the clangor of the bells!

4

    Hear the tolling of the bells—
      Iron bells!
What a world of solemn thought their monody compels!
    In the silence of the night,
    How we shiver with affright
At the melanchony menace of their tone!
  For every sound that floats
  From the rust within their throats
      Is a groan.
  And the people—ah, the people—

They that dwell up in the steeple,
    All alone,
And who tolling, tolling, tolling,
    In that muffled monotone,
Feel a glory in so rolling
    On the human heart a stone—
They are neither man nor woman—
They are neither brute nor human—
      They are ghouls:—
    And their king it is who tolls:—
    And he rolls, rolls, rolls,
      Rolls
    A paean from the bells!
And his merry bosom swells
With the paean of the bells!
And he dances, and he yells;
Keeping time, time, time,
In a sort of runic rhyme,
    To the paean of the bells—
      Of the bells—
Keeping time, time, time,
In a sort of runic rhyme,
    To the throbbing of the bells—
    Of the bells, bells, bells—
    To the sobbing of the bells;
Keeping time, time, time,
    As he knells, knells, knells,
In a happy runic rhyme,
    To the rolling of the bells—
    Of the bells, bells, bells:—
    To the tolling of the bells—
Of the bells, bells, bells, bells,
    Bells, bells, bells—
To the moaning and the groaning of the bells.

EDGAR ALLEN POE

Questions

1. It is quite common for a reader of poetry to slight the sound of the words in favor of their sense. In this poem, however, the poet is obviously making more use of the sound than of the sense in describing the various sounds of the bells. How do the sounds of the bells change with each section of the poem:

    1. "Silver bells" with "jingling and tinkling"
    2. "Golden bells" with "rhyming and chiming"

3. "Brazen bells" with "clamor and clangor"
4. "Iron bells" with "moaning and groaning"

What emotions are associated with the different sounds of the bells in the different sections?
2. How does Poe use rhythm and meter to vary this poem enough so that it is not monotonous, with all its bells, bells, bells?

THE ALTAR

A broken ALTAR, Lord, Thy servant rears,
Made of a HEART, and cemented with tears;
Whose parts are as Thy hand did frame;
No workman's tool hath touched the same.
　A　　HEART　　alone
　Is　such　a　stone
　As　nothing　but
　Thy power doth cut.
　Wherefore each part
　Of my hard HEART
　Meets in this frame,
　To praise Thy name:
That, if I chance to hold my peace,
These stones to praise Thee may not cease.
O, let Thy blessed SACRIFICE be mine,
And sanctify this ALTAR to be Thine.

GEORGE HERBERT

Questions

1. This poem uses a visual arrangement of its words to achieve some of its effects. How does the arrangement of the words represent the subject of the poem?
2. What does the poet mean by "this frame" in line 11? What does he mean by "these stones" in line 14?
3. What is the basic meter of the poem? How many different line lengths are used?

[THE GRASSHOPPER]

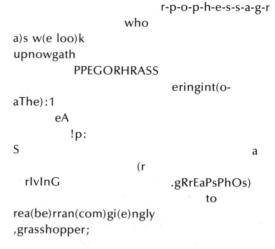

E. E. CUMMINGS

Questions

1. *A grasshopper obviously looks different when it is leaping and when it is sitting, yet the word "grasshopper" covers the creature in both positions. In this poem cummings has rearranged the letters of the word, and has interrupted the customary word order of the sentence, to present visually the whirring, gathering, leaping, and settling grasshopper, so that the poem visually represents the* becoming *of the grasshopper. What is the sense of the sentence of the poem?*
2. *What two words constitute the second-to-last line? Why is there a comma before the final word "grasshopper"? Why does the poem end with a semicolon rather than with a period?*

GOSSIP

RICHARD KOSTELANETZ

Questions

1. *This is an example of* concrete poetry, *a recent attempt to utilize more fully the visual and spatial aspects of language, apart from the sound and meaning of words. How does the spatial arrangement of words in "Gossip" contribute to the effect of the poem?*
2. *What is the effect of using stenciled lettering for the title?*
3. *What is the effect of changing the size of the letters in the poem?*

THE OLD ADAM

A photo of someone else's childhood,
a garden in another country—world
he had no part in and has no power to imagine:

yet the old man who has failed his memory
keens over the picture—'Them happy days—
gone—gone for ever!'—glad for a moment to suppose

a focus for unspent grieving, his floating
sense of loss.
He wanders

asking the day of the week, the time,
over and over the wrong questions.
Missing his way in the streets

he acts out
the bent of his life,
the lost way

never looked for, life
unlived, of which he is dying
very slowly.

'A man,'
says his son, 'who never
made a right move in all his life.' A man

who thought the dollar was sweet and
couldn't make a buck, riding the subway
year after year to untasted sweetness,

loving his sons obscurely, incurious
who they were, these men, his sons—
a shadow of love, for love longs

to know the beloved, and a light goes with it
into the dark mineshafts of feeling . . . A man
who now, without knowing,

in endless concern for the smallest certainties,
looking again and again at a paid bill,
inquiring again and again, 'When was I here last?'

asks what it's too late to ask:
'Where is my life? Where is my life?
What have I done with my life?'

DENISE LEVERTOV

Questions

1. *The poem's title and the first stanza introduce an allusion linking the old man with Adam. What is the Garden of Eden which the old man can no longer remember? What is "the lost way" back to paradise which the man mistakenly followed? What is the right way back (see stanza ten)?*
2. *Explain the paradox of stanza six.*
3. *In an essay Levertov writes that sound and measure in an organic poem imitate "the feeling of an experience, its emotional tone, its texture." How is this notion illustrated in this poem? (Consider the varying line lengths, as in stanzas three, four and five, and consider the use of repetition of such phrases as "A man" and "Where is my life.")*

THE MUTES

Those groans men use
passing a woman on the street
or on the steps of the subway

to tell her she is a female
and their flesh knows it,

are they a sort of tune,
an ugly enough song, sung
by a bird with a slit tongue

but meant for music?

Or are they the muffled roaring
of deafmutes trapped in a building that is
slowly filling with smoke?

Perhaps both.

Such men most often
look as if groan were all they could do,
yet a woman, in spite of herself,

knows it's a tribute:
if she were lacking all grace
they'd pass her in silence:

so it's not only to say she's
a warm hole. It's a word

in grief-language, nothing to do with
primitive, not an ur-language:
language stricken, sickened, cast down

in decrepitude. She wants to
throw the tribute away, dis-
gusted, and can't,

it goes on buzzing in her ear,
it changes the pace of her walk,
the torn posters in echoing corridors

spell it out, it
quakes and gnashes as the train comes in.
Her pulse sullenly

had picked up speed,
but the cars slow down and
jar to a stop while her understanding

keeps on translating:
'Life after life after life goes by

without poetry,
without seemliness,
without love.'

DENISE LEVERTOV

1. *What is the difference between the language of the "mutes" and an original "ur-language"? What verbs describe the reaction of the woman to the groans? Why had her pulse "sullenly" responded to the groan?*
2. *What is the difference between her "pulse" and her "understanding," which "keeps on translating" after the groan and her pulse reaction have stopped? Is her understanding a mute?*
3. *In an essay Levertov declares that "Form is never more than a revelation of content." With this in mind explain the connections between "poetry," "seemliness," and the "love," which the poem suggests is lacking in the groans of the "mutes."*

THE SECRET

Two girls discover
the secret of life
in a sudden line of
poetry.

I who don't know the
secret wrote
the line. They
told me

(through a third person)
they had found it
but not what it was
not even

what line it was. No doubt
by now, more than a week
later, they have forgotten
the secret,

the line, the name of
the poem. I love them
for finding what
I can't find,

and for loving me
for the line I wrote,
and for forgetting it
so that

a thousand times, till death
finds them, they may
discover it again, in other
lines

in other
happenings. And for
wanting to know it,
for

assuming there is
such a secret, yes,
for that
most of all.

DENISE LEVERTOV

Questions

1. *What is the "secret of life" that the poet sees in the girls' discovery? Why do they find it in a "sudden" line of poetry?*
2. *Why does the poet love the girls most for "assuming there is/such a secret, yes"? Why does she end the second line of the last stanza with "yes"?*
3. *In an essay on organic form Levertov states that organic poetry "is based on an intuition of an order, a form beyond forms, in which forms partake, and of which man's creative works are analogies, resemblances, natural allegories." Does this idea relate to the "secret of life" which the girls discover? What does the connection in the poem of "other lines" and "other happenings" suggest about the relationship of poetry and life? In what way is the process of "finding," "loving," and then "forgetting" an organic one?*

THOSE BEING EATEN BY AMERICA

The cry of those being eaten by America,
Others pale and soft being stored for later eating

And Jefferson
Who saw hope in new oats

The wild houses go on
With long hair growing from between their toes
The feet at night get up
And run down the long white roads by themselves

The dams reverse themselves and want to go stand alone in the desert

Ministers who dive headfirst into the earth
The pale flesh
Spreading guiltily into new literatures

That is why these poems are so sad
The long dead running over the fields

The mass sinking down
The light in children's faces fading at six or seven

The world will soon break up into small colonies of the saved

ROBERT BLY

Questions

1. *In his essay "Looking For Dragon Smoke" Robert Bly asserts that our task is "to continue to open new corridors into the psyche by association." What logic of association is there between the first and second stanzas (Jefferson declared that America should have a revolution every twenty years. He also wrote the Declaration of Independence.)*
2. *How does the absence of punctuation and logically rational development contribute to the freedom of the imaginative process in this poem? How do the variations in line and stanza length suggest an associational progression?*
3. *Is the form of this poem organic in the most fundamental sense in which Levertov uses that term? Read this poem seven times and close your eyes. See anything?*

THE EXECUTIVE'S DEATH

Merchants have multiplied more than the stars of heaven.
Half the population are like the long grasshoppers
That sleep in the bushes in the cool of the day:
The sound of their wings is heard at noon, muffled, near the earth.
The crane handler dies, the taxi driver dies, slumped over
In his taxi. Meanwhile, high in the air, executives
Walk on cool floors, and suddenly fall:
Dying, they dream they are lost in a snowstorm in mountains,
On which they crashed, carried at night by great machines.
As he lies on the wintry slope, cut off and dying,
A pine stump talks to him of Goethe and Jesus.
Commuters arrive in Hartford at dusk like moles
Or hares flying from a fire behind them,
And the dusk in Hartford is full of their sighs;
Their trains come through the air like a dark music,
Like the sound of horns, the sound of thousands of small wings.

ROBERT BLY

Questions

1. *What do the first five lines have to do with the executive's death? How is the comparison of "Half the population" to "long grasshoppers" returned to at the end of the poem?*
2. *What is suggested by "Goethe and Jesus"? What comments have they made on worlds and people cut off from each other? Why does a "pine stump" invoke their names?*
3. *What is the relationship between the "great machines," the "trains," and the "Commuters"? Does the poet's "leaping about the psyche" in this poem have any coherence?*

AFTER DRINKING ALL NIGHT WITH A FRIEND, WE GO OUT IN A BOAT AT DAWN TO SEE WHO CAN WRITE THE BEST POEM

These pines, these fall oaks, these rocks,
This water dark and touched by wind—
I am like you, you dark boat,
Drifting over water fed by cool springs.

Beneath the waters, since I was a boy,
I have dreamt of strange and dark treasures,
Not of gold, or strange stones, but the true
Gift, beneath the pale lakes of Minnesota.

This morning also, drifting in the dawn wind,
I sense my hands, and my shoes, and this ink—
Drifting, as all of this body drifts,
Above the clouds of the flesh and the stone.

A few friendships, a few dawns, a few glimpses of grass,
A few oars weathered by the snow and the heat,
So we drift toward shore, over cold waters,
No longer caring if we drift or go straight.

ROBERT BLY

Questions

1. *In this poem about writing a poem, how does the drifting of the boat become integrated with, and in fact a basis for, the form of the poem? Why is it appropriate that this occur?*
2. *In his essay Bly talks about the need for the poet to tap the resources of the unconscious. How is the image of drifting over the "true/Gift" in this poem related to this idea? In this poem how does the poet propose to capture the true gift, how does he approach it?*
3. *How would you compare and contrast the "secret" that Levertov talks about with the "true gift" mentioned in Bly's poem?*

Bibliography: Denise Levertov, Robert Bly, and Open-Form Poetry

Bowering, George. "Denise Levertov." *Antigonish Review* 7 (1971):76–87.
Burrows, E. G. "An Interview with Denise Levertov." *Michigan Quarterly Review* 7 (1968):239–42.
Crunk [pseud.]. "The Work of Denise Levertov." *Sixties* 9 (1967):48–65.
Duddy, Thomas A. "To Celebrate: A Reading of Denise Levertov." *Criticism* 10 (1968):138–52.
Friedman, Norman. "The Wesleyan Poets—III: The Experimental Poets." *Chicago Review* 19 (1967):64–90.
Heyen, William. "Inward to the World: The Poetry of Robert Bly." *The Far Point* 3 (1969):42–50.
Hughes, Daniel. "American Poetry 1969: From B to Z." *Massachusetts Review* 11 (1970):650–86.

Hungerford, Edward, ed. *Poets in Progress: Critical Prefaces to Thirteen Contemporary Americans.* Evanston, Ill.: Northwestern University Press, 1967.

Janssens, G. A. M. "The Present State of American Poetry: Robert Bly and James Wright." *English Studies* 51 (1970):112–37.

Kostelanetz, Richard. "Reactions and Alternatives: Post-World War II American Poetry." *Chelsea* 26 (1969):7–34.

Mills, Ralph, Jr. "Denise Levertov: Poetry of the Immediate." *Tri-Quarterly* 4 (1962):31–37.

————. *Contemporary American Poetry.* New York: Random House, 1965.

Moran, Ronald, and Lensing, George. "The Emotive Imagination: A New Departure in American Poetry." *Southern Review* 3 (1967):51–67.

Nelson, Rudolph L. "Edge of the Transcendent: The Poetry of Levertov and Duncan." *Southwest Review* 54 (1969):188–202.

Rosenthal, Macha L. *The New Poets: American and British Poetry Since World War II.* New York: Oxford University Press, 1967.

Wagner, Linda W. *Denise Levertov.* New York: Twayne Publishers, 1967.

Topics for Writing

1. Select a contemporary song that uses the ballad form and explain precisely in what ways the song achieves its effects. Compare the ballad song with a lyric song on the same subject.

2. Using Dudley Randall's "Ballad of Birmingham" as a model, compose a ballad on some contemporary subject or incident. If possible, find a newspaper clipping on the same subject and compare the different treatments which the different forms encourage.

3. Compare and contrast the form of Sonnet 73 by Shakespeare with the form of the poems of Levertov and Bly.

4. Compare Bly's use of association in his poetry with other, similar uses by artists working in different mediums. You might consider the Surrealist painters, for example, or the lyrics of some of Bob Dylan's songs.

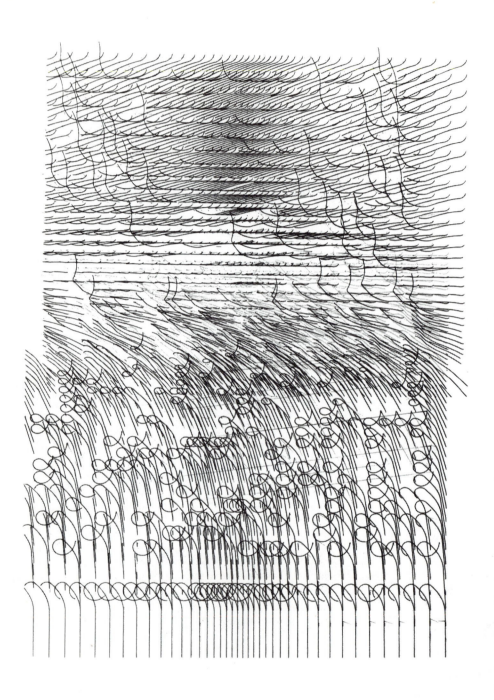

9 Poems for Additional Reading, Topically Arranged

Love

MADRIGAL

My love in her attire doth show her wit,
  It doth so well become her;
For every season she hath dressings fit,
  For winter, spring, and summer.
  No beauty she doth miss
  When all her robes are on;
  But beauty's self she is
  When all her robes are gone.

ANONYMOUS

THEY FLEE FROM ME

They flee from me, that sometime did me seek
With naked foot, stalking in my chamber.
I have seen them gentle, tame, and meek
That now are wild, and do not remember
That sometime they put themselves in danger
To take bread at my hand; and now they range
Busily seeking with a continual change.

Thanked be fortune it hath been otherwise
Twenty times better; but once, in special,
In thin array, after a pleasant guise,
When her loose gown from her shoulders did fall,
And she me caught in her arms long and small,
Therewith all sweetly did me kiss
And softly said, "Dear heart, how like you this?"

It was no dream: I lay broad waking.
But all is turnèd, thorough my gentleness,
Into a strange fashion of forsaking;
And I have leave to go of her goodness,
And she also to use newfangleness.
But since that I so kindely am served,
I would fain know what she hath deserved.

THOMAS WYATT

THE PASSIONATE SHEPHERD TO
HIS LOVE

Come live with me, and be my love,
And we will all the pleasures prove
That valleys, groves, hills and fields,
Woods, or steepy mountain yields.

And we will sit upon the rocks,
Seeing the shepherds feed their flocks,
By shallow rivers, to whose falls
Melodious birds sing madrigals.

And I will make thee beds of roses,
And a thousand fragrant posies,
A cap of flowers, and a kirtle,
Embroider'd all with leaves of myrtle;

A gown made of the finest wool,
Which from our pretty lambs we pull,
Fair-linèd slippers for the cold,
With buckles of the purest gold;

A belt of straw, and ivy-buds,
With coral clasps and amber studs;
And if these pleasures may thee move,
Come live with me, and be my love.

The shepherd-swains shall dance and sing
For they delight each May morning;
If these delights thy mind may move,
Then live with me and be my love.

CHRISTOPHER MARLOWE

SONNET 116

Let me not to the marriage of true minds
Admit impediments. Love is not love
Which alters when it alteration finds,
Or bends with the remover to remove.
O no! it is an ever-fixed mark
That looks on tempests, and is never shaken;
It is the star to every wandering bark,
Whose worth's unknown, although his height be taken.
Love's not Time's fool, though rosy lips and cheeks
Within his bending sickle's compass come;
Love alters not with his brief hours and weeks,
But bears it out even to the edge of doom.
    If this be error and upon me proved,
    I never writ, nor no man ever loved.

WILLIAM SHAKESPEARE

WHY SO PALE AND WAN?

Why so pale and wan, fond lover?
  Prithee, why so pale?
Will, when looking well can't move her,
  Looking ill prevail?
  Prithee, why so pale?

Why so dull and mute, young sinner?
  Prithee, why so mute?
Will, when speaking well can't win her,
  Saying nothing do't?
  Prithee, why so mute?

Quit, quit for shame, this will not move:
  This cannot take her.
If of herself she will not love,
  Nothing can make her:
  The devil take her!

SIR JOHN SUCKLING

THE CANONIZATION

For Godsake hold your tongue, and let me love,
  Or chide my palsy, or my gout,
My five grey hairs, or ruined fortune flout;
  With wealth your state, your mind with arts improve,
    Take you a course, get you a place,
    Observe his Honor, or his Grace;
Or the king's real, or his stamped face
  Contemplate; what you will, approve,
    So you will let me love.

Alas, alas, who's injured by my love?
　　What merchant's ships have my sighs drowned?
Who says my tears have overflowed his ground?
　　When did my colds a forward spring remove?
　　　When did the heats which my veins fill
　　　Add one more to the plaguy bill?
Soldiers find wars, and lawyers find out still
　　Litigious men, which quarrels move,
　　Though she and I do love.

Call us what you will, we are made such by love;
　　Call her one, me another fly,
We're tapers too, and at our own cost die,
　　And we in us find the eagle and the dove.
　　　The Phoenix riddle hath more wit
　　　By us; we two being one are it.
So to one neutral thing both sexes fit,
　　We die and rise the same, and prove
　　Mysterious by this love.

We can die by it, if not live by love,
　　And if unfit for tombs and hearse
Our legend be, it will be fit for verse;
　　And if no piece of chronicle we prove,
　　　We'll build in sonnets pretty rooms;
　　　As well a well-wrought urn becomes
The greatest ashes, as half-acre tombs,
　　And by these hymns all shall approve
　　Us canonized for love:

And thus invoke us; You, whom reverend love
　　Made one another's hermitage;
You, to whom love was peace, that now is rage;
　　Who did the whole world's soul contract, and drove
　　　Into the glasses of your eyes,
　　　So made such mirrors, and such spies,
That they did all to you epitomize;
　　Countries, towns, courts: beg from above
　　A pattern of your love.

JOHN DONNE

TO CELIA

Drink to me only with thine eyes,
   And I will pledge with mine;
Or leave a kiss but in the cup
   And I'll not look for wine.
The thirst that from the soul doth rise
   Doth ask a drink divine;
But might I of Jove's nectar sup.
   I would not change for thine.

I sent thee late a rosy wreath,
   Not so much honoring thee
As giving it a hope that there
   It could not withered be;
But thou thereon didst only breathe
   And sent'st it back to me;
Since when it grows, and smells, I swear,
   Not of itself but thee!

BEN JONSON

GO, LOVELY ROSE

Go, lovely Rose—
Tell her that wastes her time and me
   That now she knows,
When I resemble her to thee,
How sweet and fair she seems to be.

   Tell her that's young,
And shuns to have her graces spied,
   That hadst thou sprung
In deserts, where no men abide,
Thou must have uncommended died.

Small is the worth
Of beauty from the light retired:
  Bid her come forth,
Suffer herself to be desired,
And not blush so to be admired.

  Then die—that she
The common fate of all things rare
  May read in thee:
How small a part of time they share
That are so wondrous sweet and fair.

EDMUND WALLER

SHE WALKS IN BEAUTY

She walks in beauty, like the night
  Of cloudless climes and starry skies;
And all that's best of dark and bright
  Meet in her aspect and her eyes:
Thus mellow'd to that tender light
  Which heaven to gaudy day denies.

One shade the more, one ray the less,
  Had half impair'd the nameless grace
Which waves in every raven tress,
  Or softly lightens o'er her face;
Where thoughts serenely sweet express
  How pure, how dear their dwelling-place.

And on that cheek, and o'er that brow,
  So soft, so calm, yet eloquent,
The smiles that win, the tints that glow,
  But tell of days in goodness spent,
A mind at peace with all below,
  A heart whose love is innocent!

LORD BYRON

FIRST LOVE

I ne'er was struck before that hour
  With love so sudden and so sweet,
Her face it bloomed like a sweet flower
  And stole my heart away complete.
My face turned pale as deadly pale.
  My legs refused to walk away,
And when she looked, what could I ail?
  My life and all seemed turned to clay.

And then my blood rushed to my face
  And took my eyesight quite away,
The trees and bushes round the place
  Seemed midnight at noonday.
I could not see a single thing,
  Words from my eyes did start—
They spoke as chords do from the string,
  And blood burnt round my heart.

Are flowers the winter's choice?
  Is love's bed always snow?
She seemed to hear my silent voice,
  Not love's appeals to know.
I never saw so sweet a face
  As that I stood before.
My heart has left its dwelling-place
  And can return no more.

JOHN CLARE

HOW DO I LOVE THEE?

How do I love thee? Let me count the ways.
I love thee to the depth and breadth and height
My soul can reach, when feeling out of sight
For the ends of Being and ideal Grace.
I love thee to the level of everyday's
Most quiet need, by sun and candle-light.

I love thee freely, as men strive for Right;
I love thee purely, as they turn from Praise.
I love thee with the passion put to use
In my old griefs, and with my childhood's faith.
I love thee with a love I seemed to lose
With my lost saints,—I love thee with the breath,
Smiles, tears, of all my life!—and, if God choose,
I shall but love thee better after death.

ELIZABETH BARRETT BROWNING

A DEEP-SWORN VOW

Others because you did not keep
That deep-sworn vow have been friends of mine;
Yet always when I look death in the face,
When I clamber to the heights of sleep,
Or when I grow excited with wine,
Suddenly I meet your face.

WILLIAM BUTLER YEATS

LULLABY

Lay your sleeping head, my love,
Human on my faithless arm;
Time and fevers burn away
Individual beauty from
Thoughtful children, and the grave
Proves the child ephemeral:
But in my arms till break of day
Let the living creature lie,
Mortal, guilty, but to me
The entirely beautiful.

Soul and body have no bounds:
To lovers as they lie upon
Her tolerant enchanted slope
In their ordinary swoon,
Grave the vision Venus sends
Of supernatural sympathy,
Universal love and hope;
While an abstract insight wakes
Among the glaciers and the rocks
The hermit's carnal ecstasy.

Certainty, fidelity
On the stroke of midnight pass
Like vibrations of a bell
And fashionable madmen raise
Their pedantic boring cry:
Every farthing of the cost,
All the dreaded cards foretell,
Shall be paid, but from this night
Not a whisper, not a thought,
Not a kiss nor look be lost.

Beauty, midnight, vision dies:
Let the winds of dawn that blow
Softly round your dreaming head
Such a day of welcome show
Eye and knocking heart may bless,
Find our mortal world enough;
Noons of dryness find you fed
By the involuntary powers,
Nights of insult let you pass
Watched by every human love.

W. H. AUDEN

[YOU SHALL ABOVE ALL THINGS BE GLAD AND YOUNG]

you shall above all things be glad and young.
For if you're young, whatever life you wear

it will become you;and if you are glad
whatever's living will yourself become.
Girlboys may nothing more than boygirls need:
i can entirely her only love

whose any mystery makes every man's
flesh put space on;and his mind take off time

that you should ever think,may god forbid
and(in his mercy)your true lover spare:
for that way knowledge lies,the foetal grave
called progress,and negation's dead undoom.

I'd rather learn from one bird how to sing
than teach ten thousand stars how not to dance

E. E. CUMMINGS

UNWANTED

The poster with my picture on it
Is hanging on the bulletin board in the Post Office.

I stand by it hoping to be recognized
Posing first full face and then profile

But everybody passes by and I have to admit
The photograph was taken some years ago.

I was unwanted then and I'm unwanted now
Ah guess ah'll go up echo mountain and crah.

I wish someone would find my fingerprints somewhere
Maybe on a corpse and say, You're it.

Description: Male, or reasonably so
White, but not lily-white and usually deep-red

Thirty-fivish, and looks it lately
Five-feet-nine and one-hundred-thirty pounds: no physique

Black hair going gray, hairline receding fast
What used to be curly, now fuzzy

Brown eyes starey under beetling brow
Mole on chin, probably will become a wen

It is perfectly obvious that he was not popular at school
No good at baseball, and wet his bed.

His aliases tell his history: Dumbell, Good-for-nothing,
Jewboy, Fieldinsky, Skinny, Fierce Face, Greaseball, Sissy.

Warning: This man is not dangerous, answers to any name
Responds to love, don't call him or he will come.

EDWARD FIELD

MARRIAGE

Should I get married? Should I be good?
Astound the girl next door with my velvet suit and faustus hood?
Don't take her to movies but to cemeteries
tell all about werewolf bathtubs and forked clarinets
then desire her and kiss her and all the preliminaries
and she going just so far and I understanding why
not getting angry saying You must feel! It's beautiful to feel!
Instead take her in my arms lean against an old crooked tombstone
and woo her the entire night the constellations in the sky—

When she introduces me to her parents
back straightened, hair finally combed, strangled by a tie,
should I sit knees together on their 3rd degree sofa
and not ask Where's the bathroom?
How else to feel other than I am,
often thinking Flash Gordon soap—
O how terrible it must be for a young man
seated before a family and the family thinking
We never saw him before! He wants our Mary Lou!
After tea and homemade cookies they ask What do you do for a living?

Should I tell them? Would they like me then?
Say All right get married, we're losing a daughter
but we're gaining a son—
And should I then ask Where's the bathroom?

O God, and the wedding! All her family and her friends
and only a handful of mine all scroungy and bearded
just wait to get at the drinks and food—
And the priest! he looking at me as if I masturbated
asking me Do you take this woman for your lawful wedded wife?
And I trembling what to say say Pie Glue!
I kiss the bride all those corny men slapping me on the back
She's all yours, boy! Ha-ha-ha!
And in their eyes you could see some obscene honeymoon going on—

Then all that absurd rice and clanky cans and shoes
Niagara Falls! Hordes of us! Husbands! Wives! Flowers! Chocolates!

All streaming into cozy hotels
All going to do the same thing tonight
The indifferent clerk he knowing what was going to happen
The lobby zombies they knowing what
The whistling elevator man he knowing
The winking bellboy knowing
Everybody knowing! I'd be almost inclined not to do anything!
Stay up all night! Stare that hotel clerk in the eye!
Screaming: I deny honeymoon! I deny honeymoon!
running rampant into those almost climactic suites
yelling Radio belly! Cat shovel!
O I'd live in Niagara forever! in a dark cave beneath the Falls
I'd sit there the Mad Honeymooner
devising ways to break marriages, a scourge of bigamy
a saint of divorce—

But I should get married I should be good
How nice it'd be to come home to her
and sit by the fireplace and she in the kitchen
aproned young and lovely wanting my baby
and so happy about me she burns the roast beef
and comes crying to me and I get up from my big papa chair
saying Christmas teeth! Radiant brains! Apple deaf!
God what a husband I'd make! Yes, I should get married!
So much to do! like sneaking into Mr. Jones' house late at night

and cover his golf clubs with 1920 Norwegian books
Like hanging a picture of Rimbaud on the lawnmower
like pasting Tannu Tuva postage stamps all over the picket fence
like when Mrs Kindhead comes to collect for the Community Chest
grab her and tell her There are unfavorable omens in the sky!
And when the mayor comes to get my vote tell him
When are you going to stop people killing whales!
And when the milkman comes leave him a note in the bottle
Penguin dust, bring me penguin dust, I want penguin dust—

Yet if I should get married and it's Connecticut and snow
and she gives birth to a child and I am sleepless, worn,
up for nights, head bowed against a quiet window, the past behind me,
finding myself in the most common of situations a trembling man
knowledged with responsibility not twig-smear nor Roman coin soup—
O what would that be like!
Surely I'd give it for a nipple a rubber Tacitus
For a rattle a bag of broken Bach records
Tack Della Francesca all over its crib
Sew the Greek alphabet on its bib
And build for its playpen a roofless Parthenon

No, I doubt I'd be that kind of father
not rural not snow no quiet window
but hot smelly tight New York City
seven flights up roaches and rats in the walls
a fat Reichian wife screeching over potatoes Get a job!
And five nose running brats in love with Batman
And the neighbors all toothless and dry haired
like those hag masses of the 18th century
all wanting to come in and watch TV
The landlord wants his rent
Grocery store Blue Cross Gas & Electric Knights of Columbus
Impossible to lie back and dream Telephone snow, ghost parking—
No! I should not get married I should never get married!
But—imagine If I were married to a beautiful sophisticated woman
tall and pale wearing an elegant black dress and long black gloves
holding a cigarette holder in one hand and a highball in the other
and we lived high up in a penthouse with a huge window
from which we could see all of New York and even farther on clearer
    days
  No, can't imagine myself married to that pleasant prison dream—

O but what about love? I forget love
not that I am incapable of love
it's just that I see love as odd as wearing shoes—
I never wanted to marry a girl who was like my mother
And Ingrid Bergman was always impossible
And there's maybe a girl now but she's already married
And I don't like men and—
but there's got to be somebody!
Because what if I'm 60 years old and not married,
all alone in a furnished room with pee stains on my underwear
and everybody else is married! All the universe married but me!

Ah, yet well I know that were a woman possible as I am possible
then marriage would be possible—
Like SHE in her lonely alien gaud waiting her Egyptian lover
so I wait—bereft of 2,000 years and the bath of life.

GREGORY CORSO

Death

Adieu! farewell earth's bliss!
This world uncertain is:
Fond are life's lustful joys,
Death proves them all but toys.
None from his darts can fly:
I am sick, I must die.
   Lord, have mercy on us!

Rich men, trust not in wealth!
Gold cannot buy you health;
Physic himself must fade;
All things to end are made;
The plague full swift goes by;
I am sick, I must die.
   Lord, have mercy on us!

Beauty is but a flower
Which wrinkles will devour:
Brightness falls from the air;
Queens have died young and fair;
Dust hath closed Helen's eye;
I am sick, I must die.
   Lord, have mercy on us!

Strength stoops unto the grave:
Worms feed on Hector brave;
Swords may not fight with fate;
Earth still holds ope her gate;
'Come! come!' the bells do cry.
I am sick, I must die.
   Lord, have mercy on us!

Wit with his wantonness
Tasteth death's bitterness:
Hell's executioner
Hath no ears for to hear
What vain art can reply:
I am sick, I must die.
    Lord, have mercy on us!

THOMAS NASHE

from KING RICHARD THE SECOND

Let's talk of graves, of worms, and epitaphs.
Make dust our paper, and with rainy eyes
Write sorrow on the bosom of the earth . . .
For God's sake, let us sit upon the ground,
And tell sad stories of the death of kings:
How some have been deposed; some slain in war;
Some haunted by the ghosts they have deposed;
Some poisoned by their wives; some sleeping killed;
All murdered: for within the hollow crown
That rounds the mortal temples of a king
Keeps Death his court; and there the antick sits,
Scoffing his state, and grinning at his pomp;
Allowing him a breath, a little scene,
To monarchize, be feared, and kill with looks;
Infusing him with self and vain conceit—
As if this flesh which walls about our life,
Were brass impregnable; and humoured thus,
Comes at the last, and with a little pin
Bores through his castle-wall, and—farewell king!

WILLIAM SHAKESPEARE

THEY ARE ALL GONE INTO THE WORLD OF LIGHT!

They are all gone into the world of light!
    And I alone sit lingering here;
Their very memory is fair and bright,
    And my sad thoughts doth clear.

It glows and glitters in my cloudy breast
    Like stars upon some gloomy grove,
Or those faint beams in which this hill is dressed
    After the sun's remove.

I see them walking in an air of glory,
    Whose light doth trample on my days;
My days, which are at best but dull and hoary,
    Mere glimmering and decays.

O holy hope, and high humility,
    High as the heavens above!
These are your walks, and you have showed them me
    To kindle my cold love.

Dear, beauteous death! the jewel of the just,
    Shining nowhere but in the dark;
What mysteries do lie beyond thy dust,
    Could man outlook that mark?

He that hath found some fledged bird's nest may know
    At first sight if the bird be flown;
But what fair well or grove he sings in now,
    That is to him unknown.

And yet, as angels in some brighter dreams
    Call to the soul when man doth sleep,
So some strange thoughts transcend our wonted themes,
    And into glory peep.

If a star were confined into a tomb,
    Her captive flames must needs burn there;
But when the hand that locked her up gives room,
    She'll shine through all the sphere.

O Father of eternal life, and all
    Created glories under Thee!
Resume Thy spirit from this world of thrall
    Into true liberty!

Either disperse these mists, which blot and fill
   My perspective still as they pass;
Or else remove me hence unto that hill
   Where I shall need no glass.

HENRY VAUGHAN

TO THE MEMORY OF MR. OLDHAM

Farewell, too little and too lately known,
Whom I began to think and call my own;
For sure our souls were near allied, and thine
Cast in the same poetic mould with mine.
One common note on either lyre did strike,
And knaves and fools we both abhorred alike.
To the same goal did both our studies drive:
The last set out the soonest did arrive.
Thus Nisus fell upon the slippery place,
Whilst his young friend performed and won the race.
O early ripe! to thy abundant store
What could advancing age have added more?
It might (what nature never gives the young)
Have taught the numbers of thy native tongue.
But satire needs not those, and wit will shine
Through the harsh cadence of a rugged line.
A noble error, and but seldom made,
When poets are by too much force betrayed.
Thy gen'rous fruits, though gathered ere their prime,
Still shewed a quickness; and maturing time
But mellows what we write to the dull sweets of rhyme.
Once more, hail, and farewell! farewell, thou young
But ah! too short, Marcellus of our tongue!
Thy brows with ivy and with laurels bound;
But fate and gloomy night encompass thee around.

JOHN DRYDEN

ODE: INTIMATIONS OF IMMORTALITY

FROM RECOLLECTIONS OF EARLY CHILDHOOD

The Child is father of the Man;
And I could wish my days to be
Bound each to each by natural piety.

1

There was a time when meadow, grove, and stream,
The earth, and every common sight,
  To me did seem
 Apparelled in celestial light,
The glory and the freshness of a dream.
It is not now as it hath been of yore—
 Turn wheresoe'er I may,
  By night or day,
The things which I have seen I now can see no more.

2

 The rainbow comes and goes,
 And lovely is the rose,
 The moon doth with delight
Look round her when the heavens are bare,
  Waters on a starry night
  Are beautiful and fair;
 The sunshine is a glorious birth;
 But yet I know, where'er I go,
That there hath passed away a glory from the earth.

3

Now, while the birds thus sing a joyous song,
 And while the young lambs bound
 As to the tabor's sound,
To me alone there came a thought of grief:
A timely utterance gave that thought relief,
 And I again am strong:
The cataracts blow their trumpets from the steep;
No more shall grief of mine the season wrong;
I hear the Echoes through the mountains throng,
The Winds come to me from the fields of sleep,
 And all the earth is gay;
  Land and sea
 Give themselves up to jollity,

And with the heart of May
Doth every Beast keep holiday—
Thou Child of Joy,
Shout round me, let me hear thy shouts, thou happy Shepherd-boy!

4

Ye blesséd Creatures, I have heard the call
Ye to each other make; I see
The heavens laugh with you in your jubilee;
My heart is at your festival,
My head hath its coronal,
The fullness of your bliss, I feel—I feel it all.
Oh, evil day! if I were sullen
While Earth herself is adorning,
This sweet May morning,
And the Children are culling
On every side,
In a thousand valleys far and wide,
Fresh flowers; while the sun shines warm,
And the Babe leaps up on his Mother's arm—
I hear, I hear, with joy I hear!
—But there's a Tree, of many, one,
A single Field which I have looked upon,
Both of them speak of something that is gone:
The Pansy at my feet
Doth the same tale repeat:
Whither is fled the visionary gleam?
Where is it now, the glory and the dream?

5

Our birth is but a sleep and a forgetting:
The Soul that rises with us, our life's Star,
Hath had elsewhere its setting,
And cometh from afar:
Not in entire forgetfulness,
And not in utter nakedness,
But trailing clouds of glory do we come
From God, who is our home:
Heaven lies about us in our infancy!
Shades of the prison-house begin to close
Upon the growing Boy
But he

Beholds the light, and whence it flows,
    He sees it in his joy;
The Youth, who daily farther from the east
      Must travel, still is Nature's Priest,
      And by the vision splendid
      Is on his way attended;
At length the Man perceives it die away,
And fade into the light of common day.

6

Earth fills her lap with pleasures of her own;
Yearnings she hath in her own natural kind,
And, even with something of a Mother's mind,
      And no unworthy aim,
      The homely Nurse doth all she can
To make her foster child, her Inmate Man,
      Forget the glories he hath known,
And that imperial palace whence he came.

7

Behold the Child among his newborn blisses,
A six-years' Darling of a pygmy size!
see, where 'mid work of his own hand he lies,
Fretted by sallies of his mother's kisses,
With light upon him from his father's eyes!
See, at his feet, some little plan or chart,
Some fragment from his dream of human life,
Shaped by himself with newly-learnéd art;
      A wedding or a festival,
      A mourning or a funeral;
        And this hath now his heart,
      And unto this he frames his song;
        Then will he fit his tongue
To dialogues of business, love, or strife;
      But it will not be long
      Ere this be thrown aside,
      And with new joy and pride
The little Actor cons another part;
Filling from time to time his "humorous stage"
With all the Persons, down to palsied Age,
That Life brings with her in her equipage;
      As if his whole vocation
      Were endless imitation.

8

Thou, whose exterior semblance doth belie
       Thy Soul's immensity;
Thou best Philosopher, who yet dost keep
Thy heritage, thou Eye among the blind,
That, deaf and silent, read'st the eternal deep,
Haunted forever by the eternal mind—
       Mighty Prophet! Seer blest!
       On whom those truths do rest,
Which we are toiling all our lives to find,
In darkness lost, the darkness of the grave;
Thou, over whom thy Immortality
Broods like the Day, a Master o'er a Slave,
A Presence which is not to be put by;
Thou little Child, yet glorious in the might
Of heaven-born freedom on thy being's height,
Why with such earnest pains dost thou provoke
The years to bring the inevitable yoke,
Thus blindly with thy blessedness at strife?
Full soon thy Soul shall have her earthly freight,
And custom lie upon thee with a weight,
Heavy as frost, and deep almost as life!

9

       O joy! that in our embers
       Is something that doth live,
       That nature yet remembers
       What was so fugitive!
The thought of our past years in me doth breed
Perpetual benediction: not indeed
For that which is most worthy to be blest;
Delight and liberty, the simple creed
Of Childhood, whether busy or at rest,
With new-fledged hope still fluttering in his breast—
    Not for these I raise
    The song of thanks and praise;
  But for those obstinate questionings
  Of sense and outward things,
  Fallings from us, vanishings;
  Blank misgivings of a creature
Moving about in worlds not realized,
High instincts before which our mortal nature
Did tremble like a guilty thing surprised;

But for those first affections,
Those shadowy recollections,
Which, be they what they may,
Are yet the fountain light of all our day,
Are yet a master light of all our seeing;
Uphold us, cherish, and have power to make
Our noisy years seem moments in the being
Of our eternal silence: truths that wake,
To perish never;
Which neither listlessness, nor mad endeavor,
Nor man nor boy,
Nor all that is at enmity with joy,
Can utterly abolish or destroy!
Hence in a season of calm weather
Though inland far we be,
Our souls have sight of that immortal sea
Which brought us hither,
Can in a moment travel thither,
And see the children sport upon the shore,
And hear the mighty waters rolling evermore.

10

Then sing, ye birds, sing, sing a joyous song!
And let the young lambs bound
As to the tabor's sound!
We in thought will join your throng,
Ye that pipe and ye that play,
Ye that through your hearts today
Feel the gladness of the May!
What though the radiance which was once so bright
Be now forever taken from my sight,
Though nothing can bring back the hour
Of splendor in the grass, of glory in the flower;
We will grieve not, rather find
Strength in what remains behind;
In the primal sympathy
Which having been must ever be;
In the soothing thoughts that spring
Out of human suffering;
In the faith that looks through death,
In years that bring the philosophic mind.

11

And O, ye fountains, meadows, hills, and groves,
Forebode not any severing of our loves!
Yet in my heart of hearts I feel your might;
I only have relinquished one delight
To live beneath your more habitual sway.
I love the brooks which down their channels fret,
Even more than when I tripped lightly as they;
The innocent brightness of a newborn day
    Is lovely yet;
The clouds that gather round the setting sun
Do take a sober coloring from an eye
That hath kept watch o'er man's mortality;
Another race hath been, and other palms are won.
Thanks to the human heart by which we live,
Thanks to its tenderness, its joys, and fears,
To me the meanest flower that blows can give
Thoughts that do often lie too deep for tears.

WILLIAM WORDSWORTH

from SONG OF MYSELF

A child said *What is the grass?* fetching it to me with full hands,
How could I answer the child? I do not know what it is any more than he.
I guess it must be the flag of my disposition, out of hopeful green stuff
    woven.
Or I guess it is the handkerchief of the Lord,
A scented gift and remembrancer designedly dropped,
Bearing the owner's name someway in the corners, that we may see and
    remark, and say *Whose?*

Or I guess the grass is itself a child, the produced babe of the vegetation.

Or I guess it is a uniform hieroglyphic,
And it means, Sprouting alike in broad zones and narrow zones,
Growing among black folks as among white,
Canuck, Tuckahoe, Congressman, Cuff, I give them the same, I receive
    them the same.

And now it seems to me the beautiful uncut hair of graves.
Tenderly will I use you curling grass,
It may be you transpire from the breasts of young men,
It may be if I had known them I would have loved them,
It may be you are from old people, or from offspring taken soon out of their
 mothers' laps,
And here you are the mothers' laps.
This grass is very dark to be from the white heads of old mothers,
Darker than the colorless beards of old men,
Dark to come from under the faint red roof of mouths.
O I perceive after all so many uttering tongues,
And I perceive they do not come from the roofs of mouths for nothing.
I wish I could translate the hints about the dead young men and women,
And the hints about old men and mothers, and the offspring taken soon out
 of their laps.
What do you think has become of the young and old men?
And what do you think has become of the women and children?
They are alive and well somewhere,
The smallest sprout shows there is really no death,
And if ever there was it led forward life, and does not wait at the end to
 arrest it,
And ceased the moment life appeared.
All goes onward and outward, nothing collapses,
And to die is different from what anyone supposed, and luckier.

WALT WHITMAN

BECAUSE I COULD NOT STOP FOR DEATH

Because I could not stop for Death—
He kindly stopped for me—
The Carriage held but just Ourselves—
And Immortality.

We slowly drove—He knew no haste
And I had put away
My labor and my leisure too,
For His Civility—

We passed the School, where Children strove
At Recess—in the Ring—
We passed the Fields of Gazing Grain—
We passed the Setting Sun—

Or rather—He passed Us—
The Dews drew quivering and chill—
For only Gossamer, my Gown—
My Tippet—only Tulle—

We paused before a House that seemed
A Swelling of the Ground—
The Roof was scarcely visible—
The Cornice—in the Ground—

Since then—'tis Centuries—and yet
Feels shorter than the Day
I first surmised the Horses' Heads
Were toward Eternity—

EMILY DICKINSON

HARD CANDY

You were not my mother I
told the nurse, and did not cry
for curious relatives,
miss a day of school, or meet
my father's eyes. But with sleep
came dreams you had come back.

The day they took your clothes
from the closet, I tore down
all the naked hangers;
then sat on the porch eating
hard candy.

RICHARD MESSER

ELEGY FOR JANE

My Student, Thrown by a Horse

I remember the neckcurls, limp and damp as tendrils;
And her quick look, a sidelong pickerel smile;
And how, once startled into talk, the light syllables leaped for her,
And she balanced in the delight of her thought,
A wren, happy, tail into the wind,
Her song trembling the twigs and small branches.
The shade sang with her;
The leaves, their whispers turned to kissing;
And the mold sang in the bleached valleys under the rose.

Oh, when she was sad, she cast herself down into such a pure depth,
Even a father could not find her:
Scraping her cheek against straw;
Stirring the clearest water.

My sparrow, you are not here,
Waiting like a fern, making a spiny shadow.
The sides of wet stones cannot console me,
Nor the moss, wound with the last light.

If only I could nudge you from this sleep,
My maimed darling, my skittery pigeon.
Over this damp grave I speak the words of my love:
I, with no rights in this matter,
Neither father nor lover.

THEODORE ROETHKE

FOR THE ANNIVERSARY OF MY DEATH

Every year without knowing it I have passed the day
When the last fires will wave to me
And the silence will set out
Tireless traveller
Like the beam of a lightless star

Then I will no longer
Find myself in life as in a strange garment
Surprised at the earth
And the love of one woman
And the shamelessness of men
As today writing after three days of rain
Hearing the wren sing and the falling cease
And bowing not knowing what to what

W. S. MERWIN

LADY LAZARUS

I have done it again.
One year in every ten
I manage it—

A sort of walking miracle, my skin
Bright as a Nazi lampshade,
My right foot

A paperweight,
My face a featureless, fine
Jew linen.

Peel off the napkin
O my enemy.
Do I terrify?—

The nose, the eye pits, the full set of teeth?
The sour breath
Will vanish in a day.

Soon, soon the flesh
The grave cave ate will be
At home on me

And I a smiling woman.
I am only thirty.
And like the cat I have nine times to die.

This is Number Three.
What a trash
To annihilate each decade.

What a million filaments.
The peanut-crunching crowd
Shoves in to see

Them unwrap me hand and foot—
The big strip tease.
Gentleman, ladies,

These are my hands,
My knees.
I may be skin and bone,

Nevertheless, I am the same, identical woman.
The first time it happened I was ten.
It was an accident.

The second time I meant
To last it out and not come back at all.
I rocked shut

As a seashell.
They had to call and call
And pick the worms off me like sticky pearls.

Dying
Is an art, like everything else.
I do it exceptionally well.

I do it so it feels like hell.
I do it so it feels real.
I guess you could say I've a call.

It's easy enough to do it in a cell.
It's easy enough to do it and stay put.
It's the theatrical

Comeback in broad day
To the same place, the same face, the same brute
Amused shout:

"A miracle!"
That knocks me out.
There is a charge

For the eyeing of my scars, there is a charge
For the hearing of my heart—
It really goes.

And there is a charge, a very large charge,
For a word or a touch
Or a bit of blood

Or a piece of my hair or my clothes.
So, so, Herr Doktor.
So, Herr Enemy.

I am your opus,
I am your valuable,
The pure gold baby

That melts to a shriek.
I turn and burn.
Do not think I underestimate your great concern.

Ash, ash—
You poke and stir.
Flesh, bone, there is nothing there—

A cake of soap,
A wedding ring,
A gold filling.

Herr God, Herr Lucifer,
Beware
Beware.

Out of the ash
I rise with my red hair
And I eat men like air.

SYLVIA PLATH

FREEDOM, NEW HAMPSHIRE

1

We came to visit the cow
Dying of fever,
Towle said it was already
Shovelled under, in a secret
Burial-place in the woods.
We prowled through the woods
Weeks, we never

Found where. Other
Kids other summers
Must have found the place
And asked, Why is it
Green here? The rich
Guess a grave, maybe,
The poor think a pit

For dung, like the one
We shovelled in in the fall
That came up green
The next year, that may as well
Have been the grave
Of a cow or something
For all that shows. A kid guesses
By whether his house has a bathroom.

2

We found a cowskull once; we thought it was
From one of the asses in the Bible, for the sun
Shone into the holes through which it had seen
Earth as an endless belt carrying gravel, had heard
Its truculence cursed, had learned how sweat
Stinks, and had brayed—shone into the holes
With solemn and majestic light, as if some
Skull somewhere could be Baalbek or the Parthenon.

That night passing Towle's Barn
We saw lights. Towle had lassoed a calf
By its hind legs, and he tugged against the grip
Of the darkness. The cow stood by chewing millet.
Derry and I took hold, too, and hauled.
It was sopping with darkness when it came free.
It was a bullcalf. The cow mopped it awhile,
And we walked around it with a lantern,

And it was sunburned, somehow, and beautiful.
It took a dug as the first business
And sneezed and drank at the milk of light.
When we got it balanced on its legs, it went wobbling
Towards the night. Walking home in darkness
We saw the July moon looking on Freedom New Hampshire,
We smelled the fall in the air, it was the summer,
We thought, Oh this is but the summer!

3
Once I saw the moon
Drift into the sky like a bright
Pregnancy pared
From a goddess who thought
To be beautiful she must keep slender—
Cut loose, and drifting up there
To happen by itself—
And waning, in lost labor;

As we lost our labor
Too—afternoons
When we sat on the gate
By the pasture, under the Ledge,
Buzzing and skirling on toilet-
papered combs tunes
To the rumble-seated cars
Taking the Ossipee Road

On Sundays; for
Though dusk would come upon us
Where we sat, and though we had
Skirled out our hearts in the music,
Yet the dandruffed
Harps we skirled it on
Had done not much better than
Flies, which buzzed, when quick

We trapped them in our hands,
Which went silent when we
Crushed them, which we bore
Downhill to the meadowlark's
Nest full of throats
Which Derry charmed and combed
With an Arabian air, while I
Chucked crushed flies into

Innards I could not see,
For the night had fallen
And the crickets shrilled on all sides
In waves, as if the grassleaves
Shrieked by hillsides
As they grew, and the stars
Made small flashes in the sky,
Like mica flashing in rocks

On the chokecherried Ledge
Where bees I stepped on once
Hit us from behind like a shotgun,
And where we could see
Windowpanes in Freedom flash
And Loon Lake and Winnipesaukee
Flash in the sun
And the blue world flashing.

4
The fingerprints of our eyeballs would zigzag
On the sky; the clouds that came drifting up
Our fingernails would drift into the thin air;
In bed at night there was music if you listened,
Of an old surf breaking far away in the blood.

Kids who come by chance on grass green for a man
Can guess cow, dung, man, anything they want,
To them it is the same. To us who knew him as he was
After the beginning and before the end, it is green
For a name called out of the confusions of the earth—

Winnipesaukee coined like a moon, a bullcalf
Dragged from the darkness where it breaks up again,
Larks which long since have crashed for good in the grass
To which we fed the flies, buzzing ourselves like flies,
While the crickets shrilled beyond us, in July . . .

The mind may sort it out and give it names—
When a man dies he dies trying to say without slurring
The abruptly decaying sounds. It is true
That only flesh dies, and spirit flowers without stop
For men, cows, dung, for all dead things; and it is good, yes—

But an incarnation is in particular flesh
And the dust that is swirled into a shape
And crumbles and is swirled again had but one shape
That was this man. When he is dead the grass
Heals what he suffered, but he remains dead,
And the few who loved him know this until they die.

For my brother, 1925–1957

GALWAY KINNELL

Nature

SPRING

Spring, the sweet spring, is the year's pleasant king;
Then blooms each thing, then maids dance in a ring,
Cold doth not sting, the pretty birds do sing:
   Cuckoo, jug-jug, pu-we, to-witta-woo!

The palm and may make country houses gay,
Lambs frisk and play, the shepherds pipe all day,
And we hear aye birds tune this merry lay:
   Cuckoo, jug-jug, pu-we, to-witta-woo!

The fields breathe sweet, the daisies kiss our feet,
Young lovers meet, old wives a-sunning sit,
In every street these tunes our ears do greet:
   Cuckoo, jug-jug, pu-we, to-witta-woo!
     Spring, the sweet spring!

THOMAS NASHE

THE SPRING

Now that the winter's gone, the earth hath lost
Her snow-white robes; and now no more the frost
Candies the grass, or casts an icy cream
Upon the silver lake or crystal stream:
But the warm sun thaws the benumbed earth,
And makes it tender; gives a sacred birth
To the dead swallow; wakes in hollow tree
The drowsy cuckoo and the humble-bee.
Now do a choir of chirping minstrels bring,
In triumph to the world, the youthful spring:
The valleys, hills, and woods in rich array
Welcome the coming of the long'd-for May.

Now all things smile: only my love doth lower,
Nor hath the scalding noon-day sun the power
To melt that marble ice, which still doth hold
Her heart congeal'd, and makes her pity cold.
The ox, which lately did for shelter fly
Into the stall, doth now securely lie
In open fields; and love no more is made
By the fire-side, but in the cooler shade
Amyntas now doth with his Chloris sleep
Under a sycamore, and all things keep
   Time with the season: only she doth carry
   June in her eyes, in her heart January.

THOMAS CAREW

OF JEOFFRY, HIS CAT

For I will consider my Cat Jeoffry.
For he is the servant of the Living God, duly and daily
   serving him.
For at the first glance of the glory of God in the East he
   worships in his way.
For is this done by wreathing his body seven times round
   with elegant quickness.
For then he leaps up to catch the musk, which is the
   blessing of God upon his prayer.
For he rolls upon prank to work it in.
For having done duty and received blessing he begins to
   consider himself.
For this he performs in ten degrees.
For first he looks upon his fore-paws to see if they are
   clean.
For secondly he kicks up behind to clear away there.
For thirdly he works it upon stretch with the fore-paws
   extended.
For fourthly he sharpens his paws by wood.
For fifthly he washes himself.
For sixthly he rolls upon wash.
For seventhly he fleas himself, that he may not be inter-
   rupted upon the beat.
For eighthly he rubs himself against a post.

For ninthly he looks up for his instructions.

For tenthly he goes in quest of food.

For having consider'd God and himself he will consider his neighbour.

For if he meets another cat he will kiss her in kindness.

For when he takes his prey he plays with it to give it chance.

For one mouse in seven escapes by his dallying.

For when his day's work is done his business more properly begins.

For [he] keeps the Lord's watch in the night against the adversary.

For he counteracts the powers of darkness by his electrical skin and glaring eyes.

For he counteracts the Devil, who is death, by brisking about the life.

For in his morning orisons he loves the sun and the sun loves him.

For he is of the tribe of Tiger.

For the Cherub Cat is a term of the Angel Tiger.

For he has the subtlety and hissing of a serpent, which in goodness he suppresses.

For he will not do destruction, if he is well-fed, neither will he spit without provocation.

For he purrs in thankfulness, when God tells him he's a good Cat.

For he is an instrument for the children to learn benevolence upon.

For every house is incompleat without him and a blessing is lacking in the spirit.

For the Lord commanded Moses concerning the cats at the departure of the Children of Israel from Egypt.

For every family had one cat at least in the bag.

For the English Cats are the best in Europe.

For he is the cleanest in the use of his fore-paws of any quadrupede.

For the dexterity of his defence is an instance of the love of God to him exceedingly.

For he is the quickest to his mark of any creature.

For he is tenacious of his point.

For he is a mixture of gravity and waggery.

For he knows that God is his Saviour.

For there is nothing sweeter than his peace when at rest.

For there is nothing brisker than his life when in motion.

For he is of the Lord's poor and so indeed is he called
    by benevolence perpetually—Poor Jeoffry! poor
    Jeoffry! the rat has bit thy throat.

For I bless the name of the Lord Jesus that Jeoffry is
    better.

For the divine spirit comes about his body to sustain it in
    compleat cat.

For his tongue is exceeding pure so that it has in purity
    what it wants in musick.

For he is docile and can learn certain things.

For he can set up with gravity which is patience upon
    approbation.

For he can fetch and carry, which is patience in employ-
    ment.

For he can jump over a stick which is patience upon proof
    positive.

For he can spraggle upon waggle at the word of
    command.

For he can jump from an eminence into his master's
    bosom.

For he can catch the cork and toss it again.

For he is hated by the hypocrite and miser.

For the former is affraid of detection.

For the latter refuses the charge.

For he camels his back to bear the first notion of
    business.

For he is good to think on, if a man would express himself
    neatly.

For he made a great figure in Egypt for his signal
    services.

For he killed the Icneumon-rat very pernicious by land.

For his ears are so acute that they sting again.

For from this proceeds the passing quickness of his
    attention.

For by stroaking of him I have found out electricity.

For I perceived God's light about him both wax and fire.

For the Electrical fire is the spiritual substance, which
    God sends from heaven to sustain the bodies both
    of man and beast.

For God has blessed him in the variety of his movements.

For, tho' he cannot fly, he is an excellent clamberer.
For his motions upon the face of the earth are more than
    any other quadrupede.
For he can tread to all the measures upon the musick.
For he can swim for life.
For he can creep.

CHRISTOPHER SMART

LINES

Composed a few miles above Tintern Abbey, on revisiting the Banks of the Wye during a tour, July 13, 1798

Five years have past; five summers, with the length
Of five long winters! and again I hear
These waters, rolling from their mountain-springs
With a soft inland murmur.—Once again
Do I behold these steep and lofty cliffs,
That on a wild secluded scene impress
Thoughts of more deep seclusion; and connect
The landscape with the quiet of the sky.
The day is come when I again repose
Here, under this dark sycamore, and view
These plots of cottage-ground, these orchard-tufts,
Which at this season, with their unripe fruits,
Are clad in one green hue, and lose themselves
'Mid groves and copses. Once again I see
These hedge-rows, hardly hedge-rows, little lines
Of sportive wood run wild: these pastoral farms,
Green to the very door; and wreaths of smoke
Sent up, in silence, from among the trees!
With some uncertain notice, as might seem
Of vagrant dwellers in the houselsss woods,
Or of some hermit's cave, where by his fire
The hermit sits alone.
                These beauteous forms,
Through a long absence, have not been to me
As is a landscape to a blind man's eye:
But oft, in lonely rooms, and 'mid the din
Of towns and cities, I have owed to them

In hours of weariness, sensations sweet,
Felt in the blood, and felt along the heart;
And passing even into my purer mind,
With tranquil restoration:—feelings too
Of unremembered pleasure: such, perhaps,
As have no slight or trivial influence
On that best portion of a good man's life,
His little, nameless, unremembered, acts
Of kindness and of love. Nor less, I trust,
To them I may have owed another gift,
Of aspect more sublime; that blessèd mood,
In which the burthen of the mystery,
In which the heavy and the weary weight
Of all this unintelligible world,
Is lightened:—that serene and blessèd mood,
In which the affections gently lead us on,—
Until, the breath of this corporeal frame
And even the motion of our human blood
Almost suspended, we are laid asleep
In body, and become a living soul:
While with an eye made quiet by the power
Of harmony, and the deep power of joy,
We see into the life of things.
                                    If this
Be but a vain belief, yet, oh! how oft—
In darkness and amid the many shapes
Of joyless daylight; when the fretful stir
Unprofitable, and the fever of the world,
Have hung upon the beatings of my heart—
How oft, in spirit, have I turned to thee,
O sylvan Wye! thou wanderer thro' the woods,
How often has my spirit turned to thee!
   And now, with gleams of half-extinguished thought,
With many recognitions dim and faint,
And somewhat of a sad perplexity,
The picture of the mind revives again:
While here I stand, not only with the sense
Of present pleasure, but with pleasing thoughts
That in this moment there is life and food
For future years. And so I dare to hope,
Though changed, no doubt, from what I was when first
I came among these hills; when like a roe
I bounded o'er the mountains, by the sides

Of the deep rivers, and the lonely streams,
Wherever nature led: more like a man
Flying from something that he dreads, than one
Who sought the thing he loved. For nature then
(The coarser pleasures of my boyish days,
And their glad animal movements all gone by)
To me was all in all. I cannot paint
What then I was. The sounding cataract
Haunted me like a passion: the tall rock,
The mountain, and the deep and gloomy wood,
Their colors and their forms, were then to me
An appetite; a feeling and a love,
That had no need of a remoter charm,
By thought supplied, nor any interest
Unborrowed from the eye.—That time is past,
And all its aching joys are now no more,
And all its dizzy raptures. Not for this
Faint I, nor mourn nor murmur; other gifts
Have followed; for such loss, I would believe,
Abundant recompense. For I have learned
To look on nature, not as in the hour
Of thoughtless youth; but hearing oftentimes
The still, sad music of humanity,
Nor harsh nor grating, though of ample power
To chasten and subdue. And I have felt
A presence that disturbs me with the joy
Of elevated thoughts; a sense sublime
Of something far more deeply interfused,
Whose dwelling is the light of setting suns,
And the round ocean and the living air,
And the blue sky, and in the mind of man;
A motion and a spirit, that impels
All thinking things, all objects of all thought,
And rolls through all things. Therefore am I still
A lover of the meadows and the woods,
And mountains; and of all that we behold
From this green earth; of all the mighty world
Of eye, and ear—both what they half create,
And what perceive; well pleased to recognize
In nature and the language of the sense
The anchor of my purest thoughts, the nurse,
The guide, the guardian of my heart, and soul
Of all my moral being.

Nor perchance,
If I were not thus taught, should I the more
Suffer my genial spirits to decay:
For thou art with me here upon the banks
Of this fair river; thou my dearest Friend,
My dear, dear Friend; and in thy voice I catch
The language of my former heart, and read
My former pleasures in the shooting lights
Of thy wild eyes. Oh! yet a little while
May I behold in thee what I was once,
My dear, dear Sister! and this prayer I make,
Knowing that Nature never did betray
The heart that loved her; 'tis her privilege,
Through all the years of this our life, to lead
From joy to joy: for she can so inform
The mind that is within us, so impress
With quietness and beauty, and so feed
With lofty thoughts, that neither evil tongues,
Rash judgments, nor the sneers of selfish men,
Nor greetings where no kindness is, nor all
The dreary intercourse of daily life,
Shall e'er prevail against us, or disturb
Our cheerful faith, that all which we behold
Is full of blessings. Therefore let the moon
Shine on thee in thy solitary walk;
And let the misty mountain winds be free
To blow against thee: and, in after years,
When these wild ecstasies shall be matured
Into a sober pleasure; when thy mind
Shall be a mansion for all lovely forms,
Thy memory be as a dwelling place
For all sweet sounds and harmonies; oh! then,
If solitude, or fear, or pain, or grief
Should be thy portion, with what healing thoughts
Of tender joy wilt thou remember me,
And these my exhortations! Nor, perchance—
If I should be where I no more can hear
Thy voice, nor catch from thy wild eyes these gleams
Of past existence—wilt thou then forget
That on the banks of this delightful stream
We stood together; and that I, so long
A worshiper of Nature, hither came
Unwearied in that service; rather say

With warmer love—oh! with far deeper zeal
Of holier love. Nor wilt thou then forget,
That after many wanderings, many years
Of absence, these steep woods and lofty cliffs,
And this green pastoral landscape, were to me
More dear, both for themselves and for thy sake!

WILLIAM WORDSWORTH

from SONG OF MYSELF

I think I could turn and live with animals, they are so placid and self-
    contained,
I stand and look at them long and long.
They do not sweat and whine about their condition,
They do not lie awake in the dark and weep for their sins,
They do not make me sick discussing their duty to God,
Not one is dissatisfied, not one is demented with the mania of owning
    things,
Not one kneels to another, nor to his kind that lived thousands of years ago,
Not one is respectable or unhappy over the whole earth.
So they show their relations to me and I accept them,
They bring me token of myself, they evince them plainly in their possession.

I wonder where they get those tokens,
Did I pass that way huge times ago and negligently drop them?
Myself moving forward then and now and forever,
Gathering and showing more always and with velocity,
Infinite and omnigenous, and the like of these among them,
Not too exclusive toward the reachers of my remembrancers,
Picking out here one that I love, and now go with him on brotherly terms.
A gigantic beauty of a stallion, fresh and responsive to my caresses,
Head high in the forehead, wide between the ears,
Limbs glossy and supple, tail dusting the ground,
Eyes full of sparkling wickedness, ears finely cut, flexibly moving.
His nostrils dilate as my heels embrace him,
His well-built limbs tremble with pleasure as we race around and return.

I but use you a minute, then I resign you, stallion,
Why do I need your paces when I myself outgallop them?
Even as I stand or sit passing faster than you.

WALT WHITMAN

ON THE SEA

It keeps eternal whisperings around
  Desolate shores, and with its mighty swell
  Gluts twice ten thousand Caverns, till the spell
Of Hecate leaves them their old shadowy sound.
Often 'tis in such gentle temper found,
  That scarcely will the very smallest shell
  Be moved for days from where it sometime fell,
When last the winds of Heaven were unbound.
Oh ye! who have your eyeballs vexed and tired,
  Feast them upon the wideness of the Sea;
    Oh ye! whose ears are dinned with uproar rude,
  Or fed too much with cloying melody—
    Sit ye near some old Cavern's Mouth and brood,
Until ye start, as if the sea nymphs quired!

JOHN KEATS

VOYAGES II

—And yet this great wink of eternity,
Of rimless floods, unfettered leewardings,
Samite sheeted and processioned where
Her undinal vast belly moonward bends,
Laughing the wrapt inflections of our love;

Take this Sea, whose diapason knells
On scrolls of silver snowy sentences,
The sceptred terror of whose sessions rends
As her demeanors motion well or ill,
All but the pieties of lovers' hands.

And onward, as bells off San Salvador
Salute the crocus lustres of the stars,
In these poinsettia meadows of her tides,—
Adagios of islands, O my Prodigal,
Complete the dark confessions her veins spell.

Mark how her turning shoulders wind the hours,
And hasten while her penniless rich palms
Pass superscription of bent foam and wave,—
Hasten, while they are true,—sleep, death, desire,
Close round one instant in one floating flower.

Bind us in time, O Seasons clear, and awe.
O minstrel galleons of Carib fire,
Bequeath us to no earthly shore until
Is answered in the vortex of our grave
The seal's wide spindrift gaze toward paradise.

HART CRANE

WHALES WEEP NOT!

They say the sea is cold, but the sea contains
the hottest blood of all, and the wildest, the most urgent.

All the whales in the wider deeps, hot are they, as they urge
on and on, and dive beneath the icebergs.
The right whales, the sperm-whales, the hammer-heads, the killers
there they blow, there they blow, hot wild white breath out of the
   sea!

And they rock, and they rock, through the sensual ageless ages
on the depths of the seven seas,
and through the salt they reel with drunk delight
and in the tropics tremble they with love

and roll with massive, strong desire, like gods.
Then the great bull lies up against his bride
in the blue deep of the sea.
as mountain pressing on mountain, in the zest of life:
and out of the inward roaring of the inner red ocean of whale blood
the long tip reaches strong, intense, like the maelstrom-tip, and
   comes to rest
in the clasp and the soft, wild clutch of a she-whale's fathomless
   body.

And over the bridge of the whale's strong phallus, linking the
   wonder of whales
the burning archangels under the sea keep passing, back and forth,
keep passing archangels of bliss
from him to her, from her to him, great Cherubim
that wait on whales in mid-ocean, suspended in the waves of the sea
great heaven of whales in the waters, old hierarchies.

And enormous mother whales lie dreaming suckling their whale-
   tender young
and dreaming with strange whale eyes wide open in the waters of
   the beginning and the end.

And bull-whales gather their women and whale-calves in a ring
when danger threatens, on the surface of the ceaselsss flood
and range themselves like great fierce Seraphim facing the threat
encircling their huddled monsters of love.
and all this happiness in the sea, in the salt
where God is also love, but without words:
and Aphrodite is the wife of whales
most happy, happy she!

and Venus among the fishes skips and is a she-dolphin
she is the gay, delighted porpoise sporting with love and the sea
she is the female tunny-fish, round and happy among the males
and dense with happy blood, dark rainbow bliss in the sea.

D. H. LAWRENCE

THE HORSES

Barely a twelvemonth after
The seven days war that put the world to sleep,
Late in the evening the strange horses came.
By then we had made our covenant with silence,
But in the first few days it was so still
We listened to our breathing and were afraid.
On the second day
The radios failed; we turned the knobs; no answer.
On the third day a warship passed us, heading north,
Dead bodies piled on the deck. On the sixth day
A plane plunged over us into the sea. Thereafter
Nothing. The radios dumb;
And still they stand in corners of our kitchens,
And stand, perhaps, turned on, in a million rooms
All over the world. But now if they should speak,
If on a sudden they should speak again,
If on the stroke of noon a voice should speak,
We would not listen, we would not let it bring
That old bad world that swallowed its children quick
At one great gulp. We would not have it again.
Sometimes we think of the nations lying asleep,
Curled blindly in impenetrable sorrow,
And then the thought confounds us with its strangeness.
The tractors lie about our fields; at evening
They look like dank sea-monsters couched and waiting.
We leave them where they are and let them rust:
'They'll moulder away and be like other loam.'
We make our oxen drag our rusty ploughs,
Long laid aside. We have gone back
Far past our fathers' land.
                                    And then, that evening
Late in the summer the strange horses came.
We heard a distant tapping on the road,
A deepening drumming; it stopped, went on again
And at the corner changed to hollow thunder.
We saw the heads
Like a wild wave charging and were afraid.
We had sold our horses in our fathers' time
To buy new tractors. Now they were strange to us
As fabulous steeds set on an ancient shield

Or illustrations in a book of knights.
We did not dare go near them. Yet they waited,
Stubborn and shy, as if they had been sent
By an old command to find our whereabouts
And that long-lost archaic companionship.
In the first movement we had never a thought
That they were creatures to be owned and used.
Among them were some half-a-dozen colts
Dropped in some wilderness of the broken world,
Yet new as if they had come from their own Eden.
Since then they have pulled our ploughs and borne our loads
But that free servitude still can pierce our hearts.
Our life is changed; their coming our beginning.

EDWIN MUIR

REPOSE OF RIVERS

The willows carried a slow sound,
A sarabande the wind mowed on the mead.
I could never remember
That seething, steady leveling of the marshes
Till age had brought me to the sea.

Flags, weeds. And remembrance of steep alcoves
Where cypresses shared the noon's
Tyranny; they drew me into hades almost.
And mammoth turtles climbing sulphur dreams
Yielded, while sun-silt rippled them
Asunder . . .

How much I would have bartered! the black gorge
And all the singular nestings in the hills
Where beavers learn stitch and tooth.
The pond I entered once and quickly fled—
I remember now its singing willow rim.

And finally, in that memory all things nurse;
After the city that I finally passed
With scalding unguents spread and smoking darts
The monsoon cut across the delta
At gulf gates . . . There, beyond the dykes

I heard wind flaking sapphire, like this summer,
And willows could not hold more steady sound.

HART CRANE

SPRING IS LIKE A PERHAPS HAND

Spring is like a perhaps hand
(which comes carefully
out of Nowhere)arranging
a window,into which people look(while
people stare
arranging and changing placing
carefully there a strange
thing and a known thing here)and

changing everything carefully

spring is like a perhaps
Hand in a window
(carefully to
and fro moving New and
Old things,while
people stare carefully
moving a perhaps
fraction of flower here placing
an inch of air there)and

without breaking anything.

E. E. CUMMINGS

THE PEACE OF WILD THINGS

When despair for the world grows in me
and I wake in the night at the least sound
in fear of what my life and my children's lives may be,
I go and lie down where the wood drake
rests in his beauty on the water, and the great heron feeds.
I come into the peace of wild things
who do not tax their lives with forethought
of grief. I come into the presence of still water.
And I feel above me the day-blind stars
waiting with their light. For a time
I rest in the grace of the world, and am free.

WENDELL BERRY

THE HEAVEN OF ANIMALS

Here they are. The soft eyes open.
If they have lived in a wood
It is a wood.
If they have lived on plains
It is grass rolling
Under their feet forever.

Having no souls, they have come,
Anyway, beyond their knowing.
Their instincts wholly bloom
And they rise.
The soft eyes open.

To match them, the landscape flowers,
Outdoing, desperately
Outdoing what is required:
The richest wood,
The deepest field.

For some of these,
It could not be the place
It is, without blood.
These hunt, as they have done,
But with claws and teeth grown perfect,

More deadly than they can believe.
They stalk more silently,
And crouch on the limbs of trees,
And their descent
Upon the bright backs of their prey

May take years
In a sovereign floating of joy.
And those that are hunted
Know this as their life,
Their reward: to walk

Under such trees in full knowledge
Of what is in glory above them,
And to feel no fear,
But acceptance, compliance.
Fulfilling themselves without pain

At the cycle's center,
They tremble, they walk
Under the tree,
They fall, they are torn,
They rise, they walk again.

JAMES DICKEY

NAVAJO CORRESPONDENCES

(First Set)
1. red willow
    Sun
    yellow

2. arrow
   Wind
   Cicada
   arrow-crossing
   life

3. aspen
   white
   summer
   pink

4. Bat
   Darkness
   wing feather
   Big Fly

5. Big Fly
   feather
   Wind
   skin at tip of tongue
   speech

(Second Set)
1. black
   Darkness
   Black Wind
   yellow squash

2. Black God
   Black Star
   Darkness

3. bull-roarer
   lightning
   snakes
   pokers
   danger line
   hoops

4. ambush woods
   emetic frames
   pokers

5. cane
   digging stick
   arrow
   water

(Third Set)
1. cotton
   motion
   clouds

2. Earth
   Yellow Wind
   Pink Thunder
   Reared-in-the-earth
   Pink Snake
   rainbow
   redshell
   sunglow
   Holy Girl

3. feather cloak
   yellow lightning

4. Frog
   hail
   potatoes
   dumplings

5. Old Age
   ax
   Frog

(Fourth Set)
1. cloud water
   fog
   moss

2. smoke
   cloud
   rain
   acceptance
   breathing in

3. spiderweb
   nerves & veins
   marrow
   conveyances

4. red willow
   water
   blue

5. yellow
   Yellow-evening-light
   Yellow Wind
   black squash

(arranged by Jerome Rothenberg)

A BLESSING

Just off the highway to Rochester, Minnesota,
Twilight bounds softly forth on the grass.
And the eyes of those two Indian ponies
Darken with kindness.
They have come gladly out of the willows
To welcome my friend and me.
We step over the barbed wire into the pasture
Where they have been grazing all day, alone.
They ripple tensely, they can hardly contain their happiness
That we have come.
They bow shyly as wet swans. They love each other.
There is no loneliness like theirs.
At home once more,
They begin munching the young tufts of spring in the darkness.
I would like to hold the slenderer one in my arms,
For she has walked over to me
And nuzzled my left hand.
She is black and white,
Her mane falls wild on her forehead,
And the light breeze moves me to caress her long ear
That is delicate as the skin over a girl's wrist.

Suddenly I realize
That if I stepped out of my body I would break
Into blossom.

JAMES WRIGHT

THE ELWHA RIVER

1

I was a girl waiting by the roadside for my boyfriend to come
in his car. I was pregnant, I should have been going to high
school. I walked up the road when he didn't come, over a bridge;
I saw a sleeping man. I came to the Elwha River—grade
school—classes—I went and sat down with the children.
The teacher was young and sad-looking, homely; she assigned
us an essay:
"What I Just Did."

"I was waiting for my boyfriend by the Elwha bridge. The bridge
was redwood, a fresh bridge with inner bark still clinging on
some logs—it smelled good. There was a man there sleeping
under redwood trees. He had a box of flies by his head; he was
on the ground. I crossed the Elwha River by a meadow; it had
a flat stony prong between two river forks . . ."

Thinking this would please the teacher. We handed all the
papers in, and got them back—mine was C minus. The children
then went home; the teacher came to me and said "I don't
like you." "Why?"
—"Because I used to be a whore."

The Elwha River, I explained, is a real river, but not the river I
described. Where I had just walked was real but for the dream
river—actually the Elwha doesn't fork at that point.

As I write this I must remind myself that there is another Elwha,
the actual Olympic peninsula river, which is not the river I took
pains to recollect as real in the dream.

There are no redwoods north of southern
Curry County, Oregon.

2

Marble hollow-ground hunting knife;

    pigleather tobacco pouch
left on the ground at Whiskey Bend along
the Elwha, 1950—

Sewing kit. Blown off the cot beside me
on the boatdeck by a sudden wind
                           South China Sea;

A black beret Joanne had given me for my birthday
left in some
Kawaramachi bar.

Swiss army knife stole from my pants
   at Juhu Beach outside Bombay,
     a fine italic pen,

Theodora, Kitty-chan,
   bottle of wine got broke.
   things left on the sand.

Lost things.

3

Elwha, from its source. Threadwhite falls
out of snow-tunnel mouths with
cold mist-breath
saddles of deep snow on the ridges—

    o wise stream—o living flow
  o milky confluence, bank cutter
        alder toppler
        make meander,
swampy acres   elk churned mud

The big Douglas fir in this valley.
Nobly groovd bark, it adapts: where Sitka spruce
cannot.
   Redwood and sequoia
resisting and enduring, as against adaptation;
one mind.

   Trail crew foreman says they finally got wise
to making trails low on the outside, so water
can run off good—before they were worried because
packstock always walks the outside of the trail
because they don't want to bump their loads on rocks
or trees.   "punching out all the way from N Fork
over Low Divide & clear back here, this punchin gets
mighty old"

Puncheon slab saw cut *wowed*

"They got rip-cut chains now maybe different rakers
   this here punchin gets old"

   About 12:30 come to Whiskey Bend.
   That lowland smell.

GARY SNYDER

STAYING ALIVE

   Staying alive in the woods is a matter of calming down
   At first and deciding whether to wait for rescue,
   Trusting to others,
   Or simply to start walking and walking in one direction
   Till you come out—or something happens to stop you.
   By far the safer choice
   Is to settle down where you are, and try to make a living
   Off the land, camping near water, away from shadows.
   Eat no white berries;
   Spit out all bitterness. Shooting at anything
   Means hiking further and further every day
   To hunt survivors;
   It may be best to learn what you have to learn without a gun,

Not killing but watching birds and animals go
In and out of shelter
At will. Following their example, build for a whole season:
Facing across the wind in your lean-to,
You may feel wilder,
And nothing, not even you, will have to stay in hiding.
If you have no matches, a stick and a fire-bow
Will keep you warmer,
Or the crystal of your watch, filled with water, held up to the
    sun
Will do the same, in time. In case of snow,
Drifting toward winter,
Don't try to stay awake through the night, afraid of
    freezing—
The bottom of your mind knows all about zero;
It will turn you over
And shake you till you waken. If you have trouble sleeping
Even in the best of weather, jumping to follow
The unidentifiable noises of the night and feeling
Bears and packs of wolves nuzzling your elbow,
Remember the trappers
Who treated them indifferently and were left alone.
If you hurt yourself, no one will comfort you
Or take your temperature,
So stumbling, wading, and climbing are as dangerous as
    flying.
But if you decide, at last, you must break through
In spite of all danger,
Think of yourself by time and not by distance, counting
Wherever you're going by how long it takes you;
No other measure
Will bring you safe to nightfall. Follow no streams: they run
Under the ground or fall into wilder country.
Remember the stars
And moss when your mind runs into circles. If it should rain,
Or the fog should roll the horizon in around you,
Hold still for hours
Or days, if you must, or weeks, for seeing is believing
In the wilderness. And if you find a pathway,
Wheel rut, or fence wire,
Retrace it left or right—someone knew where he was going
Once upon a time, and you can follow

Hopefully, somewhere,
Just in case. There may even come, on some uncanny
    evening,
A time when you're warm and dry, well fed, not thirsty,
Uninjured, without fear,
When nothing, either good or bad, is happening.
This is called staying alive. It's temporary.
What occurs after
Is doubtful. You must always be ready for something to
    come bursting
Through the far edge of a clearing, running toward you,
Grinning from ear to ear
And hoarse with welcome. Or something crossing and
    hovering
Overhead, as light as air, like a break in the sky,
Wondering what you are.
Here you are face to face with the problem of recognition.
Having no time to make smoke, too much to say,
You should have a mirror
With a tiny hole in the back for better aiming, for reflecting
Whatever disaster you can think of, to show
The way you suffer.
These body signals have universal meaning: If you are lying
Flat on your back with arms outstretched behind you,
You say you require
Emergency treatment; if you are standing erect and holding
Arms horizontal, you mean you are not ready;
If you hold them over
Your head, you want to be picked up. Three of anything
Is a sign of distress. Afterward, if you see
No ropes, no ladders,
No maps or messages falling, no searchlights or trails blazing,
Then chances are, you should be prepared to burrow
Deep for a deep winter.

DAVID WAGONER

THE BEAR

1

In late winter
I sometimes glimpse bits of steam
coming up from
some fault in the old snow
and bend close and see it is lung-colored
and put down my nose
and know
the chilly, enduring odor of bear.

2

I take a wolf's rib and whittle
it sharp at both ends
and coil it up
and freeze it in blubber and place it out
on the fairway of the bears.

And when it has vanished
I move out on the bear tracks,
roaming in circles
until I come to the first, tentative, dark
splash on the earth.

And I set out
running, following the splashes
of blood wandering over the world.
At the cut, gashed resting places
I stop and rest,
at the crawl-marks
where he lay out on his belly
to overpass some stretch of bauchy ice
I lie out
dragging myself forward with bear-knives in my fists.

3

On the third day I begin to starve,
at nightfall I bend down as I knew I would
at a turd sopped in blood,
and hesitate, and pick it up,
and thrust it in my mouth, and gnash it down,
and rise
and go on running.

4

On the seventh day,
living by now on bear blood alone,
I can see his upturned carcass far out ahead, a scraggled,
steamy hulk,
the heavy fur riffling in the wind.

I come up to him
and stare at the narrow-spaced, petty eyes,
the dismayed
face laid back on the shoulder, the nostrils
flared, catching
perhaps the first taint of me as he
died.

I hack
a ravine in his thigh, and eat and drink,
and tear him down his whole length
and open him and climb in
and close him up after me, against the wind,
and sleep.

5

And dream
of lumbering flatfooted
over the tundra,
stabbed twice from within,
splattering a trail behind me,
splattering it out no matter which way I lurch,
no matter which parabola of bear-transcendence,
which dance of solitude I attempt,
which gravity-clutched leap,
which trudge, which groan.

6

Until one day I totter and fall—
fall on this
stomach that has tried so hard to keep up,
to digest the blood as it leaked in,
to break up
and digest the bone itself: and now the breeze
blows over me, blows off
the hideous belches of ill-digested bear blood
and rotted stomach
and the ordinary, wretched odor of bear,

blows across
my sore, lolled tongue a song
or screech, until I think I must rise up
and dance. And I lie still.

7

I awaken I think. Marshlights
reappear, geese
come trailing again up the flyway.
In her ravine under old snow the dam-bear
lies, licking
lumps of smeared fur
and drizzly eyes into shapes
with her tongue. And one
hairy-soled trudge stuck out before me,
the next groaned out,
the next,
the next,
the rest of my days I spend
wandering: wondering
what, anyway,
was that sticky infusion, that rank flavor of blood, that
  poetry, by which I lived?

GALWAY KINNELL

Society

LONDON

I wander thro' each charter'd street,
Near where the charter'd Thames does flow,
And mark in every face I meet
Marks of weakness, marks of woe.

In every cry of every man,
In every Infant's cry of fear,
In every voice, in every ban,
The mind-forg'd manacles I hear.

How the Chimney-sweeper's cry
Every blackning Church appalls;
And the hapless Soldier's sigh
Runs in blood down Palace walls.

But most thro' midnight streets I hear
How the youthful Harlot's curse
Blasts the new-born Infant's tear,
And blights with plagues the Marriage hearse.

WILLIAM BLAKE

BADGER

When midnight comes a host of dogs and men
Go out and track the badger to his den,
And put a sack within the hole, and lie
Till the old grunting badger passes by.
He comes and hears—they let the strongest loose.
The old fox hears the noise and drops the goose.
The poacher shoots and hurries from the cry,

And the old hare half wounded buzzes by.
They get a forkéd stick to bear him down
And clap the dogs and take him to the town,
And bait him all the day with many dogs,
And laugh and shout and fright the scampering hogs.
He runs along and bites at all he meets:
They shout and hollo down the noisy streets.

He turns about to face the loud uproar
And drives the rebels to their very door.
The frequent stone is hurled where'er they go;
When badgers fight, then everyone's a foe.
The dogs are clapped and urged to join the fray;
The badger turns and drives them all away.
Though scarcely half as big, demure and small,
He fights with dogs for hours and beats them all.
The heavy mastiff, savage in the fray,
Lies down and licks his feet and turns away.
The bulldog knows his match and waxes cold,
The badger grins and never leaves his hold.
He drives the crowd and follows at their heels
And bites them through—the drunkard swears and reels.
The frighted women take the boys away,
The blackguard laughs and hurries on the fray.
He tries to reach the woods, an awkward race,
But sticks and cudgels quickly stop the chase.
He turns again and drives the noisy crowd
And beats the many dogs in noises loud.
He drives away and beats them every one,
And then they loose them all and set them on.
He falls as dead and kicked by boys and men,
Then starts and grins and drives the crowd again;
Till kicked and torn and beaten out he lies
And leaves his hold and crackles, groans, and dies.

JOHN CLARE

DISABLED

He sat in a wheeled chair, waiting for dark,
And shivered in his ghastly suit of grey,
Legless, sewn short at elbow. Through the park
Voices of boys rang saddening like a hymn,
Voices of play and pleasure after day,
Till gathering sleep had mothered them from him.

About this time Town used to swing so gay
When glow-lamps budded in the light blue trees,
And girls glanced lovelier as the air grew dim,—
In the old times, before he threw away his knees.
Now he will never feel again how slim
Girls' waists are, or how warm their subtle hands;
All of them touch him like some queer disease.

There was an artist silly for his face,
For it was younger than his youth, last year.
Now, he is old; his back will never brace;
He's lost his colour very far from here,
Poured it down shell-holes till the veins ran dry,
And half his lifetime lapsed in the hot race,
And leap of purple spurted from his thigh.

One time he liked a blood-smear down his leg,
After the matches, carried shoulder-high.
It was after football, when he'd drunk a peg,
He thought he'd better join.—He wonders why.
Someone had said he'd look a god in kilts,
That's why; and may be, too, to please his Meg;
Aye, that was it, to please the giddy jilts
He asked to join. He didn't have to beg;
Smiling they wrote his lie; aged nineteen years.
Germans he scarcely thought of; all their guilt,
And Austria's, did not move him. And no fears
Of Fear came yet. He thought of jewelled hilts
For daggers in plaid socks; of smart salutes;
And care of arms; and leave; and pay arrears;
Esprit de corps; and hints for young recruits.
And soon, he was drafted out with drums and cheers.

Some cheered him home, but not as crowds cheer Goal.
Only a solemn man who brought him fruits
Thanked him; and then inquired about his soul.

. . .

Now, he will spend a few sick years in Institutes,
And do what things the rules consider wise,
And take whatever pity they may dole.
To-night he noticed how the women's eyes
Passed from him to the strong men that were whole.
How cold and late it is! Why don't they come
And put him into bed? Why don't they come?

WILFRED OWEN

THEME FOR ENGLISH B

The instructor said,

> *Go home and write*
> *a page tonight.*
> *And let that page come out of you—*
> *Then, it will be true.*

I wonder if it's that simple?
I am twenty-two, colored, born in Winston-Salem.
I went to school there, then Durham, then here
to this college on the hill above Harlem.
I am the only colored student in my class.
The steps from the hill lead down into Harlem,
through a park, then I cross St. Nicholas,
Eighth Avenue, Seventh, and I come to the Y,
the Harlem Branch Y, where I take the elevator
up to my room, sit down, and write this page:

It's not easy to know what is true for you or me
at twenty-two, my age. But I guess I'm what
I feel and see and hear, Harlem, I hear you:
hear you, hear me—we two—you, me, talk on this page.
(I hear New York, too.) Me—who?

Well, I like to eat, sleep, drink, and be in love.
I like to work, read, learn, and understand life.
I like a pipe for a Christmas present,
or records—Bessie, bop, or Bach.
I guess being colored doesn't make me *not* like
the same things other folks like who are other races.
So will my page be colored that I write?

Being me, it will not be white.
But it will be
a part of you, instructor.
You are white—
yet a part of me, as I am a part of you.
That's American.
Sometimes perhaps you don't want to be a part of me.
Nor do I often want to be a part of you.
But we are, that's true!
As I learn from you,
I guess you learn from me—
although you're older—and white—
and somewhat more free.

This is my page for English B.

LANGSTON HUGHES

INCIDENT

(for Eric Walrond)

Once riding in old Baltimore,
    Heart-filled, head-filled with glee,
I saw the whole of Baltimore
    Keep looking straight at me.

Now I was eight and very small,
    And he was no whit bigger,
And so I smiled, but he poked out
    His tongue, and called me, "Nigger."

I saw the whole of Baltimore
  From May until December;
Of all the things that happened there
  That's all that I remember.

COUNTEE CULLEN

BEVERLY HILLS, CHICAGO

"and the people live till they have white hair"
E. M. Price

The dry brown coughing beneath their feet,
(Only a while, for the handyman is on his way)
These people walk their golden gardens.
We say ourselves fortunate to be driving by today.

That we may look at them, in their gardens where
The summer ripeness rots. But not raggedly.
Even the leaves fall down in lovelier patterns here.
And the refuse, the refuse is a neat brilliancy.

When they flow sweetly into their houses
With softness and slowness touched by that everlasting gold,
We know what they go to. To tea. But that does not mean
They will throw some little black dots into some water and add sugar and
   the juice of the cheapest lemons that are sold,

While downstairs that woman's vague phonograph bleats, "Knock me a
   kiss."
And the living all to be made again in the sweatingest physical manner
Tomorrow . . . . Not that anybody is saying that these people have no trou-
   ble.
Merely that it is trouble with a gold-flecked beautiful banner.

Nobody is saying that these people do not ultimately cease to be. And
Sometimes their passings are even more painful than ours.
It is just that so often they live till their hair is white.
They make excellent corpses, among the expensive flowers . . . .

Nobody is furious. Nobody hates these people.
At least, nobody driving by in this car.
It is only natural, however, that it should occur to us
How much more fortunate they are than we are.

It is only natural that we should look and look
At their wood and brick and stone
And think, while a breath of pine blows,
How different these are from our own.

We do not want them to have less.
But it is only natural that we should think we have not enough.
We drive on, we drive on.
When we speak to each other our voices are a little gruff.

GWENDOLYN BROOKS

SINKING OF THE TITANIC

It was 1912 when the awful news got around
That the great Titanic was sinking down.
Shine came running up on deck, told the Captain, "Please,
The water in the boiler room is up to my knees."

Captain said, "Take your black self on back down there!
I got a hundred-fifty pumps to keep the boiler room clear."
Shine went back in the hole, started shovelling coal,
Singing, "Lord, have mercy, Lord, on my soul!"
Just then half the ocean jumped across the boiler room deck.
Shine yelled to the Captain, "The water's 'round my neck!"
Captain said, "Go back! Neither fear nor doubt!
I got a hundred more pumps to keep the water out."

"Your words sound happy and your words sound true,
But this is one time, Cap, your words won't do.
I don't like chicken and I don't like ham—
And I don't believe your pumps is worth a damn!"

The old Titanic was beginning to sink.
Shine pulled off his clothes and jumped in the brink.
He said, "Little fish, big fish, and shark fishes, too,
Get out of my way because I'm coming through."

Captain on bridge hollered, "Shine, Shine, save poor me,
And I'll make you as rich as any man can be."
Shine said, "There's more gold on land than there is on sea."
And he swimmed on.

Jay Gould's millionary daughter came running up on deck
With her suitcase in her hand and her dress 'round her neck.
She cried, "Shine, Shine, save poor me!
I'll give you everything your eyes can see."
Shine said, "There's more on land than there is on sea."
And he swimmed on.

Big fat banker begging, "Shine, Shine, save poor me!
I'll give you a thousand shares of T and T."
Shine said, "More stocks on land than there is on sea."
And he swimmed on.

When all them white folks went to heaven,
Shine was in Sugar Ray's Bar drinking Seagrams Seven.

ANONYMOUS

SHINE, PERISHING REPUBLIC

While this America settles in the mould of its vulgarity, heavily thickening to
    empire,
And protest, only a bubble in the molten mass, pops and sighs out, and the
    mass hardens,

I sadly smiling remember that the flower fades to make fruit, the fruit rots to
    make earth.
Out of the mother; and through the spring exultances, ripeness and deca-
    dence; and home to the mother.

You making haste haste on decay: not blameworthy; life is good, be it
    stubbornly long or suddenly
A mortal splendor: meteors are not needed less than mountains: shine,
    perishing republic.

But for my children, I would have them keep their distance from the
    thickening center; corruption
Never has been compulsory, when the cities lie at the monster's feet
    there are left the mountains.

And boys, be in nothing so moderate as in love of man, a clever servant,
    insufferable master.
There is the trap that catches noblest spirits, that caught—they say—
    God, when he walked on earth.

ROBINSON JEFFERS

IN GOYA'S GREATEST SCENES

In Goya's greatest scenes we seem to see
               the people of the world
   exactly at the moment when
    they first attained the title of
         'suffering humanity'
    They writhe upon the page
        in a veritable rage
          of adversity
   Heaped up
     groaning with babies and bayonets
           under cement skies
  in an abstract landscape of blasted trees
   bent statues bats' wings and beaks
      slippery gibbets
  cadavers and carnivorous cocks
  and all the final hollering monsters
    of the
      'imagination of disaster'
   they are so bloody real
       it is as if they really still existed

And they do
            Only the landscape is changed

    They still are ranged along the roads
            plagued by legionnaires
                        false windmills and demented roosters
    They are the same people
                        only further from home
    on freeways fifty lanes wide
                    on a concrete continent
                            spaced with bland billboards
            illustrating imbecile illusions of happiness

        The scene shows fewer tumbrils
                        but more maimed citizens
                                    in painted cars
            and they have strange license plates
            and engines
                    that devour America.

LAWRENCE FERLINGHETTI

from I AM JOAQUÍN

        I am Joaquín,
        lost in a world of confusion,
        caught up in the whirl of a
                    gringo society,
        confused by the rules,
        scorned by attitudes,
        suppressed by manipulation,
        and destroyed by modern society.
        My fathers
            have lost the economic battle
        and won
            the struggle of cultural survival.

And now!
   I must choose
               between
   the paradox of
victory of the spirit,
despite physical hunger,
               or
   to exist in the grasp
of American social neurosis,
sterilization of the soul
   and a full stomach.

Yes,
I have come a long way to nowhere,
unwillingly dragged by that
   monstrous, technical,
   industrial giant called
             Progress
and Anglo success. . . .

   I look at myself.
     I watch my brothers.
       I shed tears of sorrow.
       I sow seeds of hate.
   I withdraw to the safety within the
circle of life—
             MY OWN PEOPLE

I am Cuahtémoc,
proud and noble,
       leader of men,
king of an empire
civilized beyond the dreams
   of the gachupín Cortés,
who also is the blood,
   the image of myself.
I am the Maya prince.
I am Nezahualcóyotl,
great leader of the Chichimecas.
I am the sword and flame of the Cortés
             the despot.
            And
I am the eagle and serpent of
        the Aztec civilization.

. . .

I am Joaquín.
I rode with Pancho Villa,
  crude and warm,
a tornado at full strength,
nourished and inspired
  by the passion and the fire
  of all his earthy people.
I am Emiliano Zapata.
     "This land,
         this earth
           is
             OURS."

The villages
  the mountains
    the streams
      belong to Zapatistas.
     Our life
     or yours
is the only trade for soft brown earth
and maize.
All of which is our reward,
  a creed that formed a constitution
  for all who dare live free!
"This land is ours . . .
    Father, I give it back to you.
          Mexico must be free. . . ."

. . .

I stand here looking back,
and now I see
      the present,
and still
   I am the campesino,
   I am the fat political coyote—
             I,
of the same name,
     Joaquín,
in a country that has wiped out

all my history,

                        stifled all my pride,
in a country that has placed a
different weight of indignity upon

              my

                  age-

                        old

                              burdened back.

                Inferiority
is the new load. . . .

                      . . .

Here I stand

              before the court of justice,
                guilty
for all the glory of my Raza
              to be sentenced to despair.
Here I stand,
    poor in money,
    arrogant with pride,
            bold with machismo,
            rich in courage
            and
            wealthy in spirit and faith.
My knees are caked with mud.
My hands calloused from the hoe.
I have made the Anglo rich,
                  yet
    equality is but a word—
      the Treaty of Hidalgo has been broken
      and is but another treacherous promise.

My land is lost
        and stolen,
My culture has been raped.
       I lengthen
      the line at the welfare door
and fill the jails with crime.

         . . .

I shed the tears of anguish
as I see my children disappear
behind the shroud of mediocrity,
never to look back to remember me.
I am Joaquín.
       I must fight
        and win this struggle
        for my sons, and they
        must know from me
        who I am.
Part of the blood that runs deep in me
could not be vanquished by the Moors.
I defeated them after five hundred years,
and I endured.
     Part of the blood that is mine
     has labored endlessly four hundred
     years under the heel of lustful
        Europeans.
        I am still here!

I have endured in the rugged mountains
  of our country.
I have survived the toils and slavery
  of the fields.
       I have existed
in the barrios of the city

in the suburbs of bigotry
in the mines of social snobbery
in the prisons of dejection
in the muck of exploitation
and
in the fierce heat of racial hatred.

And now the trumpet sounds,
the music of the people stirs the
                    revolution.
Like a sleeping giant it slowly
rears its head
to the sound of
                    tramping feet
                    clamoring voices
                    mariachi strains
                    fiery tequila explosions
                    the smell of chile verde and
                    soft brown eyes of expectation for a
                                        better life.

And in all the fertile farmlands,
                                        the barren plains,
the mountain villages,
smoke-smeared cities,
                    we start to MOVE.

          La Raza!
          Méjicano!
          Español!
            Latino!
             Hispano!
              Chicano!
or whatever I call myself,
                I look the same
                I feel the same
                I cry
                     and
          sing the same.

I am the masses of my people and
I refuse to be absorbed.
                I am Joaquín.
The odds are great
but my spirit is strong,
                my faith unbreakable,
                my blood is pure.
I am Aztec prince and Christian Christ.
                I SHALL ENDURE!
                I WILL ENDURE!

RODOLFO GONZALES

IN PRAISE OF LIMESTONE

If it form the one landscape that we, the inconstant ones,
    Are consistently homesick for, this is chiefly
Because it dissolves in water. Mark these rounded slopes
    With their surface fragrance of thyme and, beneath,
A secret system of caves and conduits; hear the springs
    That spurt out everywhere with a chuckle,
Each filling a private pool for its fish and carving
    Its own little ravine whose cliffs entertain
The butterfly and the lizard; examine this region
    Of short distances and definite places:
What could be more like Mother or a fitter background
    For her son, the flirtatious male who lounges
Against a rock in the sunlight, never doubting
    That for all his faults he is loved; whose works are but
Extensions of his power to charm? From weathered outcrop
    To hill-top temple, from appearing waters to
Conspicuous fountains, from a wild to a formal vineyard,
    Are ingenious but short steps that a child's wish
To receive more attention than his brothers, whether
    By pleasing or teasing, can easily take.
Watch, then, the band of rivals as they climb up and down
    Their steep stone gennels in twos and threes, at times
Arm in arm, but never, thank God, in step; or engaged
    On the shady side of a square at midday in

Voluble discourse, knowing each other too well to think
    There are any important secrets, unable
To conceive a god whose temper-tantrums are moral
    And not to be pacified by a clever line
Or a good lay: for, accustomed to a stone that responds,
    They have never had to veil their faces in awe
Of a crater whose blazing fury could not be fixed;
    Adjusted to the local needs of valleys
Where everything can be touched or reached by walking,
    Their eyes have never looked into infinite space
Through the lattice-work of a nomad's comb; born lucky,
    Their legs have never encountered the fungi
And insects of the jungle, the monstrous forms and lives
    With which we have nothing, we like to hope, in common.
So, when one of them goes to the bad, the way his mind works
    Remains comprehensible: to become a pimp
Or deal in fake jewellery or ruin a fine tenor voice
    For effects that bring down the house, could happen to all
But the best and the worst of us . . .
                                    That is why, I suppose,
    The best and worst never stayed here long but sought
Immoderate soils where the beauty was not so external,
    The light less public and the meaning of life
Something more than a mad camp. 'Come!' cried the granite wastes,
    'How evasive is your humour, how accidental
Your kindest kiss, how permanent is death.' (Saints-to-be
    Slipped away sighing.) 'Come!' purred the clays and gravels.
'On our plains there is room for armies to drill; rivers
    Wait to be tamed and slaves to construct you a tomb
In the grand manner: soft as the earth is mankind and both
    Need to be altered.' (Intendant Caesars rose and
Left, slamming the door.) But the really reckless were fetched
    By an older colder voice, the oceanic whisper:
'I am the solitude that asks and promises nothing;
    That is how I shall set you free. There is no love;
There are only the various envies, all of them sad.'
    They were right, my dear, all those voices were right

And still are; this land is not the sweet home that it looks,
    Nor its peace the historical calm of a site
Where something was settled once and for all: A backward
    And dilapidated province, connected
To the big busy world by a tunnel, with a certain
    Seedy appeal, is that all it is now? Not quite:
It has a worldly duty which in spite of itself
    It does not neglect, but calls into question
All the Great Powers assume; it disturbs our rights. The poet,
    Admired for his earnest habit of calling
The sun the sun, his mind Puzzle, is made uneasy
    By these marble statues which so obviously doubt
His antimythological myth; and these gamins,
    Pursuing the scientist down the tiled colonnade
With such lively offers, rebuke his concern for Nature's
    Remotest aspects: I, too, am reproached, for what
And how much you know. Not to lose time, not to get caught,
    Not to be left behind, not, please! to resemble
The beasts who repeat themselves, or a thing like water
    Or stone whose conduct can be predicted, these
Are our Common Prayer, whose greatest comfort is music
    Which can be made anywhere, is invisible,
And does not smell. In so far as we have to look forward
    To death as a fact, no doubt we are right: But if
Sins can be forgiven, if bodies rise from the dead,
    These modifications of matter into
Innocent athletes and gesticulating fountains,
    Made solely for pleasure, make a further point:
The blessed will not care what angle they are regarded from,
    Having nothing to hide. Dear, I know nothing of
Either, but when I try to imagine a faultless love
    Or the life to come, what I hear is the murmur
Of underground streams, what I see is a limestone landscape.

W. H. AUDEN

MAN, MAN, MAN

Man, man, man is for the woman made,
And the woman made for man;
As the spur is for the jade,
As the scabbard for the blade,
As for digging is the blade,
  As for liquor is the can,
So man, man, man, is for the woman made,
  And the woman made for man.

As the sceptre's to be swayed,
As for Night's the serenade,
  As for pudding is the pan,
  As to cool us is the fan,
So man, man, man, is for the woman made,
  And the woman made for man.

Be she widow, wife or maid,
Be she wanton, be she staid,
Be she well or ill-arrayed,
  Shrew, slut, or harridan,
Yet man, man, man, is for the woman made,
  And the woman made for man.

ANONYMOUS

WOMAN WITH GIRDLE

Your Midriff sags toward your knees;
your breasts lie down in air,
their nipples as uninvolved
as warm starfish.
You stand in your elastic case,
still not giving up the new-born
and the old-born cycle.
Moving, you roll down the garment,
down that pink snapper and hoarder,
as your belly, soft as pudding,

slops into the empty space;
down, over the surgeon's careful mark,
down over hips, those head cushions
and mouth cushions,
slow motion like a rolling pin,
over crisp hairs, that amazing field
that hides your genius from your patron;
over thighs, thick as young pigs,
over knees like saucers,
over calves, polished as leather,
down toward the feet.
You pause for a moment,
tying your ankles into knots.
Now you rise,
a city from the sea,
born long before Alexandria was,
straightway from God you have come
into your redeeming skin.

ANNE SEXTON

MOTHERHOOD

She sat on a shelf,
her breasts two bellies
on her poked-out belly,
on which the navel looked
like a sucked-in mouth—
her knees bent and apart,
her long left arm raised,
with the large hand knuckled
to a bar in the ceiling—
her right hand clamping
the skinny infant to her chest—
its round, pale, new,
soft muzzle hunting
in the brown hair for a nipple,
its splayed, tiny hand picking
at her naked, dirty ear.
Twisting its little neck,

with tortured, ecstatic eyes
the size of lentils, it looked
into her severe, close-set,
solemn eyes, that beneath bald
eyelids glared—dull lights
in sockets of leather.

She twitched some chin-hairs,
with pain or pleasure,
as the baby-mouth found and
yanked at her nipple;
its pink-nailed, jointless
fingers, wandering her face,
tangled in the tufts
of her cliffy brows.
She brought her big
hand down from the bar—
with pretended exasperation
unfastened the little hand,
and locked it within her palm—
while her right hand,
with snag-nailed forefinger
and short, sharp thumb, raked
the new orange hair
of the infant's skinny flank—
and found a louse,
which she lipped, and
thoughtfully crisped
between broad teeth.
She wrinkled appreciative
nostrils, which, without a nose,
stood open—damp, holes
above the poke of her mouth.

She licked her lips, flicked
her leather eyelids—
then, suddenly flung
up both arms and grabbed
the bars overhead.
The baby's scrabbly fingers
instantly caught the hair—
as if there were metal rings there—

in her long, stretched armpits.
And, as she stately swung,
and then proudly, more swiftly
slung herself from corner
to corner of her cell—
arms longer than her round
body, short knees bent—
her little wild-haired,
poke-mouthed infant hung,
like some sort of trophy,
or decoration, or shaggy medal—
shaped like herself—but new,
clean, soft and shining
on her chest.

MAY SWENSON

THE VOW

for Anne Hutchinson

sister,
your name is not a household word.
maybe you had a 2 line description
in 8th grade history.
more likely you were left out,
as i am when men converse in my presence.
Anne Hutchinson:
"a woman of haughty & fierce carriage."
my shoulders straighten.
you are dead, but not as dead as you
have been, we will avenge you.
you and all the nameless brave spirits,
my mother, my grandmothers,
great grandmothers (Breen Northcott, butcher's wife,
the others forgotten.) who bore me?
generations of denial & misuse
who bore those years of waste? sisters & mothers
it is too late for all of you. waste

& waste again, life after life,
shot to hell. it will take more
than a husband with a nation behind him
to stop me now.

ALTA

THE PURE PRODUCTS OF AMERICA

The pure products of America
go crazy—
mountain folk from Kentucky

or the ribbed north end of
Jersey
with its isolate lakes and

valleys, its deaf-mutes, thieves
old names
and promiscuity between

devil-may-care men who have taken
to railroading
out of sheer lust of adventure—

and young slatterns, bathed
in filth
from Monday to Saturday

to be tricked out that night
with gauds
from imaginations which have no

peasant traditions to give them
character
but flutter and flaunt

sheer rags—succumbing without
emotion
save numbed terror

under some hedge of choke-cherry
or viburnum—
which they cannot express—

Unless it be that marriage
perhaps
with a dash of Indian blood

will throw up a girl so desolate
so hemmed round
with disease or murder

that she'll be rescued by an
agent—
reared by the state and

sent out at fifteen to work in
some hard-pressed
house in the suburbs—

some doctor's family, some Elsie—
voluptuous water
expressing with broken

brain the truth about us—
her great
ungainly hips and flopping breasts

addressed to cheap
jewelry
and rich young men with fine eyes

as if the earth under our feet
were
an excrement of some sky

and we degraded prisoners
destined
to hunger until we eat filth

while the imagination strains
after deer
going by fields of goldenrod in

the stifling heat of September
Somehow
it seems to destroy us

It is only in isolate flecks that
something
is given off

No one
to witness
and adjust, no one to drive the car

WILLIAM CARLOS WILLIAMS

GREENS

A boy stoops, picking greens with his mother—
This is the scene in the great elm-shadows.
A pail stands by her feet, her dress conceals
Her chill knees, made bitter by the tall man
Who now lifts a glass, she thinks, with his friends,
Or worse, seeks a younger love in the town
While she with her fading muslin aprons
And her dented tin pail seeks greens, always
Greens, and wins, with her intermittent sighs,
Sympathy, love forever from the boy.
He does not know, this sharp-boned boy who bends
To his mother, that he has been seduced
Already, that he has known anguish, bliss
Of sex—as much as he will ever know.
He does not know, here in the bees' shadow,
He has become the tall and angry man,
The husband wounding the woman who bends,
Sighs and is ecstatic in her clutching
Of sons—bending, dark of brow, by her pail,
Stooped, brushing back the long, complaining strands
Of her hair. She is now too proud to weep,
But not to read the law, to reap greens, greens
Forever in her small pathetic pail.

DAVID RAY

AUTUMN BEGINS IN MARTINS FERRY, OHIO

In the Shreve High football stadium,
I think of Polacks nursing long beers in Tiltonsville,
And gray faces of Negroes in the blast furnace at Benwood,
And the ruptured night watchman of Wheeling Steel,
Dreaming of heroes.

All the proud fathers are ashamed to go home.
Their women cluck like starved pullets,
Dying for love.

Therefore,
Their sons grow suicidally beautiful
At the beginning of October,
And gallop terribly against each other's bodies.

JAMES WRIGHT

THE CAMPUS ON THE HILL

Up the reputable walks of old established trees
They stalk, children of the *nouveaux riches;* chimes
Of the tall Clock Tower drench their heads in blessing:
"I don't wanna play at your house;
I don't like you any more."
My house stands opposite, on the other hill,
Among meadows, with the orchard fences down and falling;
Deer come almost to the door.
You cannot see it, even in this clearest morning.
White birds hang in the air between
Over the garbage landfill and those homes thereto adjacent,
Hovering slowly, turning, settling down
Like the flakes sifting imperceptibly onto the little town
In a waterball of glass.
And yet, this morning, beyond this quiet scene,
The floating birds, the backyards of the poor,
Beyond the shopping plaza, the dead canal, the hillside lying tilted in
    the air,

Tomorrow has broken out today:
Riot in Algeria, in Cyprus, in Alabama;
Aged in wrong, the empires are declining,
And China gathers, soundlessly, like evidence.
What shall I say to the young on such a morning?—
Mind is the one salvation?—also grammar?—
No; my little ones lean not toward revolt. They
Are the Whites, the vaguely furiously driven, who resist
Their souls with such passivity
As would make Quakers swear. All day, dear Lord, all day
They wear their godhead lightly.
They look out from their hill and say,
To themselves, "We have nowhere to go but down;
The great destination is to stay."
Surely the nations will be reasonable;
They look at the world—don't they?—the world's way?
The clock just now has nothing more to say.

W. D. SNODGRASS

WHEN THE DUMB SPEAK

There is a joyful night in which we lose
Everything, and drift
Like a radish
Rising and falling, and the ocean
At last throws us into the ocean,
And on the water we are sinking
As if floating on darkness.
The body raging
And driving itself, disappearing in smoke,
Walks in large cities late at night,
Or reading the Bible in Christian Science windows,
Or reading a history of Bougainville.
Then the images appear:
Images of death,
Images of the body shaken in the grave,
And the graves filled with seawater;
Fires in the sea,
The ships smoldering like bodies,

Images of wasted life,
Life lost, imagination ruined,
The house fallen,
The gold sticks broken,
Then shall the talkative be silent,
And the dumb shall speak.

ROBERT BLY

God

A HYMN TO GOD THE FATHER

Wilt thou forgive that sin where I begun,
   Which is my sin though it were done before?
Wilt thou forgive those sins through which I run,
   And do them still, though still I do deplore?
     When thou hast done, thou hast not done,
      For I have more.

Wilt thou forgive that sin by which I won
   Others to sin? and made my sin their door?
Wilt thou forgive that sin which I did shun
   A year or two, but wallowed in a score?
     When thou hast done, thou hast not done,
      For I have more.

I have a sin of fear, that when I've spun
   My last thread, I shall perish on the shore;
Swear by thyself that at my death thy sun
   Shall shine as it shines now, and heretofore;
     And having done that, thou hast done.
      I have no more.

JOHN DONNE

GOOD FRIDAY, 1613. RIDING WESTWARD

Let man's soul be a sphere, and then, in this
The intelligence that moves, devotion is;
And as the other spheres, by being grown
Subject to foreign motion, lose their own,
And being by others hurried every day
Scarce in a year their natural form obey,
Pleasure or business, our souls admit

For their first mover, and are whirled by it.
Hence is't that I am carried towards the west
This day, when my soul's form bends towards the east.
There I should see a sun, by rising set,
And by that setting, endless day beget;
But that Christ on this cross did rise and fall,
Sin had eternally benighted all.
Yet dare I' almost be glad I do not see
That spectacle of too much weight for me.
Who sees God's face, that is self life must die;
What a death were it then to see God die!
It made his own lieutenant, nature, shrink;
It made his footstool crack, and the sun wink.
Could I behold those hands which span the poles
And tune all spheres at once, pierced with those holes?
Could I behold that endless height, which is
Zenith to us and our antipodes,
Humbled below us? or that blood which is
The seat of all our souls, if not of his,
Made dirt of dust, or that flesh which was worn
By God for his apparel, ragg'd and torn?
If on these things I durst not look, durst I
Upon his miserable mother cast mine eye,
Who was God's partner here, and furnished thus
Half of that sacrifice which ransomed us?
Though these things, as I ride, be from mine eye,
They'are present yet unto my memory,
For that looks towards them; and thou look'st towards me,
O Savior, as thou hang'st upon the tree;
I turn my back to thee but to receive
Corrections, till thy mercies bid thee leave.
Oh, think me worth thine anger, punish me,
Burn off my rusts, and my deformity;
Restore thine image, so much, by thy grace,
That thou mayst know me, and I'll turn my face.

JOHN DONNE

THE PULLEY

When God at first made man,
Having a glass of blessings standing by,
Let us, said he, pour on him all we can:
Let the world's riches, which dispersèd lie,
    Contract into a span.

So strength first made a way;
Then beauty flow'd, then wisdom, honour, pleasure.
When almost all was out, God made a stay,
Perceiving that alone of all his treasure
    Rest in the bottom lay.

For if I should, said he,
Bestow this jewel also on my creature,
He would adore my gifts instead of me,
And rest in nature, not the God of nature:
    So both should losers be.

Yet let him keep the rest,
But keep them with repining restlessness:
Let him be rich and weary, that at least,
If goodness lead him not, yet weariness
    May toss him to my breast.

GEORGE HERBERT

PARADISE

I bless thee, Lord, because I GROW
Among thy trees, which in a ROW
To thee both fruit and order OW.

What open force, or hidden CHARM
Can blast my fruit, or bring me HARM
While the inclosure is thine ARM?

Inclose me still for fear I START.
Be to me rather sharp and TART,
Than let me want thy hand and ART.

When thou dost greater judgments SPARE,
And with thy knife but prune and PARE,
Ev'n fruitful trees more fruitful ARE.

Such sharpness shows the sweetest FREND:
Such cuttings rather heat than REND:
And such beginnings touch their END.

GEORGE HERBERT

BERMUDAS

Where the remote Bermudas ride
In th' ocean's bosom unespy'd,
From a small boat that row'd along,
The list'ning winds receiv'd this song:
    "What should we do but sing His praise,
That led us through the watery maze,
Unto an isle so long unknown,
And yet far kinder than our own?
Where He the huge sea-monsters wracks,
That lift the deep upon their backs.
He lands us on a grassy stage,
Safe from the storms, and prelate's rage.
He gave us this eternal spring,
Which here enamels everything;
And sends the fowls to us in care,
On daily vists through the air.
He hangs in shades the orange bright,
Like golden lamps in a green night;
And does in the pomegranates close
Jewels more rich than Ormus shows.
He makes the figs our mouths to meet,
And throws the melons at our feet.
But apples plants of such a price,
No tree could ever bear them twice.
With cedars, chosen by His hand,

From Lebanon, He stores the land,
And makes the hollow seas, that roar
Proclaim the ambergris on shore.
He cast (of which we rather boast)
The Gospel's pearl upon our coast
And in these rocks for us did frame
A temple, where to sound His name.
Oh let our voice His praise exalt,
Till it arrive at Heaven's vault,
Which thence (perhaps) rebounding, may
Echo beyond the Mexique Bay."
    Thus sung they, in the English boat,
An holy and a cheerful note;
And all the way, to guide their chime,
With falling oars they kept the time.

ANDREW MARVELL

PIED BEAUTY

Glory be to God for dappled things—
    For skies of couple-colour as a brinded cow;
      For rose-moles all in stipple upon trout that swim;
Fresh-firecoal chestnut-falls; finches' wings;
    Landscape plotted and pieced—fold, fallow, and plough;
      And áll trádes, their gear and tackle and trim.

All things counter, original, spare, strange;
    Whatever is fickle, freckled (who knows how?)
      With swift, slow; sweet, sour; adazzle, dim;
He fathers-forth whose beauty is past change:
                Praise him.

GERARD MANLEY HOPKINS

GOD'S GRANDEUR

The world is charged with the grandeur of God.
　It will flame out, like shining from shook foil;
　It gathers to a greatness, like the ooze of oil
Crushed. Why do men then now not reck his rod?
Generations have trod, have trod, have trod;
　And all is seared with trade; bleared, smeared with toil;
　And wears man's smudge and shares man's smell: the soil
Is bare now, nor can foot feel, being shod.

And for all this, nature is never spent;
　There lives the dearest freshness deep down things;
And though the last lights off the black West went
　Oh, morning, at the brown brink eastward, springs—
Because the Holy Ghost over the bent
　World broods with warm breast and with ah! bright wings.

GERARD MANLEY HOPKINS

A GOD IN WRATH

A god in wrath
Was beating a man;
He cuffed him loudly
With thunderous blows
That rang and rolled over the earth.
All people came running.
The man screamed and struggled,
And bit madly at the feet of the god.
The people cried:
"Ah, what a wicked man!"
And—
"Ah, what a redoubtable god!"

STEPHEN CRANE

CHRIST CLIMBED DOWN

Christ climbed down
from His bare Tree
this year
and ran away to where
there were no rootless Christmas trees
hung with candycanes and breakable stars

Christ climbed down
from His bare Tree
this year
and ran away to where
there were no gilded Christmas trees
and no tinsel Christmas trees
and no tinfoil Christmas trees
and no pink plastic Christmas trees
and no gold Christmas trees
and no black Christmas trees
and no powerblue Christmas trees
hung with electric candles
and encircled by tin electric trains
and clever cornball relatives

Christ climbed down
from His bare Tree
this year
and ran away to where
no intrepid Bible salesmen
covered the territory
in two-tone cadillacs
and where no Sears Roebuck creches
complete with plastic babe in manger
arrived by parcel post
the babe by special delivery
and where no televised Wise Men
praised the Lord Calvert Whiskey

Christ climbed down
from His bare Tree
this year
and ran away to where
no fat handshaking stranger
in a red flannel suit
and a fake white beard
went around passing himself off
as some sort of North Pole saint
crossing the desert to Bethlehem
Pennsylvania
in a Volkswagen sled
drawn by rollicking Adirondack reindeer
with German names
and bearing sacks of Humble Gifts
from Saks Fifth Avenue
for everybody's imagined Christ child

Christ climbed down
from His bare Tree
this year
and ran away to where
no Bing Crosby carollers
groaned of a tight Christmas
and where no Radio City angels
iceskated wingless
thru a winter wonderland
into a jinglebell heaven
daily at 8:30
with Midnight Mass matinees

Christ climbed down
from His bare Tree
this year
and softly stole away into
some anonymous Mary's womb again
where in the darkest night

of everybody's anonymous soul
He awaits again
un unimaginable
and impossibly
Immaculate Reconception
the very craziest
of Second Comings

LAWRENCE FERLINGHETTI

JOURNEY OF THE MAGI

'A cold coming we had of it,
Just the worst time of the year
For a journey, and such a long journey:
The ways deep and the weather sharp,
The very dead of winter.'
And the camels galled, sore-footed, refractory,
Lying down in the melting snow.
There were times we regretted
The summer palaces on slopes, the terraces,
And the silken girls bringing sherbet.
Then the camel men cursing and grumbling
And running away, and wanting their liquor and women,
And the night-fires going out, and the lack of shelters,
And the cities hostile and the towns unfriendly
And the villages dirty and charging high prices:
A hard time we had of it.
At the end we preferred to travel all night,
Sleeping in snatches,
With the voices singing in our ears, saying
That this was all folly.
Then at dawn we came down to a temperate valley,
Wet, below the snow line, smelling of vegetation;
With a running stream and a water-mill beating the darkness,
And three trees on the low sky,
And an old white horse galloped away in the meadow.
Then we came to a tavern with vine-leaves over the lintel,

Six hands at an open door dicing for pieces of silver,
And feet kicking the empty wine-skins.
But there was no information, and so we continued
And arrived at evening, not a moment too soon
Finding the place; it was (you may say) satisfactory.

   All this was a long time ago, I remember,
And I would do it again, but set down
This set down
This: were we led all that way for
Birth or Death? There was a Birth, certainly,
We had evidence and no doubt. I had seen birth and death,
But had thought they were different; this Birth was
Hard and bitter agony for us, like Death, our death.
We returned to our places, these Kingdoms,
But no longer at ease here, in the old dispensation,
With an alien people clutching their gods.
I should be glad of another death.

T. S. ELIOT

SUNDAY MORNING

1

Complacencies of the peignoir, and late
Coffee and oranges in a sunny chair,
And the green freedom of a cockatoo
Upon a rug mingle to dissipate
The holy hush of ancient sacrifice.
She dreams a little, and she feels the dark
Encroachment of that old catastrophe,
As a calm darkens among water-lights.
The pungent oranges and bright, green wings
Seem things in some procession of the dead,
Winding across wide water, without sound.
The day is like wide water, without sound,
Stilled for the passing of her dreaming feet
Over the seas, to silent Palestine,
Dominion of the blood and sepulchre.

2

Why should she give her bounty to the dead?
What is divinity if it can come
Only in silent shadows and in dreams?
Shall she not find in comforts of the sun,
In pungent fruit and bright, green wings, or else
In any balm or beauty of the earth,
Things to be cherished like the thought of heaven?
Divinity must live within herself:
Passions of rain, or moods in falling snow;
Grievings in loneliness, or unsubdued
Elations when the forest blooms; gusty
Emotions on wet roads on autumn nights;
All pleasures and all pains, remembering
The bough of summer and the winter branch.
These are the measures destined for her soul.

3

Jove in the clouds had his inhuman birth.
No mother suckled him, no sweet land gave
Large-mannered motions to his mythy mind
He moved among us, as a muttering king,
Magnificent, would move among his hinds,
Until our blood, commingling, virginal,
With heaven, brought such requital to desire
The very hinds discerned it, in a star.
Shall our blood fail? Or shall it come to be
The blood of paradise? And shall the earth
Seem all of paradise that we shall know?
The sky will be much friendlier then than now,
A part of labor and a part of pain,
And next in glory to enduring love,
Not this dividing and indifferent blue.

4

She says, "I am content when wakened birds,
Before they fly, test the reality
Of misty fields, by their sweet questionings;
But when the birds are gone, and their warm fields
Return no more, where, then, is paradise?"
There is not any haunt of prophecy,
Nor any old chimera of the grave,
Neither the golden underground, nor isle
Melodious, where spirts gat them home,
Nor visionary south, nor cloudy palm
Remote on heaven's hill, that has endured
As April's green endures; or will endure
Like her remembrance of awakened birds,
Or her desire for June and evening, tipped
By the consummation of the swallow's wings.

5

She says, "But in contentment I still feel
The need of some imperishable bliss."
Death is the mother of beauty; hence from her,
Alone, shall come fulfilment to our dreams
And our desires. Although she strews the leaves
Of sure obliteration on our paths,
The path sick sorrow took, the many paths
Where triumph rang its brassy phrase, or love
Whispered a little out of tenderness,
She makes the willow shiver in the sun
For maidens who were wont to sit and gaze
Upon the grass, relinquished to their feet.
She causes boys to pile new plums and pears
On disregarded plate. The maidens taste
And stray impassioned in the littering leaves.

6

Is there no change of death in paradise?
Does ripe fruit never fall? Or do the boughs
Hang always heavy in that perfect sky,
Unchanging, yet so like our perishing earth,
With rivers like our own that seek for seas
They never find, the same receding shores
That never touch with inarticulate pang?
Why set the pear upon those river-banks
Or spice the shores with odors of the plum?
Alas, that they should wear our colors there,
The silken weavings of our afternoons,
And pick the strings of our insipid lutes!
Death is the mother of beauty, mystical,
Within whose burning bosom we devise
Our earthly mothers waiting, sleeplessly.

7

Supple and turbulent, a ring of men
Shall chant in orgy on a summer morn
Their boisterous devotion to the sun,
Not as a god, but as a god might be,
Naked among them, like a savage source.
Their chant shall be a chant of paradise,
Out of their blood, returning to the sky;
And in their chant shall enter, voice by voice,
The windy lake wherein their lord delights,
The trees, like serafin, and echoing hills,
That choir among themselves long afterward.
They shall know well the heavenly fellowship
Of men that perish and of summer morn.
And whence they came and whither they shall go
The dew upon their feet shall manifest.

8

She hears, upon that water without sound,
A voice that cries, "The tomb in Palestine
Is not the porch of spirits lingering.
It is the grave of Jesus, where he lay."
We live in an old chaos of the sun,
Or old dependency of day and night,
Or island solitude, unsponsored, free,
Of that wide water, inescapable.
Deer walk upon our mountains, and the quail
Whistle about us their spontaneous cries;
Sweet berries ripen in the wilderness;
And, in the isolation of the sky,
At evening, casual flocks of pigeons make
Ambiguous undulations as they sink,
Downward to darkness, on extended wings.

WALLACE STEVENS

Change

RICH MEN, TRUST NOT

Rich men, trust not in wealth,
Gold cannot buy you health:
Physic himself must fade;
All things to end are made;
The plague full swift goes by.
I am sick, I must die—
    Lord have mercy on us!

Beauty is but a flower
Which wrinkles will devour;
Brightness falls from the air;
Queens have died young, and fair;
Dust hath closed Helen's eye.
I am sick, I must die—
    Lord have mercy on us!

Strength stoops unto the grave,
Worms feed on Hector brave;
Swords may not fight with fate;
Earth still holds ope her gate;
Come, come, the bells do cry.
I am sick, I must die—
    Lord have mercy on us!

THOMAS NASHE

SONNET 12

When I do count the clock that tells the time
And see the brave day sunk in hideous night,
When I behold the violet past prime
And sable curls all silver'd o'er with white,

When lofty trees I see barren of leaves,
Which erst from heat did canopy the herd,
And summer's green all girded up in sheaves
Borne on the bier with white and bristly beard—
Then of thy beauty do I question make
That thou among the wastes of time must go,
Since sweets and beauties do themselves forsake
And die as fast as they see others grow,
    And nothing 'gainst Time's scythe can make defence
    Save breed, to brave him when he takes thee hence.

WILLIAM SHAKESPEARE

BRIGHT STAR, WOULD I WERE STEADFAST AS THOU ART

Bright star, would I were steadfast as thou art—
    Not in lone splendour hung aloft the night
And watching, with eternal lids apart,
    Like nature's patient, sleepless Eremite,
The moving waters at their priestlike task,
    Of pure ablution round earth's human shores,
Or gazing on the new soft-fallen mask
    Of snow upon the mountains and the moors.
No—yet still steadfast, still unchangeable,
    Pillowed upon my fair love's ripening breast,
To feel for ever its soft fall and swell,
    Awake for ever in a sweet unrest,
Still, still to hear her tender-taken breath,
And so live ever—or else swoon to death.

JOHN KEATS

MUTABILITY

From low to high doth dissolution climb,
And sink from high to low, along a scale
Of awful notes, whose concord shall not fail;
A musical but melancholy chime,

Which they can hear who meddle not with crime,
Nor avarice, nor over-anxious care.
Truth fails not; but her outward forms that bear
The longest date do melt like frosty rime
That in the morning whitened hill and plain
And is no more; drop like the tower sublime
Of yesterday, which royally did wear
His crown of weeds, but could not even sustain
Some casual shout that broke the silent air,
Or the unimaginable touch of Time.

WILLIAM WORDSWORTH

REMEMBER

Remember me when I am gone away,
Gone far away into the silent land;
When you can no more hold me by the hand,
Nor I half turn to go yet turning stay.
Remember me when no more day by day
You tell me of our future that you planned:
Only remember me; you understand
It will be late to counsel then or pray.
Yet if you should forget me for a while
And afterwards remember, do not grieve:
For if the darkness and corruption leave
A vestige of the thoughts that once I had,
Better by far you should forget and smile
Than that you should remember and be sad.

CHRISTINA ROSSETTI

THE SOUL SELECTS HER OWN SOCIETY

The soul selects her own society,
Then shuts the door;
On her divine majority
Obtrude no more.

Unmoved, she notes the chariot's pausing
At her low gate;
Unmoved, an emperor is kneeling
Upon her mat.

I've known her from an ample nation
Choose one;
Then close the valves of her attention
Like stone.

EMILY DICKINSON

CROSSING BROOKLYN FERRY

1

Flood-tide below me! I see you face to face!
Clouds of the west—sun there half an hour high—I see you also
   face to face.

Crowds of men and women attired in the usual costumes, how curious you
   are to me!
On the ferry-boats the hundreds and hundreds that cross, returning home,
   are more curious to me than you suppose,
And you that shall cross from shore to shore years hence are more to me,
   and more in my meditations, than you might suppose.

2

The impalpable sustenance of me from all things at all hours of the day,
The simple, compact, well-join'd scheme, myself disintegrated, every one disintegrated yet part of the scheme,
The similitudes of the past and those of the future,
The glories strung like beads on my smallest sights and hearings, on the walk in the street and the passage over the river,
The current rushing so swiftly and swimming with me far away,
The others that are to follow me, the ties between me and them,
The certainty of others, the life, love, sight, hearing of others.

Others will enter the gates of the ferry and cross from shore to shore,
Others will watch the run of the flood-tide,
Others will see the shipping of Manhattan north and west, and the heights of Brooklyn to the south and east,
Others will see the islands large and small;
Fifty years hence, others will see them as they cross, the sun half an hour high,
A hundred years hence, or ever so many hundred years hence, others will see them,
Will enjoy the sunset, the pouring-in of the flood-tide, the falling-back to the sea of the ebb-tide.

3

It avails not, time nor place—distance avails not,
I am with you, you men and women of a generation, or ever so many generations hence,
Just as you feel when you look on the river and sky, so I felt,
Just as any of you is one of a living crowd, I was one of a crowd,
Just as you are refresh'd by the gladness of the river and the bright flow, I was refresh'd,
Just as you stand and lean on the rail, yet hurry with the swift current, I stood yet was hurried,
Just as you look on the numberless masts of ships and the thick-stemm'd pipes of steamboats, I look'd.

I too many and many a time cross'd the river of old,
Watched the Twelfth-month sea-gulls, saw them high in the air floating with motionless wings, oscillating their bodies,

Saw how the glistening yellow lit up parts of their bodies and left the rest in
    strong shadow,
Saw the slow-wheeling circles and the gradual edging toward the south,
Saw the reflection of the summer sky in the water,
Had my eyes dazzled by the shimmering track of beams,
Look'd at the fine centrifugal spokes of light round the shape of my head in
    the sunlit water.
Look'd on the haze on the hills southward and south-westward,
Look'd on the vapor as it flew in fleeces tinged with violet,
Look'd toward the lower bay to notice the vessels arriving,
Saw their approach, saw aboard those that were near me,
Saw the white sails of schooners and sloops, saw the ships at anchor,
The sailors at work in the rigging or out astride the spars,
The round masts, the swinging motion of the hulls, the slender serpentine
    pennants,
The large and small steamers in motion, the pilots in their pilot-houses,
The white wake left by the passage, the quick tremulous whirl of the
    wheels,
The flags of all nations, the falling of them at sunset,
The scallop-edged waves in the twilight, the ladled cups, the frolicsome
    crests and glistening,
The stretch afar growing dimmer and dimmer, the gray walls of the granite
    storehouses by the docks,
On the river the shadowy group, the big steam-tug closely flank'd on each
    side by the barges, the hay-boat, the belated lighter,
On the neighboring shore the fires from the foundry chimneys burning
    high and glaringly into the night,
Casting their flicker of black contrasted with wild red and yellow light over
    the tops of houses, and down into the clefts of streets.

4
These and all else were to me the same as they are to you,
I loved well those cities, loved well the stately and rapid river,
The men and women I saw were all near to me,
Others the same—others who look back on me because I look'd forward to
    them,
(The time will come, though I stop here to-day and to-night.)

5
What is it then between us?
What is the count of the scores or hundreds of years between us?

Whatever it is, it avails not—distance avails not, and place avails not,
I too lived, Brooklyn of ample hills was mine,
I too walk'd the streets of Manhattan island, and bathed in the waters
    around it,
I too felt the curious abrupt questionings stir within me,
In the day among crowds of people sometimes they came upon me,
In my walks home late at night or as I lay in my bed they came upon me,
I too had been struck from the float forever held in solution,
I too had receiv'd identity by my body,
That I was I knew was of my body, and what I should be I knew I should be
    of my body.

6

It is not upon you alone the dark patches fall,
The dark threw its patches down upon me also,
The best I had done seem'd to me blank and suspicious,
My great thoughts as I supposed them, were they not in reality meagre?
Nor is it you alone who know what it is to be evil,
I am he who knew what it was to be evil,
I too knitted the old knot of contrariety,
Blabb'd, blush'd, resented, lied, stole, grudg'd,
Had guile, anger, lust, hot wishes I dared not speak,
Was wayward, vain, greedy, shallow, sly, cowardly, malignant,
The wolf, the snake, the hog, not wanting in me,
The cheating look, the frivolous word, the adulterous wish, not wanting,
Refusals, hates, postponements, meanness, laziness, none of these
    wanting,
Was one with the rest, the days and haps of the rest,
Was call'd by my nighest name by clear loud voices of young men as they
    saw me approaching or passing,
Felt their arms on my neck as I stood, or the negligent leaning of their flesh
    against me as I sat,
Saw many I loved in the street or ferry-boat or public assembly, yet never
    told them a word,
Lived the same life with the rest, the same old laughing, gnawing, sleeping,
Play'd the part that still looks back on the actor or actress,
The same old role, the role that is what we make it, as great as we like,
Or as small as we like, or both great and small.

7

Closer yet I approach you,
What thought you have of me now, I had as much of you—I laid in my stores
 in advance,
I consider'd long and seriously of you before you were born.

Who was to know what should come home to me?
Who knows but I am enjoying this?
Who knows, for all the distance, but I am as good as looking at you now, for
 all you cannot see me?

8

Ah, what can ever be more stately and admirable to me than mast-hemm'd
 Manhattan?
River and sunset and scallop-edg'd waves of flood-tide?
The sea-gulls oscillating their bodies, the hay-boat in the twilight, and the
 belated lighter?
What gods can exceed these that clasp me by the hand, and with voices I
 love call me promptly and loudly by my nighest name as I approach?
What is more subtle than this which ties me to the woman or man that looks
 in my face?
Which fuses me into you now, and pours my meaning into you?

We understand then do we not?
What I promis'd without mentioning it, have you not accepted?
What the study could not teach—what the preaching could not accomplish
 is accomplish'd, is it not?

9

Flow on, river! flow with the flood-tide, and ebb with the ebb-tide!
Frolic on, crested and scallop-edg'd waves!
Gorgeous clouds of the sunset! drench with your splendor me, or the men
 and women generations after me!
Cross from shore to shore, countless crowds of passengers!
Stand up, tall masts of Mannahatta! stand up, beautiful hills of Brooklyn!
Throb, baffled and curious brain! throw out questions and answers!
Suspend here and everywhere, eternal float of solution!
Gaze, loving and thirsting eyes, in the house or street or public assembly!
Sound out, voices of young men! loudly and musically call me by my nigh-
 est name!
Live, old life! play the part that looks back on the actor or actress!

Play the old role, the role that is great or small according as one makes it!

Consider, you who peruse me, whether I may not in unknown ways be looking upon you;

Be firm, rail over the river, to support those who lean idly, yet haste with the hasting current;

Fly on, sea-birds! fly sideways, or wheel in large circles high in the air;

Receive the summer sky, you water, and faithfully hold it till all downcast eyes have time to take it from you!

Diverge, fine spokes of light, from the shape of my head, or any one's head, in the sunlit water!

Come on, ships from the lower bay! pass up or down, white-sail'd schooners, sloops, lighters!

Flaunt away, flags of all nations! be duly lower'd at sunset!

Burn high your fires, foundry chimneys! cast black shadows at nightfall! cast red and yellow light over the tops of the houses!

Appearances, now or henceforth, indicate what you are,

You necessary film, continue to envelop the soul,

About my body for me, and your body for you, be hung our divinest aromas,

Thrive, cities—bring your freight, bring your shows, ample and sufficient rivers,

Expand, being than which none else is perhaps more spiritual,

Keep your places, objects than which none else is more lasting.

You have waited, you always wait, you dumb, beautiful ministers,

We receive you with free sense at last, and are insatiate hence forward,

Not you any more shall be able to foil us, or withhold yourselves from us,

We use you, and do not cast you aside—we plant you permanently within us,

We fathom you not—we love you—there is perfection in you also,

You furnish your parts toward eternity,

Great or small, you furnish your parts toward the soul.

WALT WHITMAN

GRASS

Pile the bodies high at Austerlitz and Waterloo.
Shovel them under and let me work—
                    I am the grass; I cover all.

And pile them high at Gettysburg
And pile them high at Ypres and Verdun.

Shovel them under and let me work.
Two years, ten years, and passengers ask the conductor:
                    What place is this?
                    Where are we now?

                    I am the grass.
                    Let me work.

CARL SANDBURG

FOR THE GRAVE OF DANIEL BOONE

The farther he went the farther home grew.
Kentucky became another room;
the mansion arched over the Mississippi;
flowers were spread all over the floor.
He traced ahead a deepening home,
and better, with goldenrod:

Leaving the snakeskin of place after place,
going on—after the trees
the grass, a bird flying after a song.
Rifle so level, sighting so well
his picture freezes down to now,
a story-picture for children.

They go over the velvet falls
into the tapestry of his time,
heirs to the landscape, feeling no jar:
it is like evening; they are the quail
surrounding his fire, coming in for the kill;
their little feet move sacred sand.

Children, we live in a barbwire time
but like to follow the old hands back—
the ring in the light, the knuckle, the palm,
all the way to Daniel Boone,
hunting our own kind of deepening home.
From the land that was his I heft this rock.

Here on his grave I put it down.

WILLIAM STAFFORD

ON THE MOVE

'Man, you gotta Go.'

The blue jay scuffling in the bushes follows
Some hidden purpose, and the gust of birds
That spurts across the field, the wheeling swallows,
Have nested in the trees and undergrowth.
Seeking their instinct, or their poise, or both,
One moves with an uncertain violence
Under the dust thrown by a baffled sense
Or the dull thunder of approximate words.

On motorcycles, up the road, they come:
Small, black, as flies hanging in heat, the Boys,
Until the distance throws them forth, their hum
Bulges to thunder held by calf and thigh.
In goggles, donned impersonality,
In gleaming jackets trophied with the dust,
They strap in doubt—by hiding it, robust—
And almost hear a meaning in their noise.

Exact conclusion of their hardiness
Has no shape yet, but from known whereabouts
They ride, direction where the tires press.
They scare a flight of birds across the field:
Much that is natural, to the will must yield.
Men manufacture both machine and soul,
And use what they imperfectly control
To dare a future from the taken routes.

It is a part solution, after all.
One is not necessarily discord
On earth; or damned because, half animal,
One lacks direct instinct, because one wakes
Afloat on movement that divides and breaks.
One joins the movement in a valueless world,
Choosing it, till, both hurler and the hurled,
One moves as well, always toward, toward.

A minute holds them, who have come to go:
The self-defined, astride the created will
They burst away; the towns they travel through
Are home for neither bird nor holiness,
For birds and saints complete their purposes.
At worse, one is in motion; and at best,
Reaching no absolute, in which to rest,
One is always nearer by not keeping still.

THOM GUNN

Art

from A MIDSUMMER NIGHT'S DREAM

The lunatic, the lover, and the poet
Are of imagination all compact.
One sees more devils than vast hell can hold:
That is the madman. The lover, all as frantic,
Sees Helen's beauty in a brow of Egypt.
The poet's eye, in a fine frenzy rolling,
Doth glance from heaven to earth, from earth to heaven;
And as imagination bodies forth
The forms of things unknown, the poet's pen
Turns them to shapes, and gives to airy nothing
A local habitation and a name.
Such tricks hath strong imagination
That, if it would but apprehend some joy,
It comprehends some bringer of that joy;
Or in the night, imagining some fear,
How easy is a bush suppos'd a bear!

WILLIAM SHAKESPEARE

KUBLA KHAN

In Xanadu did Kubla Khan
  A stately pleasure-dome decree;
Where Alph, the sacred river, ran
Through caverns measureless to man
  Down to a sunless sea.
So twice five miles of fertile ground
With walls and towers were girdled round:
And there were gardens bright with sinuous rills,
Where blossomed many an incense-bearing tree,
And here were forests ancient as the hills,
Enfolding sunny spots of greenery.

But oh! that deep romantic chasm which slanted
Down the green hill athwart a cedarn cover!
A savage place; as holy and enchanted
As e'er beneath a waning moon was haunted
By woman wailing for her demon-lover!
And from this chasm, with ceaseless turmoil seething,
As if this earth in fast thick pants were breathing,
A mighty fountain momently was forced:
Amid whose swift half-intermitted burst
Huge fragments vaulted like rebounding hail,
Or chaffy grain beneath the thresher's flail:
And 'mid these dancing rocks at once and ever
It flung up momently the sacred river.
Five miles meandering with a mazy motion
Through wood and dale the sacred river ran,
Then reached the caverns measureless to man,
And sank in tumult to a lifeless ocean:
And 'mid this tumult Kubla heard from far
Ancestral voices prophesying war!

    The shadow of the dome of pleasure
    Floated midway on the waves;
    Where was heard the mingled measure
    From the fountain and the caves.
It was a miracle of rare device,
A sunny pleasure-dome with caves of ice!

A damsel with a dulcimer
In a vision once I saw:
It was an Abyssinian maid,
And on her dulcimer she played,

Singing of Mount Abora.
Could I revive within me
Her symphony and song,
    To such a deep delight 'twould win me,
That with music loud and long,
I would build that dome in air,
That sunny dome! those caves of ice!
And all who heard should see them there,
And all should cry, Beware! Beware!
His flashing eyes, his floating hair!
Weave a circle round him thrice,
And close your eyes with holy dread,
For he on honey-dew hath fed,
And drunk the milk of Paradise.

SAMUEL TAYLOR COLERIDGE

ODE ON A GRECIAN URN

Thou still unravish'd bride of quietness,
    Thou foster-child of silence and slow time,
Sylvan historian, who canst thus express
    A flowery tale more sweetly than our rhyme:
What leaf-fring'd legend haunts about thy shape
    Of deities or mortals, or of both,
        In Tempe or the dales of Arcady?
    What men or gods are these? What maidens loth?
    What mad pursuit? What struggle to escape?
            What pipes and timbrels? What wild ecstasy?

Heard melodies are sweet, but those unheard
    Are sweeter; therefore, ye soft pipes, play on;
Not to the sensual ear, but, more endear'd,
    Pipe to the spirit ditties of no tone:
Fair youth, beneath the trees, thou canst not leave
    Thy song, nor ever can those trees be bare;
        Bold lover, never, never canst thou kiss,
Though winning near the goal—yet, do not grieve;
    She cannot fade, though thou hast not thy bliss,
        For ever wilt thou love, and she be fair!

Ah, happy, happy boughs! that cannot shed
    Your leaves, nor ever bid the spring adieu;
And, happy melodist, unwearièd,
    For ever piping songs for ever new;
More happy love! more happy, happy love!
    For ever warm and still to be enjoy'd,
        For ever panting, and for ever young;
All breathing human passion far above,
    That leaves a heart high-sorrowful and cloy'd,
        A burning forehead, and a parching tongue.

Who are these coming to the sacrifice?
    To what green altar, O mysterious priest,
Lead'st thou that heifer lowing at the skies,
    And all her silken flanks with garlands drest?
What little town by river or sea shore,
    Or mountain-built with peaceful citadel,
        Is emptied of this folk, this pious morn?
And, little town, thy streets for evermore
    Will silent be; and not a soul to tell
        Why thou art desolate, can e'er return.

O Attic shape! Fair attitude! with brede
    Of marble men and maidens overwrought,
With forest branches and the trodden weed;
    Thou, silent form, dost tease us out of thought
As doth eternity. Cold pastoral!
    When old age shall this generation waste,
      Thou shalt remain, in midst of other woe
Than ours, a friend to man, to whom thou say'st,
    "Beauty is truth, truth beauty," that is all
      Ye know on earth, and all ye need to know.

JOHN KEATS

POETS TO COME

Poets to come! orators, singers, musicians to come!
Not to-day is to justify me and answer what I am for,
But you, a new brood, native, athletic, continental, greater than
    before known,
Arouse! for you must justify me.

I myself but write one or two indicative words for the future,
I but advance a moment only to wheel and hurry back in the
    darkness.

I am a man who, sauntering along without fully stopping, turns a
    casual look upon you and then averts his face.
Leaving it to you to prove and define it,
Expecting the main things from you.

WALT WHITMAN

THE SONNET

A sonnet is a moment's monument—
  Memorial from the soul's eternity
  To one dead deathless hour. Look that it be,
Whether for lustral rite or dire portent,
Of its own arduous fulness reverent:
  Carve it in ivory or in ebony,
  As day or night may rule; and let time see
Its flowering crest impearled and orient.

A sonnet is a coin: its face reveals
  The soul—its converse, to what power 'tis due—
Whether for tribute to the august appeals
  Of life, or dower in love's high retinue,
It serve; or, 'mid the dark wharf's cavernous breath,
In Charon's palm it pay the toll to Death.

DANTE GABRIEL ROSSETTI

THE CIRCUS ANIMALS' DESERTION

1
I sought a theme and sought for it in vain,
I sought it daily for six weeks or so.
Maybe at last, being but a broken man,
I must be satisfied with my heart, although
Winter and summer till old age began
My circus animals were all on show,
Those stilted boys, that burnished chariot,
Lion and woman and the Lord knows what.

2

What can I but enumerate old themes?
First that sea-rider Oisin led by the nose
Through three enchanted islands, allegorical dreams,
Vain gaiety, vain battle, vain repose,
Themes of the embittered heart, or so it seems,
That might adorn old songs or courtly shows;
But what cared I that set him on to ride,
I, starved for the bosom of his faery bride?

And then a counter-truth filled out its play,
The Countess Cathleen was the name I gave it;
She, pity-crazed, had given her soul away,
But masterful Heaven had intervened to save it.
I thought my dear must her own soul destroy,
So did fanaticism and hate enslave it,
And this brought forth a dream and soon enough
This dream itself had all my thought and love.

And when the Fool and Blind Man stole the bread
Cuchulain fought the ungovernable sea;
Heart-mysteries there, and yet when all is said
It was the dream itself enchanted me:
Character isolated by a deed
To engross the present and dominate memory.
Players and painted stage took all my love,
And not those things that they were emblems of.

3

Those masterful images because complete
Grew in pure mind, but out of what began?
A mound of refuse or the sweepings of a street,
Old kettles, old bottles, and a broken can,
Old iron, old bones, old rags, that raving slut
Who keeps the till. Now that my ladder's gone,
I must lie down where all the ladders start,
In the foul rag-and-bone shop of the heart.

WILLIAM BUTLER YEATS

ARS POETICA

A poem should be palpable and mute
As a globed fruit

Dumb
As old medallions to the thumb

Silent as the sleeve-worn stone
Of casement ledges where the moss has grown—

A poem should be wordless
As the flight of birds

A poem should be motionless in time
As the moon climbs

Leaving, as the moon releases
Twig by twig the night-entangled trees,

Leaving, as the moon behind the winter leaves,
Memory by memory the mind—

A poem should be motionless in time
As the moon climbs

A poem should be equal to:
Not true

For all the history of grief
An empty doorway and a maple leaf

For love
The meaning grasses and two lights above the sea—

A poem should not mean
But be

ARCHIBALD MACLEISH

The poem of the mind in the act of finding
What will suffice. It has not always had
To find: the scene was set; it repeated what
Was in the script.
                  Then the theater was changed
To something else. Its past was a souvenir.
It has to be living, to learn the speech of the place.
It has to face the men of the time and to meet
The women of the time. It has to think about war
To construct a new stage. It has to be on that stage
And, like an insatiable actor, slowly and
With meditation, speak words that in the ear,
In the delicatest ear of the mind, repeat,
Exactly, that which it wants to hear, at the sound
Of which, an invisible audience listens,
Not to the play, but to itself, expressed
In an emotion as of two people, as of two
Emotions becoming one. The actor is
A metaphysician in the dark, twanging
An instrument, twanging a wiry string that gives
Sounds passing through sudden rightnesses, wholly
Containing the mind, below which it cannot descend,
Beyond which it has no will to rise.
                          It must
Be the finding of a satisfaction, and may
Be of a man skating, a woman dancing, a woman
Combing. The poem of the act of the mind.

WALLACE STEVENS

DIRECTIVE

Back out of all this now too much for us,
Back in a time made simple by the loss
Of detail, burned, dissolved, and broken off
Like graveyard marble sculpture in the weather,
There is a house that is no more a house

Upon a farm that is no more a farm
And in a town that is no more a town.
The road there, if you'll let a guide direct you
Who only has at heart your getting lost,
May seem as if it should have been a quarry—
Great monolithic knees the former town
Long since gave up pretense of keeping covered.
And there's a story in a book about it:
Besides the wear of iron wagon wheels
The ledges show lines ruled southeast-northwest,
The chisel work of an enormous Glacier
That braced his feet against the Arctic Pole.
You must not mind a certain coolness from him
Still said to haunt this side of Panther Mountain.
Nor need you mind the serial ordeal
Of being watched from forty cellar holes
As if by eye pairs out of forty firkins.
As for the woods' excitement over you
That sends light rustle rushes to their leaves,
Charge that to upstart inexperience.
Where were they all not twenty years ago?
They think too much of having shaded out
A few old pecker-fretted apple trees.
Make yourself up a cheering song of how
Someone's road home from work this once was,
Who may be just ahead of you on foot
Or creaking with a buggy load of grain.
The height of the adventure is the height
Of country where two village cultures faded
Into each other. Both of them are lost.
And if you're lost enough to find yourself
By now, pull in your ladder road behind you
And put a sign up CLOSED to all but me.
Then make yourself at home. The only field
Now left's no bigger than a harness gall.
First there's the children's house of make-believe,
Some shattered dishes underneath a pine,
The playthings in the playhouse of the children.
Weep for what little things could make them glad.
Then for the house that is no more a house,
But only a belilaced cellar hole,
Now slowly closing like a dent in dough.
This was no playhouse but a house in earnest.

Your destination and your destiny's
A brook that was the water of the house,
Cold as a spring as yet so near its source,
Too lofty and original to rage.
(We know the valley streams that when aroused
Will leave their tatters hung on barb and thorn.)
I have kept hidden in the instep arch
Of an old cedar at the waterside
A broken drinking goblet like the Grail
Under a spell so the wrong ones can't find it,
So can't get saved, as Saint Mark says they mustn't.
(I stole the goblet from the children's playhouse.)
Here are your waters and your watering place.
Drink and be whole again beyond confusion.

ROBERT FROST

DAYBREAK

Again this procession of the speechless
Bringing me their words
The future woke me with its silence
I join the procession
An open doorway
Speaks for me
Again

W. S. MERWIN

Discography

Caedmon 1019	Auden, W. H.
Caedmon 1101	Blake, William—(Richardson)
Verve/Fore. S-3083	Blake, William—(Ginsberg)—Songs of Innocence & Experience
Caedmon S-1244	Brooks, Gwendolyn—Reading her Poetry, with Poem by D. L. Lee
Folkways 9790	Brown, Sterling
Caedmon 1201	Browning, Robert—My Last Duchess, etc.
Argo 119	Collins/Goldsmith/Gray—(Speaight)
Caedmon 1206	Crane, Hart—Tennessee Williams Reads
Caedmon 1017	Cummings, E. E.
Caedmon 1119	Dickinson, Emily—(Harris)—Poems
Caedmon S-1333	Dickey, James—(Dickey)—Poems
Spoken Arts 984	
Argo 403	Donne, John—(Johnson, Orr)—26 Poems
Fan. 7004	Ferlinghetti, Lawrence—Poems
Caedmon 1060	Frost, Robert—Reading His Poetry
Douglas 801	Ginsberg, Allen—Thinq
Caedmon 1140	Hardy, Thomas—(Burton)—Poetry
Caedmon 1203	Housman, A. E.—Shropshire Lad, etc.
Caedmon 1087	Keats, John—(Richardson)—Poetry
Pos. 1003	Kinnell, Galway & Andrew Glaze—Poems
Caedmon 1041	Lindsay, Vachel

Caedmon S-1295	Merwin, W. S.—Reading His Poetry
Caedmon 1123	Millay, Edna St. Vincent—Reading from Her Poetry
Caedmon 1025	Moore, Marianne
Lexington 7600	Poe, Edgar A.—(Hooks)—Poems
Folkways 9736	Roethke, Theodore—(Roethke)—Words For the Wind
Caedmon 1150	Sandburg, Carl—Reading His Poetry
2-Caedmon SRS 241	Shakespeare, William—(Gielgud)—Sonnets (complete)
Spoken Arts 849	Speaight,
Speaight,	Robert—Gray,
Caedmon 1068	Stevens, Wallace
Caedmon 1080	Tennyson, Alfred, Lord—Poetry
2-Caedmon 2014	Thomas, Dylan—Complete Recorded Poetry
Caedmon S-1233	Whitman, Walt—(Begley)—Crossing Brooklyn Ferry & Other Poems
Caedmon 1047	Williams, William Carlos
Spoken Arts 860	Wordsworth, William—(Speaight)—Treasury
CMS 617	World's Great Poets—Vol. 1, Ginsberg, Ferlinghetti, Corso
Caedmon 1081	Yeats, William Butler—(McKenna, Cusack)

This list of recordings can be only partial, since new recordings constantly are appearing and old ones continually are going out of stock. Any good record store should be able to provide you with a current catalogue and, on the basis of the information provided here, should be able to order most of the recordings listed in this discography. Many libraries have collections of recordings; and if they do not have the record you want, they probably would be more than willing to either purchase or borrow it for you.

Glossary of Terms

Allegory: a narrative in which the characters, plot, and sometimes setting represent abstractions whose significance is understood best, and sometimes only, in terms of some larger philosophical or religious system. The technique of allegory is used in poems which are not themselves narrative allegories. See Chapter 4.

Alliteration: the repetition of an initial sound in words that occur close to each other in a phrase or line of poetry. The repetition of the "h" sound in the phrase "house high hay" ("Fern Hill") is an example of alliteration.

Allusion: a reference to some person, place, event, or literary work. In "She is the Helen of her town," "Helen" alludes to the beautiful Helen of Troy. See Chapter 4.

Anapest: a foot of poetry in which two unaccented syllables are followed by an accented one. See Chapter 7.

Assonance: the repetition of identical or similar vowel sounds in a line or lines of poetry. In Gray's "Elegy," for instance, the "ow" sound is repeated in the line "The lowing herd winds slowly o'er the lea."

Ballad: a short narrative song. One of the earliest forms of poetry, ballads were often composed and sung by some anonymous singer and later recorded in written form. See Chapter 8.

Blank Verse: poetry written in unrhymed iambic pentameter. See Chapter 7.

Cacophony: in poetry, the use of sounds which seem to the reader harsh, unharmonious, and dissonant. The opposite of cacophony is euphony.

Connotation: the associations implied, rather than defined, by a particular word or expression. The word "mother," for instance, may connote tenderness and apple pie. See Denotation.

Consonance: the repetition of consonants which occur at the ends of words, in a line or lines of poetry. "Fairest merriest best" is an example of consonance.

Couplet: lines of poetry which rhyme in pairs; for example, this concluding couplet of one of Shakespeare's sonnets: "So long as men can breathe or eyes can see, / So long lives this and this gives life to thee."

Dactyl: a foot of poetry in which one accented syllable is followed by two unaccented ones. See Chapter 7.

Denotation: the specific, literal meaning of a word or expression, as opposed to its implied suggestions or associations. A "mother," for instance, is a woman who has borne a child. See Connotation.

Diction: the choice of words used in a work of literature. Some possible kinds of diction are concrete or abstract, colloquial or formal, technical or commonplace. Certain kinds of diction in a poem can evoke certain kinds of reactions in the reader, as well as indicate certain kinds of things about the speaker who uses them.

Dramatic Monologue: a type of poem in which the reader is allowed to "overhear" the words of one speaker (monologue) in a dramatic moment which reveals some important aspect of that person's character. See the discussion of Browning's "My Last Duchess" in Chapter 5.

Elegy: a type of poem which presents a formal lament for the death of a particular person or persons. See the discussion of Gray's "Elegy" in Chapter 4.

Epic: a type of narrative poem which presents the story of a particular hero or group of heroes in such a way that the subject's actions reflect and comment upon the values and destiny of a particular nation or race.

Euphony: the use of sounds in poetry which are musical and pleasing to the reader. See Cacophony.

Foot: a combination of accented and unaccented syllables which forms the basic unit of a line of metrical poetry. See Chapter 7.

Free Verse: poetry which does not have a regular metric pattern. See Chapter 7.

Iamb: a foot of poetry in which an unaccented syllable is followed by an accented one. The iambic foot is the most prevalent in English poetry.

Imagery: the representation in language of any sensory experience. See Chapter 3.

Irony: an arrangement of words that presents tension or opposition between what is expressed and what is implied. See Chapter 5.

Lyric: a poem, usually short, which expresses the speaker's thoughts or feelings on a particular subject. See Chapter 7.

Metaphor: a comparison between two different things in which one thing is given characteristics usually associated with the other; for example, "My love is a flower." See Chapter 3.

Meter: the recurrence of a standard foot in a line or lines of poetry. See Chapter 7.

Metonymy: the use of the name of one thing to stand for another with which it is commonly associated. See Chapter 4.

Onomatopoeia: the use of language whose sound resembles the meanings it conveys or the things it describes.

Paradox: a statement which seems to be contradictory, but which in a given context is really true. See Chapter 5.

Pentameter: a line of poetry consisting of five metrical feet. See Chapter 7.

Persona: the speaker of a poem, as distinguished from the author of the poem. A male author, for instance, might write a poem using a female persona to express feelings about childbirth.

Personification: the attributing of human qualities to abstractions or inanimate objects. See Chapter 4.

Prosody: the study of versification, including such elements as meter, rhyme, and stanza form.

Rhyme: the identity of sounds in different words. *End rhyme* refers to the occurrence of identical sounds in the concluding syllables of two lines of poetry. *Internal rhyme* refers to the occurrence of identical sounds within a single line of poetry. Rhyme may be *perfect,* in which case the two sounds are exactly identical (fall, ball); or it may be *slant,* in which the two sounds are similar but not precisely identical. Emily Dickinson makes effective use of slant rhyme in the following stanza:

> I've known her—from an ample nation—
> Choose One—
> Then—close the valves of her attention—
> Like Stone—

Rhythm: the pace at which a particular line of poetry moves. See Chapter 7.

Scansion: the practice of marking each syllable of each foot of a line of poetry according to that syllable's accent (stressed or not) relative to the other syllables in the metrical foot. See Chapter 7.

Simile: a comparison between two different things in which some word ("like" or "as") is used to point out the comparison. See Chapter 3.

Sonnet: a fourteen-line poem which is usually of iambic pentameter and employs a set rhyme scheme. See Chapter 8.

Spondee: a metrical foot in which two stressed syllables are grouped. See Chapter 7.

Stanza: a unit of lines in a poem, indicated by a spatial division.

Structure: the most fundamental organization of a poem, the arrangement of ideas, events, images, and other various structural elements with which this book has been concerned.

Symbol: something concrete which in a given context can suggest something abstract as well as its literal meaning. See Chapter 6.

Synecdoche: the use of a part of something to signify the whole thing. See Chapter 4.

Theme: the basic concept or attitude of a poem. Most poems are not written to persuade the reader of the truth of a theme or idea, but rather to render some vision of experience. Nevertheless, in summing up your reaction to a poem you may usefully employ the term "theme" to describe the idea or message which your mind has abstracted from the imaginative experience the poem has presented you.

Trochee: a metrical foot composed of an accented syllable followed by an unaccented one. See Chapter 7.

Title and Author Index